Teaching Content Area Reading Skills

A Modular Preservice and Inservice Program

Second Edition

Teaching Content Area Reading Skills

A Modular Preservice and Inservice Program

Second Edition

Harry W. Forgan
Charles T. Mangrum II
University of Miami

Charles E. Merrill Publishing Company
A Bell & Howell Company
Columbus   Toronto   London   Sydney

The Charles E. Merrill
Comprehensive Reading Program
Arthur W. Heilman, Consulting Editor

To Ruth Ann and Jane
Whose encouragement, help, and loyalty make every
undertaking—and all of life—a joyous pursuit.

Published by
Charles E. Merrill Publishing Company
A Bell & Howell Company
Columbus, Ohio 43216

This book was set in Times Roman
Cover Design: Harlan Typographic
Production Coordination: Linda Hillis Bayma

Photo Credits: pages 43, 180, 253, 279, 285 by Alan Bagg; 142, 238 by Paul Conklin; 11 by Jean-Claude Lejeune; 7, 37, 59, 66, 93, 103, 123, 149, 187, 200, 221, 268 by David S. Strickler.

Library of Congress Catalog Card Number: 80–83544

International Standard Book Number: 0–675–08037–1

1 2 3 4 5 6 7 8 9–86 85 84 83 82 81

Printed in the United States of America

Preface

The book you are about to read may be different from textbooks you have used in college courses or for inservice programs. It is not a research textbook in which you find summaries of knowledge organized by chapter and subsections. Although there is a definite need for the research textbook, there is also a need for an alternative text that we call the *applied textbook*. The applied textbook combines experience with information commonly known from research to supply the reader with a way of performing. This applied textbook is designed to help content area teachers develop the basic competencies needed to help students read written materials used in subject areas.

We think the competencies that content area teachers need for helping students read materials are best developed through the use of a *modular* format such as the one found in this book and in our companion textbook, *Developing Competencies in Teaching Reading: A Modular Program for Preservice and Inservice Elementary and Middle School Teachers*. A module is a self-instructional package designed to assist the user in accomplishing certain objectives. An objective consists of those things you will be able to do, know, and/or feel after instruction that you may not have done, known, and/or felt before instruction. The ten modules in this book are designed to help you enable your students to read the materials you use in your content area classes.

In this second edition, we have made changes to make this modular program more readable and useful to students. The changes were suggested by the many university and college professors and inservice directors who have used the textbook during the past five years. Although we have made these changes, we have maintained the basic theme and format of the original textbook. This second edition, like the first, is designed to help content area teachers acquire the competencies they need to effectively and efficiently help their students read their textual materials.

We extend a special note of appreciation to Edward Fry for developing the Graph for Estimating Readability (extended form), to Alton Raygor for developing The Raygor Readability Estimate, and to Natividad Santos for developing the Classification Scheme for Reading Questions—all three of these devices should prove valuable to content area teachers. We appreciate the opportunity to share with our readers the devices and the suggestions for their effective use. We also acknowledge our present and past University of Miami students and in-service teachers who provided us with many excellent suggestions for the second edition. We have found that their comments and suggestions keep us thinking about the practical aspects of reading instruction. Also acknowledged are the many students at Southwood Junior High School in Miami, Florida, with whom our University of Miami undergraduate students worked to develop the competencies found in these modules.

Finally, we appreciate the continued support of our families as we proceed with our writing projects. Our children, Jennifer, Jimmy, Mykel, and Mark , have continued to show patience while their dads worked hard to prepare the second edition. At the same time, they helped us release our anxieties by going for bicycle rides and walks to help us keep our sense of reality and perspective on children. Most important, we continue to receive and appreciate the necessary encouragement and support of our wives, Ruth Ann and Jane.

Harry Forgan
Charles Mangrum

Contents

OVERVIEW   1

    Instructions and Flowchart for Completing Modules, 4
    Checklist of Terminal Objectives, 4

MODULE 1   Determining Readability Levels   7

    Fry's Graph for Estimating Readability, 16

MODULE 2   Preparing Materials at Specified
    Readability Levels   37

MODULE 3   Determining Suitability of Materials   59

MODULE 4   Diagnosing Reading Skill Needs   93

MODULE 5   Teaching Word Meanings   123

MODULE 6   Helping Students Comprehend   149

MODULE 7   Helping Students Use
    Study Skills and Strategies   187

MODULE 8   Helping Students Pronounce
    Multisyllable Words   221

MODULE 9   Motivating Reluctant Readers   253

MODULE 10   Identifying and Helping Problem Readers   279

INDEX   311

ABOUT THE AUTHORS   315

Overview

There are three basic reasons you need to acquire the competencies in this modular program. First, there is dissatisfaction with the present reading achievement levels of secondary students who live in a world in which reading is so important. Second, it is impossible for elementary-school teachers to help students develop *all* the necessary reading skills for different types of content area materials. Elementary-school children are incapable of developing some of the higher level reading skills and the specialized vocabulary required for reading content area materials. Third, it is generally agreed that the teachers who are the most effective in helping students read specialized content materials are the teachers of the content areas.

The purpose of this modular program is to enable you to help students read your content area materials. This does not mean that as content area teachers you are expected to teach beginning reading skills. We recognize that content teachers are mainly responsible for helping students meet the objectives of particular subject areas. The competencies stressed in these modules do not give you additional responsibilities, but rather enable you to be more effective as you implement the responsibilities you presently have.

Ten Basic Competencies

This program is designed to help you accomplish the ten reading competencies required of content area teachers. When you are able to perform them, you will be doing your part to help students read content area materials and thus be more likely to succeed in your classes. Specifically, you are expected to help students read content area materials by performing the following tasks:

1. Students cannot be expected to read materials written above their reading levels. Therefore, you need to be able to determine the readability of your written material to avoid frustrating your students with reading requirements they cannot handle.

2. You will frequently need to supplement the available materials and prepare written materials for your students. In order to do this you must be able to write and alter materials at specified readability levels. As a result, your resources for teaching will be increased and more appropriate for your students.

3. Often a variety of reading materials are used to teach basic concepts in content area courses. Before assigning materials to students, you must be sure the materials are suitable in reading level. You need to determine which materials are suitable for particular students.

4. Many reading skills are needed to read specialized materials. After becoming aware of the reading skills necessary in your content area, you must determine which reading skills the students have or have not acquired. You need reading skills tests to diagnose the needs of students in your content area.

5. All content areas have a specialized vocabulary. Teachers are expected to help students develop and expand word meanings at different levels. To do so, you will need guidelines and activities for teaching the specialized vocabulary of your area.

6. A student is not reading unless he or she is comprehending. Often, students need help in comprehending subject area materials. You must be able to help students develop strategies to help them comprehend the specialized reading materials in your content area.

7. Different types of study strategies are appropriate for different content areas. Since content area teachers themselves have employed study strategies, they are the most qualified persons to help students develop appropriate strategies for the specific area. You must be aware of your strategies and share them with your students.

8. Students often encounter long and difficult words when reading content area materials. You are not expected to teach the beginning word-recognition skills, but you should be able to help students develop a strategy for pronouncing multisyllable words that may at first appear unfamiliar to them.

9. There are many students who know how to read, but are reluctant to read. You should be able to use a strategy that will increase their motivation.

10. Just because students are reluctant to read does not mean they are reluctant to learn. There are some students who are far behind in reading and need assistance in order to succeed in content areas. Every content teacher is responsible for identifying and referring problem readers and for adapting instruction so problem readers can succeed. You are expected to help problem readers survive—and learn—in your classroom while they are overcoming their reading problems.

The Modular Format

You will probably notice that the format of this book is different from other textbooks you have used. The title states that this is a *modular program*. A module is a self-instructional package designed to assist the learner in accomplishing certain objectives. An objective consists of what you are able to do, know, and/or feel after instruction that you may not have done, known, and/or felt before instruction. The ten modules in this book are self-instructional packages whose purpose is to enable you to achieve the ten basic tasks required of content area teachers. You will find that there is a separate module for each of the ten major competencies that you need to help students read content materials.

In examining the modules you will notice that each module includes the following components: Prospectus, Pretest, Branching Program Alternatives for Pretest Responses, several Enabling Elements, Posttest, Posttest Answers, and a Selected Bibliography. Since you may be expected to complete the modules independently, let us take a closer look at each one of these parts.

The *Prospectus* provides an overview of the module. It includes the rationale for accomplishing the objectives of the module. After reading the rationale, you will understand why the module might be of value to you as a content area teacher. The terminal and specific objectives are also listed in the Prospectus. The terminal objective indicates the behavior you are expected to perform in the classroom. This behavior is indicated in more detail by the clearly and precisely defined specific objectives. The Prospectus also includes a description of the resources and time required to do the module so you will be able to plan its completion. Any special materials that may be required for completing the module are specified along with an estimated completion time for the most important activities.

After reading the Prospectus, turn to the Pretest to determine if there are any objectives you have accomplished. The Pretest is a simple yes–no checklist designed for self-evaluation. If you think you can perform the behavior asked for in the Pretest, choose YES. If you have any doubt, choose NO.

The *Branching Program Alternatives for Pretest Responses* is designed to provide the direction you need to go through the modules. The Branching Program will tell you which Enabling Elements are designed to help you accomplish specific objectives. The Branching Program tells you what to do for each response you made on the Pretest. The modules then take into account your individual differences in that you only work to accomplish the objectives that you have not yet developed.

The major parts of the modules are *Enabling Elements*. Each Enabling Element consists of a restatement of the specific objective and Enabling Activities designed to help you accomplish that specific objective. You will notice that some of the activities in every Enabling Element suggest that you read a study guide. Study guides include the background information you need to accomplish the objectives. In addition to the background information, many of the study guides include practicum exercises to help you actually put your new skills to work. The study guides make the modules relatively self-contained since you are not referred to other resources to accomplish the objectives.

A *Posttest* is included for each of the ten modules. You will notice that the Posttest items are based on the objectives and are used to determine whether or not you have accomplished the objectives. Posttest items vary in format. You will find that some of the items require you to list or describe, and others are simulation-type activities requiring you to apply your newly developed skills.

Posttest answers are provided in each module. You can check your responses with the answers as a method of self-evaluation. The results of your self-evaluation can then be used to determine if you have accomplished the objectives. If so, you can go on to the next module. If not, you may want to return through some of the Enabling Elements as directed.

A *Selected Bibliography* is included after each module. In some cases you may want more information or may wish to consult other sources for different ideas. The references included in the bibliography have been selected because they are the ones we think are the most helpful and readily available to content area teachers.

Instructions and Flowchart for Completing the Ten Modules

Your instructor may have specific suggestions for completing the modules in this book. If not, we suggest beginning with Module 1. The following instructions and flowchart will explain the recommended procedure for completing each module. After completing Module 1, complete the remaining modules in any sequence according to your needs as a content area teacher. We hope you enjoy the modules and accomplish the objectives.

Instructions

1. Read the Prospectus to determine if this module meets your specific professional needs. If the module meets your specific needs, continue reading.
2. Self-administer the Pretest and follow the Branching Program to complete the objectives you have not accomplished.
3. Complete the Enabling Elements in sequence. Use the study guides and activities as appropriate.
4. When you have completed all activities for your selected objectives, take the Posttest to determine if you have met the evaluative criteria.
5. If satisfactory performance was not obtained, return to previous Enabling Activities as needed or consult your instructor. Retake the appropriate Posttest items.
6. When the module has been completed, you may wish to examine the Selected Bibliography for additional information or study.

You can keep records of your progress with this checklist of terminal objectives.

Checklist of Terminal Objectives

_____ *Module 1.* You will determine the readability level of passages selected from major reading sources in your content area.

_____ *Module 2.* You will write materials at specified readability levels and alter the readability levels of passages related to your content area.

_____ *Module 3.* You will use an Informal Suitability Survey to determine the suitability of content area materials.

_____ *Module 4.* You will use reading skills tests to determine if students have acquired the reading skills related to your content area.

_____ *Module 5.* You will be able to introduce and expand word meanings in your subject area.

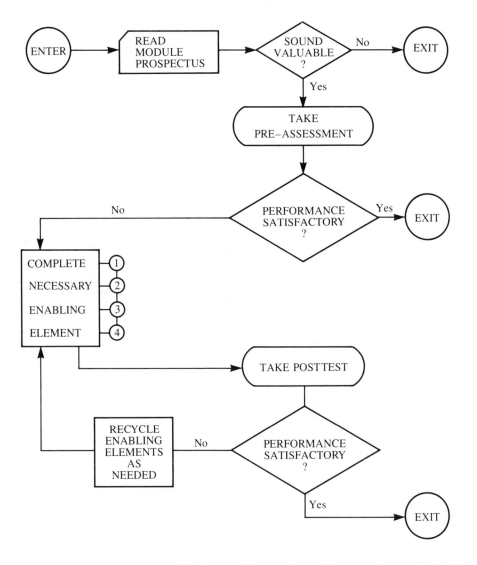

_____ *Module 6.* You will prepare a lesson plan to improve the comprehension achievement of students in your subject area.

_____ *Module 7.* You will specify the major study skills from your content area, prepare a plan for teaching a study skill, and apply three study strategies.

_____ *Module 8.* You will determine the word-pronunciation strategies used by students and help them use a strategy for pronouncing multisyllable words.

_____ *Module 9.* You will acquire and use the provided strategy for motivating reluctant readers.

_____ *Module 10.* You will identify problem readers and factors that may be interfering with their responsiveness to reading tasks and adapt your instructional procedures to help problem readers succeed in your content areas.

Determining Readability Levels

Contents

Prospectus
  Rationale
  Objectives
  Resources and Time Required
Pretest
Branching Program Alternatives for Pretest Responses
Enabling Element 1: *Factors Influencing Readability*
Enabling Element 2: *How to Use Fry's Graph for Estimating Readability*
Enabling Element 3: *Using Fry's Graph to Determine Readability*
Posttest
  Posttest Answers
Selected Bibliography

Prospectus

Rationale

As a teacher you will need to select materials for your students to read in conjunction with the course assignments. These materials may include textbooks, newspapers, magazines, and pamphlets. One of the criteria you should use for selecting these materials is readability. *Readability* is concerned with the difficulty of materials to be read. This module is designed to help you use Fry's Graph for Estimating Readability to determine the difficulty of reading materials. Its use will aid you in finding appropriate materials for the range of reading levels among students in your classes. You will be learning how to use Fry's graph to find the reading levels of textbooks, newspaper articles, magazines, and pamphlets. Fry's graph can also be used to determine the readability levels of test items that you prepare for your students. This module is extremely important for you, the content area teacher, since you will want to be able to provide students with materials that are appropriate for their reading levels.

Objectives

Terminal Objective

You will determine the readability level of passages selected from major reading sources in your content area.

Specific Objectives

1. You will list the two major factors that influence the readability of material and the two major uses of readability formulas.

2. You will state the five steps followed when using Fry's Graph for Estimating Readability to determine the reading level of specified passages.

3. You will use Fry's graph to estimate readability levels of (a) textbooks, (b) articles, and (c) selections with less than 100 words.

Resources and Time Required

Most of the materials required for completing this module are provided. You will also need textbooks, newspaper or magazine articles, and those other written materials, such as handouts, that you commonly use in teaching your classes. The estimated time to complete the starred core Enabling Activities is three to four hours.

Pretest

Directions: For each question, choose the word that indicates your belief regarding your competency. If you are in doubt, choose NO.

1. There are two major factors that influence the readability of written   YES   NO
   material and two major uses of readability formulas. Can you state the
 • two major factors influencing the readability of written material and list
   the two major uses of readability formulas?

2. Edward Fry developed the Graph for Estimating Readability. Do you   YES   NO
   know how to use Fry's graph to determine the readability level of
   written material?

3. Have you used Fry's graph to estimate readability levels of (a) text-   YES   NO
   books, (b) articles, and (c) selections with less than 100 words?

Branching Program Alternatives for Pretest Responses

1. If you can state the two major factors that influence the readability of written material and list the two major uses of readability formulas, you are ready for Enabling Element 2. If not, Enabling Element 1 will provide you with this information.

2. If you know how to use Fry's Graph for Estimating Readability, you are ready for Enabling Element 3. If not, Enabling Element 2 is designed to develop this competency.

3. If you are skillful in using Fry's graph to estimate readability levels of (a) textbooks, (b) articles, and (c) selections with less than 100 words, you have completed the objectives of this module and are ready for the Posttest. If you need to practice, or use Fry's graph to estimate readability levels of different types of written materials such as textbooks, articles, *or* other selections with fewer than 100 words, do the appropriate sections in Enabling Element 3.

Enabling Element 1
Factors Influencing Readability

Specific Objective 1

You will list the two major factors that influence the readability of material and the two major uses of readability formulas.

Enabling Activities

*1. Read Study Guide 1. Identify the two factors that influence readability and the two major uses of readability formulas.

2. Reflect upon your own reading and ask, "What makes some selections more difficult for me to comprehend?"

3. Ask your students, "Why are some materials easier to read than others?" Have you identified other factors that may make some material more difficult than others?

4. Why should you learn about the factors that influence readability and the formulas that are available to determine it? How can this information help you as a teacher? Discuss these questions with your colleagues.

5. Most of the readability formulas developed today are for the English language; however, applications are growing. Locate the Klare article, "Assessing Readability," in the Selected Bibliography for this module if you want to learn about formulas available to measure materials written in any of the following foreign languages: French, Dutch, Spanish, Hebrew, German, Hindi, Russian, and Chinese.

---

*Indicates core Enabling Activities.

Find materials at appropriate readability levels for your students.

Study Guide 1

Readability is the objective measure of the difficulty of a book or article. Readability levels are generally reported in terms of grade level. Therefore, one might find a textbook written at the ninth-grade level, fourth-grade level, and so forth. The readability of texts and supplementary reading materials should be of great concern to teachers because students are expected to gather information and develop new skills via reading. Teachers then need to know the factors that influence readability and ways of determining readability.

History

Factors that influence readability have been the subject of scholarly study for thousands of years. According to Klare, "Lorge tells of word and idea counts made by Talmudists in 900 A.D. so that they could use frequency of occurrence to distinguish from usual senses (meanings)" (1963, p. 30).

Although the study of readability has been under way for many years, little progress was made until statistical techniques were developed. Such techniques made it possible to identify important readability factors and to construct formulas for estimating passage difficulty. According to Klare (1963) early studies revealed many factors that were related to readability. Klare reported that Gray and Leary, for example, had identified 289 factors influencing readability, 20 of which were significantly related to readability.

Several dozen readability formulas have been developed over the years. Many of the earlier formulas were complex and required the user to count a number of variables. Later research revealed that the two most important factors influencing readability of commonly printed materials in the United States are *sentence length* and *word difficulty*. In general, the longer the sentences and the longer the words, the more difficult is the material to read. Conversely, if the sentences are short and the words are short, the material is easier to read.

Today, the more commonly accepted and widely used formulas use sentence length and word difficulty for estimating reading level. Examples of this method are the Spache Readability Formula (1953) for primary grade materials and the Dale-Chall Readability Formula (1947, 1948) for materials in grades four through sixteen. Because the Spache and Dale-Chall formulas require considerable time, in the last few years researchers have developed shortcut tables or charts, which facilitate the use of the Spache and Dale-Chall formulas. Others, such as Edward Fry (1968, 1977), have developed alternative formulas that are based upon the same factors but can be more simply and quickly applied. Of the less time-consuming formulas, Fry's Graph for Estimating Readability is one of the most commonly accepted.

Uses of Readability Formulas

One use of a readability formula is to estimate the reading difficulty of printed materials. Estimates of reading level are especially useful to the teacher interested in making reading assignments or in selecting textbooks and other commonly used written materials. Teachers who are given the opportunity to participate in textbook selection should consider how difficult the textbooks are to read. Likewise, many content area teachers are not bound to one textbook, but rather develop a collection of resource materials to use in teaching their classes. They use newspaper clippings, articles from journals or magazines, pamphlets, and other printed materials that correlate with the objectives of their content area classes. Before asking students to read these materials, teachers should determine just how difficult the reading levels of the materials are.

The second major use of the readability formula is to guide the teacher in preparing or altering the reading levels of materials. It is necessary for all teachers to be writers as they prepare tests, study guides, course outlines, letters to parents, and other materials. In writing materials for others to read, it is important that the content area teacher write at a readability level within the reading level range of the students and/or parents. Likewise, some teachers like to alter materials by raising or lowering the reading level to go along with the capabilities of students. For example, if you find a very technical article with a readability level above your students' level and yet desire to use this article with your students because of its content, you may want to alter the reading level to make it more readable for your students.

Limitations of Readability Formulas

Even though the readability formulas are useful, there are some limitations. First, most readability formulas do not take into consideration the concepts that are being presented in the printed materials. As mentioned earlier, the two most common criteria used in readability formulas are sentence length and word difficulty. However, some materials that are within the students' reading level according to the readability formulas may be more difficult to read than other materials because they deal with concepts that are beyond the students' understanding.

Another limitation of readability formulas is that they do not take into consideration the use of slang, satire, multiple meanings, or the interest of the reader. Likewise, readability formulas cannot be used with certain types of material such as poetry in which the sentence structure is different. These limitations must be kept in mind when applying the formulas to reading materials.

Common Formulas

For use in the primary grades, the Spache Readability Formula is the most commonly accepted formula. Developed in 1953, the formula uses two factors to estimate reading level: average sentence length and percentage of difficult words. Through use and study, this formula has been demonstrated to be valid and reliable for estimating reading level of written material; however, it is complex and time-consuming.

For grades four through sixteen the Dale-Chall Readability Formula is widely used. This formula first appeared in 1947. Like the Spache, it uses sentence length and word difficulty for estimating reading level. While it is considered to be one of the more accurate readability formulas, it is complex and time-consuming.

Fry's Graph for Estimating Readability is an outgrowth of a need for a simple and efficient technique for estimating reading difficulty. Fry's graph uses the traditional factors of sentence length and word difficulty to determine readability. However, with Fry's graph word difficulty is estimated through a count of syllables rather than through the cumbersome and lengthy technique of comparing every word to a list of words to determine its difficulty. Fry (1969, pp. 534–38) reports that the Fry Graph for Estimating Readability correlates 0.90 with the Spache Readability Formula and 0.94 with the Dale-Chall Readability Formula. These high correlations indicate considerable consistency between formulas and support the wide acceptance and use of Fry's graph.

You are ready to learn how to use Fry's Graph for Estimating Readability. The graph that you are going to use is the most recent one developed by Edward Fry. This graph, which first appeared in the *Journal of Reading* in December 1977, is an extended version of Fry's original graph, which appeared in 1968. If you know how to use Fry's extended graph, go directly to Enabling Element 3. If not, or if you need practice with the procedure, Enabling Element 2 will teach you how to use Fry's newer graph for estimating readability.

Enabling Element 2
How to Use Fry's Graph for Estimating Readability

Specific Objective 2

You will state the five steps followed when using Fry's Graph for Estimating Readability to determine the reading level of specified passages.

Enabling Activities

*1. Read Study Guide 2, "How to Use Fry's Graph for Estimating Readability," and familiarize yourself with the procedures for estimating readability.

*2. Make a list of the five steps for using Fry's graph.

*3. Do you need more practice in counting syllables? If so, read these words aloud and count the number of sound units you hear. Check your responses with those listed on page 22 of this Enabling Element.

a. very
b. telephone
c. ¢
d. environment
e. drenched
f. basketball
g. hopeful
h. ERA

i. matches
j. Washington
k. seventeenth
l. 1961
m. any
n. $4.98
o. let's

*4. When counting the number of sentences in a 100-word passage, the hundredth word is often not the last word in a sentence. The proportion of the last sentence must be determined if this is the case. What proportion (in a decimal) is each one of the following sentences?
a. The last sentence contains 8 words, 4 of which are in the 100-word count.
b. The last sentence is 15 words, and 4 of the words are part of the 100-word selection.
c. The last sentence includes 32 words, and 9 of these are in your 100-word passage.
Check your responses with those listed on page 22 of this Enabling Element.

*5. Let us suppose you find that the readability estimate of a selection is tenth grade. What is the range of the true estimate of readability? Check your response with the answer on page 22.

*6. According to Fry's graph, what are the readabilities of selections with the following counts?
a. 128 syllables in five sentences

---

*Indicates core Enabling Activities.

    b. 156 syllables in seven sentences

    c. 160 syllables in ten sentences

    Check your response with the answers on page 22 of this Enabling Element.

*7. Do the Practicum Exercise to see if you can follow the directions for using Fry's graph.

Study Guide 2

Fry's graph was developed to serve as a quick, easy, usable technique for estimating the reading difficulty of written material for grade one through graduate school. The graph incorporates two factors to be used in estimating reading level: average sentence length and total number of syllables. Examine Fry's graph (figure 1, p. 16).

    The top heading in Fry's graph is "average number of syllables per 100 words." The numerals at the top of the graph, then, refer to the number of syllables contained in a 100-word selection. A 100-word selection with short words may contain as few as 108 syllables; thus each word is only about one syllable long. A 100-word selection with long words may contain more than 182 syllables. If a 100-word selection contains 182 syllables, most of the words are more than one syllable.

    Now look at the left side of the graph and notice the statement, "average number of sentences per 100 words." As you examine the left side of the graph, you will notice that the number of sentences ranges from two (long sentences) to twenty-five sentences (short sentences). If there are only two sentences in 100 words, each sentence is about 50 words long. Likewise, if there are twenty-five sentences in 100 words, each sentence is only 4 words long. If a 100-word selection has fewer than two sentences or more than twenty-five sentences, Fry's graph cannot be used.

    As you look at the center of the graph, you will notice that grade-level bands range from first grade to seventeenth grade. Of course, thirteenth grade is the freshman year of college; the fourteenth year is the sophomore; the fifteenth is the junior year of college; and the sixteenth is the senior year of college. The seventeenth+ grade level indicates the readability would be at a level appropriate for a graduate student.

    As you continue to look at the graph, you will notice that some areas of the graph are gray. Grade-level scores in these areas are invalid because the lines converge or diverge. Readability estimates are most valid when they are near the center line on Fry's graph.

    Now that you have carefully examined Fry's Graph for Estimating Readability, you are ready for directions on how to use the graph. Refer to the graph as you read these directions.

Directions for Using Fry's Graph

Fry (1977, pp. 242–52) provides the following directions (partially adapted by the authors) for obtaining reading level estimates:

1. *Select a representative passage from written material for which you wish to know the reading level.* Since you use only a sample from the printed material for which you

Figure 1

Graph for estimating readability—extended

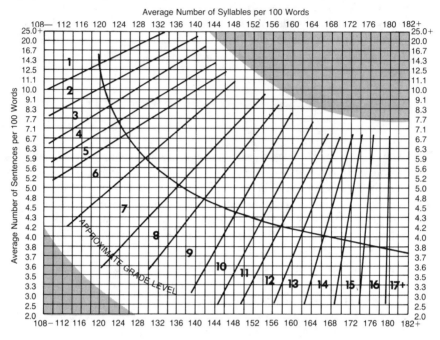

Average Number of Syllables per 100 Words

Expanded Directions for Working Readability Graph

1. Randomly select three (3) sample passages and count out exactly 100 words each, beginning with the beginning of a sentence. Do count proper nouns, initializations, and numerals.

2. Count the number of sentences in the hundred words, estimating length of the fraction of the last sentence to the nearest one-tenth.

3. Count the total number of syllables in the 100-word passage. If you don't have a hand counter available, an easy way is to simply put a mark above every syllable over one in each word; then when you get to the end of the passage, count the number of marks and add 100. Small calculators can also be used as counters by pushing numeral 1, then push the + sign for each word or syllable when counting.

4. Enter graph with *average* sentence length and *average* number of syllables; plot dot where the two lines intersect. Area where dot is plotted will give you the approximate grade level.

5. If a great deal of variability is found in syllable count or sentence count, putting more samples into the average is desirable.

6. A word is defined as a group of symbols with a space on either side; thus, *Joe, IRA, 1945,* and & are each one word.

7. A syllable is defined as a phonetic syllable. Generally, there are as many syllables as vowel sounds. For example, *stopped* is one syllable and *wanted* is two syllables. When counting syllables for numerals and initializations, count one syllable for each symbol. For example, *1945* is four syllables, *IRA* is three syllables, and & is one syllable.

Note: This "extended graph" does not outmode or render the earlier (1968) version inoperative or inaccurate; it is an extension.

Source: By Edward Fry. Reprinted from *The Journal of Reading*, December 1977. Reproduction permitted. No copyright.

want to determine readability, it is essential that the material you select is representative of the entire article or book. After you have found a representative selection, count 100 words in the sample beginning with the first word of a sentence. Do not count the words in titles or headings. Be sure to count all the words, including initials and numerals. A word is defined as a group of symbols with a space on each side of the group; thus, *Charles*, *USA*, *1980*, and + are each 1 word.

2. *Count the number of sentences in the 100-word passage.* This procedure is rather simple since you just go through the passage and look for sentences ending with a period, question mark, or exclamation mark. If the final sentence does not stop at the end of the 100 words, determine what proportion of this last sentence you are including in the 100-word count. Estimate the last sentence to the nearest tenth. For example, if the final sentence in a 100-word count has 16 words, and 8 of these are in the 100-word count, the final sentence would be counted as 0.5 sentences. For additional practice, see Enabling Activity 4.

3. *Count the number of syllables in the 100-word passage.* You do not need to decide where syllable breaks occur in each of the words. Rather, you simply read the selection aloud and put a slash above each syllable you hear in the words. For example, the word *though* has one syllable, *counted* has two syllables, *determine* has three syllables, and *appropriate* has four syllables. For our purposes, a *syllable* is a phonetic syllable that you actually hear. Usually a word has as many syllables as there are vowel sounds. When counting syllables for numerals and initializations, count one syllable for each symbol. For example, *1980* would be counted as four syllables, *USA* has three syllables, and + has one syllable. For additional practice see Enabling Activity 3.

4. *Refer to Fry's graph* (see figure 1). Notice the grid of intersecting lines. The vertical lines represent the average number of syllables per 100 words. The horizontal lines represent the average number of sentences per 100 words. Where any vertical and horizontal lines intersect, approximate grade levels are indicated. Record the level of your selection at this time. According to Fry, most of the intersecting points will fall near the curved line. If the intersecting point falls in the gray area, conclude that the results are invalid, select another 100-word sample, and refigure.

5. *Remember that these are estimates of readability.* Fry (1977) has stated that these estimates are probably within one year of true estimates of readability.

Illustrations of Each Step

Let us suppose you desire to use the following selection, "Teachers Don't Want to Be Labeled," with your students to help them realize that each person has strengths and weaknesses rather than being totally gifted, average, or slow. After reading the article, you want to know at what reading level it is written in order to determine whether or not you can require your students to read it.

Step 1: Select a Representative 100-word Selection. Usually, the first 100 words in an article are useful if they are fairly representative of the selection. You count every word, including such small words as *a* and *the*, as well as proper nouns, numerals, and initializations. If you use the first 100 words of the article, "Teachers Don't Want to Be Labeled," you will find that the one-hundredth word is *number*, which is in the first sentence of the second paragraph. Remember not to count titles in your word count.

Step 2: Count the Number of Sentences. The second step in using Fry's graph is to count the number of sentences in the 100-word selection. The one-hundredth word does not always end the selection; therefore, it is necessary to determine the proportion of the last sentence that falls within the word count. Estimate to the nearest one-tenth the fraction of the last sentence that is within the 100-word count.

In our 100-word sample there are three complete sentences and part of another sentence. The fourth sentence contains a total of 31 words, of which 24 are in our 100-word count. The fraction of the fourth sentence to be used is 24/31. The fraction 24/31 can be changed to a decimal by dividing 31 into 24. The result is the decimal 0.77, which we round off to the nearest tenth—0.8. Thus, our sentence count for the 100-word selection is 3.8. You need not do the division when you can estimate the fraction to the nearest tenth.

**Teachers Don't Want
to Be Labeled***

By Harry W. Forgan

When teaching a course on tests and measurements at Kent State University recently, I decided to administer an adult group intelligence test to the class. I wanted the students to "feel" what it was like to take such a test and realize what items we use to measure intelligence. I also thought they might be more aware of the short time it takes to obtain a number which is regarded as very important by many educators.

The students were told not to write their names on the test papers, but rather to use a code such as their house number, physical measurements, or any less obvious symbol. I explained that I really didn't have faith in IQ scores; therefore, I didn't want to know their IQs.

The administration of the test required only 50 minutes. The students seemed to enjoy taking it and chuckled at some of the tasks they were expected to perform. I had to laugh myself when I saw some of them looking at their hands and feet when responding to items concerning right and left.

Upon scoring the test I found that the lowest IQ was 87 and the highest 143. The mean IQ for the 48 students was 117. I was not astonished by the 87, even though all of the students had successfully completed the general education course and student teaching at Kent State and were ready to graduate by the end of the term. After all, IQ tests have many limitations.

Then I got an idea. I decided to prepare a report for each student, writing his code on the outside and "IQ 87" on the inside of each. I folded and stapled each paper—after all, an IQ is confidential information!

At the next class period I arranged all of the folded papers on a table at the front of the room. I wrote the range and the average IQ on the chalkboard. Many students snickered at the

*Reprinted with permission from the *Phi Delta Kappan*, vol. LV, no. 1, September 1973, p. 98.

thought of somebody getting an 87. The students were eager and afraid as I began by explaining the procedures for picking up their papers. I made a point of telling them not to tell others their IQ score, because this would make the other person feel as if he too had to divulge his ''total endowment.'' The students were then directed to come up to the table, row by row, to find their coded paper. I stood sheepishly—ready to laugh out loud as I watched the students carefully open their papers and see ''IQ 87.'' Many opened their mouths with astonishment and then smiled at their friends to indicate they were extremely happy with their scores.

There was dead silence when I began to discuss the implications of the IQ scores. I explained that in some states a person who scores below 90 on an IQ test is classified as a slow learner. The fact that group intelligence tests should not be used to make such a classification was stressed. I also emphasized the fact that *someone* in this class could have been classified as a slow learner and placed in a special class on the basis of this test.

I told how many guidance counselors would discourage a child with an 87 IQ from attending college. Again I emphasized the fact that one person in this room was ready to graduate from college having passed several courses in history, biology, English, and many other areas.

I then went on to explain that the majority of elementary and secondary school teachers believe in ability grouping. This is usually done on the basis of intelligence tests, so I explained that I would like to try ability grouping with this class—again to see ''how it feels.'' Some students objected right away, saying that ''I did not want to know their IQ scores.'' I calmed them by saying it would be a worthwhile learning experience and assured them that I really didn't believe in IQ scores.

I told the students not to move at this time, but I would like all of those with an IQ below 90 to come to the front so they could sit nearer to me for individual help. I told the students who had an average IQ (between 90–109) to go to the back of the room and then take the seats in the middle of the class. The students with an above average IQ were asked to go to the side of the room and take the seats in the back because they really didn't need much extra help.

''O.K., all those who got an IQ below 90 can come to the front of the room.'' The students looked around to find those who scored below 90. I said that I knew there was an 87 and maybe a couple of 89's. Again, there was dead silence.

''O.K., all those students whose IQ is between 90–109 go to the back of the room.'' Immediately, to my amazement, 8 or 10 students picked up their books and headed for the back of the room. Before they could get there I said, ''Wait a minute! Sit down! I don't want to embarrass you, but you would lie and cheat—the same way we make our students lie and cheat—because you don't want to be classified as 'slow.' I wrote 'IQ 87' on every paper!''

The class erupted. It was in an uproar for about five minutes. Some of the women cried. Some indicated that they needed to use the restroom. All agreed it was a horrifying and yet valuable experience.

I asked them to do one thing for me: Please don't label kids because we are all ''gifted,'' ''average,'' and ''slow,'' depending on the task at hand. They promised.

Step 3: Count the Number of Syllables. Teachers seem to prefer different ways of counting the number of syllables in a 100-word selection. Two procedures are illustrated below. Choose the one that is easier for you.

Procedure A. Read the selection subvocally and make a slash to indicate the number of syllables in each word. Keep in mind it is not necessary to divide the words into syllables. Simply note how many syllables you hear in each word. After making slashes for each syllable, count the number of syllables in each line, and record this number to the right of the line. Add the number of syllables in each line to determine the total number of syllables in the 100-word selection. An illustration follows:

	Syllables
When teaching a course on tests and measurements at Kent State Universi-	18
ty recently, I decided to administer an adult group intelligence test to the class. I	26
wanted the students to "feel" what it was like to take such a test and realize	20
what items we use to measure intelligence. I also thought they might be more	20
aware of the short time it takes to obtain a number which is regarded as very	22
important by many educators.	10
The students were told not to write their names on the test papers, but	16
rather to use a code such as their house number /physical measurements, or any	12
less obvious symbol.	
Total	144

Procedure B. Assume each word in the 100-word selection has one syllable (that's true!) and simply make slashes for or count the second, third, fourth syllable in each word. Remember to add your subtotal to 100 to determine the total number of syllables in the 100-word selection. An illustration follows:

	Syllables
When teaching a course on tests and measurements at Kent State Universi-	6
ty recently, I decided to administer an adult group intelligence test to the class. I	12
wanted the students to "feel" what it was like to take such a test and realize	4
what items we use to measure intelligence. I also thought they might be more	6
aware of the short time it takes to obtain a number which is regarded as very	6
important by many educators.	6
The students were told not to write their names on the test papers, but	2
rather to use a code such as their house number /physical measurements, or any	2
less obvious symbol.	
Subtotal	44
+ 100 =	144

Step 4: Refer to Fry's Graph. Locate the number at the top of Fry's graph that indicates the number of syllables. For our sample look at 144. Place your right index finger on the vertical line under 144. Locate the number at the left side of Fry's graph that indicates the number of sentences. Our selection has 3.8 sentences, so place your left index finger on

3.8. Move both fingers along the appropriate lines until they meet. Notice the grade level band on which the two lines intersect. For this particular selection, the reading level estimate is between ninth and tenth grade. Remember that lines intersecting in the gray areas always reveal invalid scores.

Step 5: Remember, This Is an Estimate! Because the estimate for readability when using Fry's graph is within one year of the true estimate, our sample has a true range of ninth or tenth grade since it is right in the middle. Let us suppose that the estimate was eighth grade; then the true range would have been seventh, eighth, or ninth.

Practicum Exercise

You learn by doing! Now that you know how to use Fry's Graph for Estimating Readability, try it on a passage. The selection below contains more than 100 words, so your first step is to find the one-hundredth word. Second, you will count the number of sentences in the 100 words. Third, you will count the number of syllables in the 100-words. Next, you will refer to Fry's graph to determine the readability. Finally, you will consider the estimates you obtained to be within one year of the true estimate of readability. Do this Practicum Exercise, and then compare your results with ours at the end of this Enabling Element.

Selection for Practicum Exercise

Syllables

    The purpose of this selection is to provide you with practice in using Fry's _____
Graph for Estimating Readability. The first edition of Fry's graph came out in _____
1968, and Fry extended his graph in 1977. The extended graph continues _____
through the seventeenth + grade level. The extended graph was published in an _____
IRA publication entitled *Journal of Reading* in December 1977. _____

    Because Fry did not obtain a copyright for his graph, reproduction is _____
permitted. Personally, we feel that Fry has made a worthwhile contribution to _____
the field of reading, and we thank him for it. _____

    We believe you will find Fry's graph easy to use and, after practice, will be _____
able to determine readability levels of printed materials within a few minutes. _____
This new competency will enable you to select materials that are appropriate for _____
the ranges of reading levels found among your students. _____

Total _____

1. Number of Sentences _____
2. Number of Syllables _____
3. Estimate of Readability _____

Answers

Enabling Activities 3–6

3. a. very (2)   i. matches (2)
    b. telephone (3)   j. Washington (3)
    c. ¢ (1)   k. seventeenth (3)
    d. environment (4)   l. 1961 (4)
    e. drenched (1)   m. any (2)
    f. basketball (3)   n. $4.98 (4)
    g. hopeful (2)   o. let's (1)
    h. ERA (3)

4. a. $4/8 = 0.5$
    b. $4/15 = 0.3$
    c. $9/32 = 0.3$

5. The true estimate is ninth-, tenth-, or eleventh-grade reading level.

6. a. Seventh grade
    b. Ninth grade
    c. Invalid estimate (Another sample would have to be used to find the reading level.)

Practicum Exercise

	Syllables
The purpose of this selection is to provide you with practice in using Fry's	20
Graph for Estimating Readability. The first edition of Fry's graph came out in	22
1968, and Fry extended his graph in 1977. The extended graph continues	24
through the seventeenth + grade level. The extended graph was published in an	19
IRA publication entitled *Journal of Reading* in December 1977.	23
Because Fry did not obtain a copyright for his graph, reproduction is	19
permitted. Personally, we feel that Fry has made a worthwhile contribution to	21
the field of reading, and we thank him for it.	11
We believe you will find Fry's graph easy to use and, after practice, will be	6

100 words

able to determine readability levels of printed materials within a few minutes. This new competency will enable you to select materials that are appropriate for the ranges of reading levels found among your students.

Total   165

1. Number of Sentences   6.2
2. Number of Syllables   165
3. Estimate of Readability 11th grade

Go to Enabling Element 3 to locate specific directions and practice activities for estimating readability levels of (1) textbooks, (2) articles, and (3) selections with less than 100 words. After using Fry's graph several times, you will be able to determine the readability of a selection within five to ten minutes.

Enabling Element 3
Using Fry's Graph to Determine Readability

Specific Objective 3

You will use Fry's graph to estimate readability levels of (1) textbooks, (2) articles, and (3) selections with less than 100 words.

Enabling Activities

*1. Read Study Guide 3. It is designed to acquaint you with specific directions that are necessary to use Fry's graph with different types of written materials.

*2. Do Practicum Exercises 1 and 2 to develop skill in determining readability levels of textbooks. This skill will be valuable when you evaluate textbooks for use and also as you determine the readability levels of your present texts. Check your response for Practicum Exercise 1 with the answers listed on pages 30–31 of this Enabling Element.

*3. Do Practicum Exercises 3 and 4 to practice evaluating the readability levels of articles. Check your answers for Exercise 3 with those on pages 31–32 of this Enabling Element.

*4. Do Practicum Exercises 5 and 6 to develop skill in using Fry's graph to estimate the readability of selections that have fewer than 100 words. Check your response for Exercise 5 on page 32 of the Enabling Element.

 5. You may want to duplicate Fry's graph for each of your students and teach them how to use the graph. Many secondary students can learn how to use Fry's graph and thus help you determine the readability of many of your written materials. Of course, you will want to check their work.

Study Guide 3

You can use Fry's graph to estimate the readability of several types of written materials. This Study Guide is designed to provide specific directions and practice activities for using Fry's graph to estimate readability of (1) textbooks, (2) articles, and (3) selections with less than 100 words. Refer to Enabling Element 2 for general directions.

---

*Indicates core Enabling Activities.

Using Fry's Graph with Textbooks

If you want to determine the readability level of a textbook, you will need to select a minimum of three 100-word passages. One of the selections should be from the beginning of the book, one from the middle of the book, and one from the last third of the book. Be sure to choose self-contained selections, those that do not refer to charts or illustrations.

Follow the directions in Enabling Element 2 to determine the number of syllables and sentences in each selection. After doing so, find the *average* number of syllables and sentences by adding the three passages together and dividing by three. For example:

100-Word Passages		Syllables	Sentences
First 100 Words		124	6.6
Second 100 Words		141	5.5
Third 100 Words		158	6.8
	Sums	423	18.9
	Averages	141	6.3

Plot on the graph the average number of sentences and syllables to estimate readability. The average readability in the preceding example is seventh grade.

Now it is your turn.

Practicum Exercise 1

Determine the average readability of the following three passages randomly selected from the beginning, middle, and end of a hypothetical basic health book.

1. Count 100 words in each representative passage. Always start counting at the beginning of a sentence and *do* count the proper nouns, numerals, and initializations.
2. Count the number of syllables in each passage.
3. Count the number of sentences in each passage.
4. Determine the reading level of each passage.
5. Determine the average reading level of the health textbook by finding the average number of syllables and sentences in the three selections, then using these averages as you refer to Fry's graph.
6. Check your answers with the answers on pages 30–31 of this Study Guide.

Rabies

Syllables

 Since bites by cats, dogs, or any wild animal always present the danger of   _____
infection with rabies, a biting animal should never be killed unless unavoidable   _____
as a matter of safety. It should be caught and held for observation for at least   _____
fifteen days, in order to determine whether it develops rabies.   _____
 If it is necessary to kill the animal at the time of the biting, the carcass   _____

should be sent to the state public health laboratory for an examination of its _____
brain. If the laboratory finds the animal was rabid, it is essential that treatment _____
be initiated at once. _____

Total   _____

Headache

Syllables

    The term *headache* is such a part of our everyday vocabulary that is has _____
become almost synonymous with any unpleasant situation or problem. But in a _____
medical sense the term quite literally means a head pain or an aching head and _____
is a symptom rather than itself an actual disease condition. _____
    Hence, headache can suggest the possibility of a great many underlying _____
conditions. Perhaps one of the better known types is the throbbing, devastating _____
headache that sometimes accompanies a hangover. This differs from the type _____
known as tension headache, associated with figuring out one's income tax, _____
since they arise from different causes. _____

Total   _____

Heatstroke

Syllables

    The most important feature of heatstroke, which is sometimes also re- _____
ferred to as sunstroke, is the extremely high body temperature that accompanies _____
it. It is a far more serious condition than heat exhaustion. _____
    Heatstroke occurs more often in males than in females and is more _____
common in elderly people and in those addicted to alcohol. Physical exertion is _____
a definite contributing factor; and an attack is much more likely to occur when _____
the humidity is high than when it is low, even at the same temperature. _____
    The underlying cause of heatstroke is intimately connected with a cessa- _____
tion of sweating, accounting for the excessive rise in body temperature. _____

Total   _____

	Number of Sentences	Number of Syllables	Reading Level	True Estimate Range
"Rabies"	_____	_____	_____	_____
"Headache"	_____	_____	_____	_____
"Heatstroke"	_____	_____	_____	_____
Sums	_____	_____		
Averages	_____	_____	_____	_____

    The answers are at the end of Enabling Element 3. If your answers are correct, continue reading. If not, repeat steps 1 through 6 and determine why not. Remember that your syllable count may vary by a few syllables due to dialect differences.

Practicum Exercise 2

Now try a real exercise. Randomly select at least three 100-word passages from a textbook used in your teaching area. Determine the average grade level reading ability necessary for reading this material. A chart such as follows may be helpful.

	Number of Sentences	Number of Syllables	Reading Level	True Estimate Range
First 100-word Passage	_____	_____	_____	_____
Second 100-Word Passage	_____	_____	_____	_____
Third 100-Word Passage	_____	_____	_____	_____
Sums	_____	_____		
Averages	_____	_____	_____	_____

Here are some follow-up questions you may want to ask yourself. Does the readability estimate match the reading levels of my students? If yes, then you have chosen textual material suitable for your students. If no, you may want to consider changing textual material. Is the readability range among passages less than two years for grades seven through nine and three years for grades ten through twelve? If yes, the range of reading levels should not overtax your students' reading ability. If not, many passages may frustrate your students, and it may be advisable to consider changing the textual material.

A word of caution! Sometimes a book is found with great variability either in sentence length or syllable count for all passages. If this is the case, randomly select additional sample passages; average the number of syllables and sentences; and plot as before. If the same variability occurs, conclude that the book has uneven readability and consider changing texts. This type of material is the most frustrating.

Now you know how to determine the readability level of textbooks in your subject area. Read on and you will learn how to evaluate journal articles.

Using Fry's Graph with Articles

Teachers often wish to use articles from magazines, newspapers, or other sources. They need to know if the reading levels of the materials are appropriate for their students.

The directions for using Fry's graph in Study Guide 2 can be followed exactly if the articles contain at least 100 words. One representative 100-word selection is sufficient to determine the readability unless the article is unusually long. For longer articles, two or three randomly selected passages will provide a more valid estimate.

Practice your skill in using Fry's graph by determining the readability of the following article.

Practicum Exercise 3

1. Count the number of sentences per 100 words.
2. Count the number of syllables per 100 words, including proper nouns, numerals, and initializations.
3. Refer to Fry's graph.
4. Check your answers on the last page of this Study Guide. If you have the correct answer, go to the next Practicum Exercise. If not, check to see if your numbers for syllables and sentences match ours. If not, recount your syllables and sentences and repeat step number 3. Your syllable count may be different from ours because of dialect differences; however, the syllable count should vary by only a few syllables.

New Target for Feminists: TV Kiddie Cartoons

Syllables

Women's liberation may have a new battle to fight—Saturday morning cartoon shows. According to researchers at the University of Michigan, cartoons still are entrenched firmly in traditional male-female sex roles. _____

This conclusion was drawn by analyzing twenty programs from such series as "Fat Albert," "Underdog," and "The Flintstones." Males were seen in forty-two job roles, while females appeared in only nine. Only six of the thirty-one cartoon women had jobs outside the home; whereas in reality, 50 percent of all American women are in the labor force. *100 words*
Perhaps the time has come for feminists to analyze all television shows to determine if this is how children develop stereotypes of sex roles. _____

Total _____

Practicum Exercise 4

Put your new skill into action by selecting an article you have used or would like to use with your classes. Follow the directions to estimate the readability level.

Selections with Fewer Than 100 Words

Sometimes teachers want to evaluate selections that are less than 100 words in length. This is particularly true for essay test questions, math problems, directions to an activity, or brief articles. Fry's graph can still be useful; however, the directions must be adapted because the graph is based on 100-word selections. The following procedures should be used:

1. Count the total number of words in the selection and round down to the nearest ten. For an example, if there are forty-four words in your selections, use only the first forty to make a count of the number of syllables and sentences.

2. Count the number of syllables and sentences in the selected words.

3. Multiply the total number of sentences and syllables by the number in the Conversion Chart (below) that corresponds with the number of words in your selection.

Conversion Chart for Fry's Graph
For Selections with Fewer Than 100 Words

If the number of words in the selection is:	Multiply the number of syllables and sentences by:
30	3.3
40	2.5
50	2.0
60	1.67
70	1.43
80	1.25
90	1.1

4. Refer to Fry's graph to find the grade level band that indicates the readability level. The following essay questions are used to demonstrate these directions.

Essay Questions

Syllables

1. To what extent do you believe it is possible for people of different races, religions, or political beliefs to live together in harmony? What suggestions can you make to help people become more tolerant? _22_ _23_ _13_

2. It is often said that communism develops fastest in those countries where people do not have the basic necessities of life. Why do you think this might *60 words* be possible? _20_ _20_

Total _98_

In counting the words, you will find a total of 63. Rounding this down to the nearest ten, you will be using 60 words in our sample. There are 98 syllables and 3.8 sentences in the 60 words. Both of these numbers are then multiplied by 1.67 to convert them to a scale of 100 words. Thus, we have 163 syllables and 6.3 sentences, which indicate the readability of eleventh-grade level.

Practicum Exercise 5

A sample math problem follows. Notice there are only 83 words in this selection. Estimate the readability by following these directions:

1. Count the number of words and round down to the nearest ten.

2. Count the number of syllables and sentences in the selected words.

3. To base your estimate on a 100-word passage, find the appropriate number on the Conversion Chart.

4. Multiply the appropriate number times the number of sentences and syllables.

5. Plot these numbers on Fry's graph to obtain an estimate of readability. Check your answers at the end of this Study Guide.

Math Problem

Syllables

Nancy got a job working at a local store. She makes $4.12 an hour. She is   ————
to report to work after school each afternoon and work for three hours. On   ————
Saturdays and Sundays, she works eight hours. She wanted this job so she could   ————
save money to buy a car. She hopes to be able to get a used MG car for $4000.   ————
Assuming that she does not have to pay her own taxes, how long will it take her   ————
to earn $4000?   ————

Total   ————

Record your answers and check them with the ones at the end of the Study Guide.

———— Nearest ten (number of words used in determing readability)
———— Number of syllables $\times$ ———— = ————
———— Number of sentences $\times$ ———— = ————
———— Estimate of readability

Practicum Exercise 6

If you do not use it, you will lose it! Retain your newly acquired skill by determining the readability of selections from textual material in your content areas. Find the readability levels of essay questions and other material containing less than 100 words. Many times students fail tests because the questions are written at reading levels that are too difficult.

Applying the Concept of
Fry's Graph for Estimating Readability

As a content area teacher, you probably use numerous printed materials in helping the students accomplish the objectives of your classes. We realize there is not enough time in the day for you to determine the readability of every single newspaper article, magazine article, pamphlet, or other written material that you like to use. The fact is, you would be spending too much time counting words, sentences, and syllables!

We believe that after you have completed this module on how to use Fry's Graph for Estimating Readability, you will have a better concept of readability, which you can informally apply as you select printed materials. In other words, you will be aware of the fact that the length of the sentence and the length of the words make the biggest difference in terms of readability levels. Whenever you consider an article for use with your students, you can simply glance at the sentence length and word length to get a feeling for the difficulty of the material. If you notice that the sentences are extremely long and there are many difficult words in the passages, you will know the readability level may be beyond many of your students. Our point is now that you have this competency, you can apply it informally as you make reading assignments and select reading materials for your students.

In summary, competency in using Fry's graph will be most useful when you are participating on a textbook selection committee, or when you are selecting articles to prepare and duplicate for many of your students. Otherwise, you will be applying the concept of readability on an informal basis as you peruse those reading assignments you are asking students to complete.

If you can use Fry's graph to determine the readability levels of textbooks, articles, and selections containing less than 100 words, you are ready for the Posttest. You have acquired some new skills, which will help you select appropriate materials for your students. In addition, you will be able to use this information as you write and alter reading levels of different materials. Module 2 will show you how this is done. Pass the Posttest and go on to Module 2!

Answers

Practicum Exercise 1

The average reading level of the three health book selections, "Rabies," "Headache," and "Heatstroke," is 13th level (freshman). This was found by finding the average number of sentences (4.5) and the average number of syllables (167), and then locating the intersecting point on the graph.

	Number of Sentences	*Number of Syllables	Reading Level	True Estimate Range
"Rabies"	4.0	161	12th grade	11–13
"Headache"	4.9	170	14th level	13–15
"Heatstroke"	4.7	169	14th level	13–15
Sums	13.6	500		
Averages	4.5	167	13th level	12–14
(sums divided by 3)				

Rabies

Syllables

Since bites by cats, dogs, or any wild animal always present the danger of infection with rabies, a biting animal should never be killed unless unavoidable as a matter of safety. It should be caught and held for observation for at least fifteen days, in order to determine whether it develops rabies.

20
24
21
18

---

*Caution: Remember dialects make a difference in syllable counts. Check your syllable counts with the ones listed below if there is a great variance.

If it is necessary to kill the animal at the time of the biting, the carcass   *23*

should be sent to the state public health laboratory for an examination of its   *23*

brain. If the laboratory finds the animal was rabid, it is essential that treatment   *24*

be initiated at once. / *100 words*   *8*

Total   *161*

Headache

Syllables

The term *headache* is such a part of our everyday vocabulary that it has   *22*

become almost synonymous with any unpleasant situation or problem. But in a   *24*

medical sense the term quite literally means a head pain or an aching head and   *21*

is a symptom rather than itself an actual disease condition.   *18*

Hence, headache can suggest the possibility of a great many underlying   *21*

conditions. Perhaps one of the better known types is the throbbing, devastating   *20*

headache that sometimes accompanies a hangover. This differs from the type   *19*

known as tension headache, associated with figuring out one's income tax,   *20*

since they arise from / *100 words* different causes.   *5*

Total   *170*

Heatstroke

Syllables

The most important feature of heatstroke, which is sometimes also re-   *17*

ferred to as sunstroke, is the extremely high body temperature that accompanies   *22*

it. It is a far more serious condition than heat exhaustion.   *17*

Heatstroke occurs more often in males than in females and is more   *16*

common in elderly people and in those addicted to alcohol. Physical exertion is   *25*

a definite contributing factor; and an attack is much more likely to occur when   *23*

the humidity is high than when it is low, even at the same temperature.   *21*

The underlying cause of heatstroke is intimately connected with a cessa-   *21*

tion of sweating, accounting / *100 words* for the excessive rise in body temperature.   *7*

Total   *169*

Practicum Exercise 3

The article, "New Target for Feminists: TV Kiddie Cartoons," contains 5.4 sentences and 163 syllables in the first 100 words of the passage; therefore, the readability is twelfth-grade level. The true estimate of readability is from eleventh grade to thirteenth level. If your syllable count total is different, check it line by line with the one following.

New Target for Feminists: TV Kiddie Cartoons

	Syllables
Women's liberation may have a new battle to fight—Saturday morning	19
cartoon shows. According to researchers at the University of Michigan, car-	22
toons still are entrenched firmly in traditional male-female sex roles.	17
This conclusion was drawn by analyzing twenty programs from such	17
series as "Fat Albert," "Underdog," and "The Flintstones." Males were seen	16
in forty-two job roles, while females appeared in only nine. Only six of the	20
thirty-one cartoon women had jobs outside the home; whereas, in reality, 50	22
percent of all American women are in the labor force. *100 words*	16
Perhaps the time has come for feminists to analyze/all television shows to	14
determine if this is how children develop stereotype of sex roles.	

Total   _163_

Practicum Exercise 5

_80_ Nearest ten
_104_ Number of syllables × _1.25_ = _130_ syllables
_6.8_ Number of sentences × _1.25_ = _8.6_ sentences
_4-5_ Estimate of readability

If your syllable count is extremely different, check it line by line with the one below.

Math Problem

	Syllables
Nancy got a job working at a local store. She makes $4.12 an hour. She is	22
to report to work after school each afternoon and work for three hours. On	18
Saturdays and Sundays, she works eight hours. She wanted this job so she could	18
save money to buy a car. She hopes to be able to get a used MG car for $4000,	26
Assuming that she does not have to pay her own taxes, how long will it take her / *80 words*	20
to earn $4000?	

Total   _104_

Posttest

Directions: Read each of the following statements and complete each Posttest item.

1. State the two most important of the factors that influence the readability of written material.

2. List the two major uses of readability devices such as Fry's Graph for Estimating Readability.

3. Write the five directions for estimating readability when using Fry's Graph for Estimating Readability.

4. Use Fry's graph to determine the reading level of the following selection, "The International Date Line."

The International Date Line

Syllables

The International Date Line is often referred to as the Sunday-Monday _____
line. It follows approximately the 180th meridian, on opposite sides of which _____
the reckoning of the date differs by one complete day. If you travel from west to _____
east, standard time advances one hour for each fifteen degrees, which is one _____
twenty-fourth of a circle of longitude around the earth. In passing around the _____
earth completely, you gain twenty-four hours, or one complete day. If you _____
travel from east to west, it is necessary to turn your clock back one hour for each _____
fifteen degrees of/longitude; thus, you lose twenty-four hours in passing _____
completely around the earth.   *100 words* _____

Total _____

_____ Number of sentences
_____ Number of syllables
_____ Readability level

5. Decide if the following directions for using Fry's graph are true or false.
_____ a. Skip all proper nouns when selecting a 100-word passage.
_____ b. The estimate of readability is probably within one-half year of the true estimate of readability.
_____ c. Syllable counts by various people may differ slightly.
_____ d. If the intersecting points fall in the gray areas of the graph, the results are invalid.
_____ e. Count only complete sentences when counting the number of sentences in the 100-word count.

6. What adaptations would you make if you wanted to use Fry's graph with selections containing fewer than 100 words?

7. What adaptations are necessary when using Fry's graph to determine the readability levels of textbooks?

Posttest Answers

1. The two most important of the factors that influence the readability of written material are:
   a. sentence length
   b. vocabulary (or word difficulty)

2. The two major uses of readability formulas such as Fry's Graph for Estimating Readability are:
   a. estimating reading level
   b. preparing or rewriting material

3. The general procedures for estimating the reading level of any material when using Fry's Graph for Estimating Readability are:

Step 1. Select a representative 100-word passage.

Step 2. Count the number of sentences.

Step 3. Count the number of syllables.

Step 4. Plot the number of sentences and syllables on Fry's graph to obtain an estimate of readability.

Step 5. Remember that the true estimate is in a range of one year in either direction.

4. The selection, "The International Date Line" has:

   _4.6_ Number of sentences

   _148_ Number of syllables

   _9th_ Readability level

You can check your syllable count by comparing it line by line with the sample below.

The International Date Line

	Syllables
The International Date Line is often referred to as the Sunday-Monday	20
line. It follows approximately the 180th meridian, on opposite sides of which	25
the reckoning of the date differs by one complete day. If you travel from west to	21
east, standard time advances one hour for each fifteen degrees, which is one	18
twenty-fourth of a circle of longitude around the earth. In passing around the	21
earth completely, you gain twenty-four hours or one complete day. If you	17
travel from east to west it is necessary to turn your clock back one hour for each	21
fifteen degrees of longitude; thus, you lose twenty-four hours in passing	5
completely around the earth.	

Total _148_

5. a. false
   b. false
   c. true
   d. true
   e. false

6. Count the words and round down to the nearest ten. To base your selection on a scale of 100 words, find the appropriate number on the Conversion Chart. Multiply this number times the number of syllables and sentences.

7. Make sure you include a minimum of three 100-word selections randomly selected from the beginning, middle, and end of a textbook. The readability level is found by averaging the number of syllables and sentences in the selections.

If you have completed all Posttest items with 100 percent accuracy, you are ready for another module. If not, refer to the appropriate Study Guides for clarification of your difficulty. If you cannot clarify the difficulty, contact your instructor.

Final Comment

If you have completed this module with 100 percent accuracy, congratulations! You have now acquired a useful set of skills that will enable you to more adequately meet the needs of the students you teach. One word of caution, however. Your new knowledge is of no value unless you use it to help students cope with their reading assignments. This module does not test your intentions or application of readability skills; these qualities are dependent upon your professional and ethical responsibility.

Selected Bibliography

Arnold, R. D., and Sherry, N. "A Comparison of the Reading Levels of Disabled Readers with Assigned Textbooks." *Reading Improvement* 12, no. 4 (Winter 1975): 207–11.

Dale, E., and Chall, J. S. "A Formula for Predicting Readability." *Educational Research Bulletin* 27, no. 1 (1948): 11–20.

————, and Chall, J. S. "A Formula for Predicting Readability: Instructions." *Educational Research Bulletin* 27, no. 2 (1947): 37–54.

Fry, E. "A Readability Formula that Saves Time." *Journal of Reading* 11, no. 4 (1968): 513–16, 575–78.

————. "The Readability Graph Validated at Primary Levels." *The Reading Teacher* 22, no. 3 (1969): 534–38.

————. "Fry's Readability Graph: Clarifications, Validity, and Extention to Level 17." *Journal of Reading* 21, no. 3 (1977): 242–52.

Hittleman, D. R. "Readability, Readability Formulas, and Cloze: Selecting Instructional Materials." *Journal of Reading* 22, no. 2 (1978): 117–22.

Johnson, R. E., and Vardian, E. B. "Reading, Readability, and Social Studies." *The Reading Teacher* 26, no. 2 (1973): 483–88.

Kennedy, K. "Reading Level Determination for Selected Texts." *The Science Teacher* 41 (1974): 26–27.

Klare, G. R. "Assessing Readability." *Reading Research Quarterly* 10 (1974): 62–102.

————. The Measurement of Readability. Ames, Iowa: Iowa State University, 1963.

Lorge, I. "Readability Formulas—An Evaluation." *Elementary English* 36, no. 2 (1949): 86–95.

Maxwell, M. J. "Readability: Have We Gone Too Far?" *Journal of Reading* 21, no. 6 (1978): 525–30.

Pyrczak, F. Readability of Directions on Potentially Hazardous Household Products. *Reading Improvement* 14, no. 2 (Summer 1977): 77–81.

Spache, G. D. "A New Readability Formula for Primary Grade Reading Materials." *Elementary School Journal* 53, no. 3 (1953): 410–13.

MODULE 2

Preparing Materials at Specified Readability Levels

Contents

Prospectus
  Rationale
  Objectives
  Resources and Time Required
Pretest
Branching Program Alternatives for Pretest Responses
Enabling Element 1: *Reasons for Preparing Materials for Specified Readability Levels*
Enabling Element 2: *Altering Reading Levels of Subject Area Materials*
Enabling Element 3: *Writing Materials at Specified Readability Levels*
Posttest
  Posttest Answers
Selected Bibliography

Prospectus

Rationale

Teachers often select reading material from magazines, newspapers, pamphlets, and other materials for their students to read. These materials are usually valuable, but sometimes the readability level is above the reading level of the students. To make this material useful, skill in altering readability is necessary.

Over the term of a school year, teachers prepare many tests, course syllabi, worksheets, summaries, and other instructional aids for their students. It is essential for these materials to be prepared at the reading level suitable for most, if not all, students. Therefore it is necessary when teachers write material that they be able to control readability. This module is designed to help you write and alter materials to make them appropriate for your students.

Objectives

Terminal Objective

You will write materials at specified readability levels and alter the readability levels of passages related to your content area.

Specific Objectives

1. You will state the two major reasons for writing and altering materials for specified readability levels.

2. You will take a specified passage at the twelfth-grade reading level and alter the passage for a student with a sixth-grade reading level.

3. You will select a topic from your content area and write a 100-word passage at the fifth-grade reading level.

Resources and Time Required

Most of the materials required for completing this module are provided. However, it will be valuable to have some of your content area materials available. Gather sample test items, handouts you have prepared, magazine or newspaper articles, and various content area textbooks so they are ready for use. Module 1 should be completed before this module is begun. Since skill in finding readability is a prerequisite for completing this module, we provide in this module an alternative technique (Raygor's graph) for determining readability for those who found it difficult to use Fry's graph. The estimated time for completing the starred Enabling Activities in this module is three to four hours.

Pretest

Directions: For each question, determine the word that indicates your belief regarding your competency. If you are in doubt, choose NO.

1. Many educators believe it is important for teachers to be able to write   YES   NO
   and alter materials for specified reading levels. Can you state two
   reasons why these skills are necessary?

2. Readability formulas can be used to alter the reading level of materials.   YES   NO
   Can you alter materials in your content area to change the reading level?

3. Content teachers must frequently write test items and handouts for their   YES   NO
   students. Can you use Fry's graph to write materials at specified reading
   levels?

Branching Program Alternatives
for Pretest Responses

1. If you can state the rationale that explains why teachers should be able to write and alter materials for specified readability levels, you are ready for Enabling Element 2. If not, Enabling Element 1 will provide you with this information.

2. If you can alter materials in your content area to lower reading levels, you do not need to complete Enabling Element 2. Enabling Element 2 is very helpful if you do not know how to rewrite materials to change reading levels.

3. If you can use Fry's graph for preparing materials at specified readability levels, you are ready for the Posttest. If not, Enabling Element 3 is designed to help you develop this competency.

Enabling Element 1

Reasons for Preparing Materials for
Specified Reading Levels

Specific Objective 1

You will state the two main reasons for writing and altering materials for specified readability levels.

Enabling Activities

*1. Read Study Guide 1. Identify the main reasons teachers must be able to develop skill in writing and altering materials for particular reading levels.

2. Talk with some of your students and colleagues. Do they believe it is necessary for teachers to write materials at specified readability levels? Is Raths (1964) correct in saying that one responsibility assumed by good teachers is that of preparing curriculum materials?

3. Hold a discussion with one of your classes. Ask the students why they sometimes fail tests or neglect to complete assignments. See if they mention the fact that they did not understand the test items or directions. Probe to determine what caused the lack of understanding. Is the readability level of the materials one of the factors?

*4. Teachers are often cautioned to avoid "talking over the heads" of their students. Likewise, students do not like teachers who "talk down" to them. Discuss the implications for preparation of materials.

5. Some teachers believe standards are being lowered when reading levels of materials are lowered. Evaluate this statement.

6. A prerequisite for successfully completing this module is skill in determining readability levels. If you have not completed Module 1, "Determining Readability," do so now. If you attempted Module 1 but failed to develop competency in using Fry's graph to estimate readability levels, we provide an alternative technique for determining readability at the end of Study Guide 1. Be sure to pay attention to

---

*Indicates core Enabling Activities.

"Prerequisites for Preparing Materials for Specified Readability Levels," in Study Guide 1 if you want to learn another technique—perhaps an easier technique—for determining readability levels.

Study Guide 1

Effective Communication

According to Raths, one responsibility of a good teacher is preparing materials for students. All teachers recognize the inadequacies of available materials for meeting the individual needs of each student; thus they need supplemental materials. Teachers prepare handouts, review sheets, test items, directions for assignments and activities, and summaries from magazines and newspaper articles. Since students must be able to read these materials, it is imperative that teachers be skilled in writing the materials at appropriate reading levels.

We often hear of teachers who cannot understand why their students failed an examination after hours of teaching and reviewing. Some teachers claim that the students knew the answers the day before the test, but on the day of the test they did not seem to know a thing! When one examines the test items, it is relatively easy to understand why students failed.

This same problem arises if assignment sheets, course outlines, summaries, or other handouts are written at levels too difficult for the students to read. Both teachers and students become frustrated because they are not communicating. Teachers are often warned about talking above the levels of their students, and of course this same caution should be kept in mind concerning written communication.

We are not suggesting that content teachers should lower their course standards. Rather they should do a more effective job of communicating with their students so that high standards can be achieved in the course. Just as students do not like teachers to talk down to them, neither do they enjoy materials that insult their reading capabilities. Likewise, students do not want to be confused by materials that are too difficult to understand. Somewhere between these two extremes, clear communication is possible. Clear communication makes the achievement of subject area objectives possible. Teachers are advised to identify appropriate objectives and then to do an effective job of preparing handouts, course outlines, assignment sheets, and so forth. Also, if the test items that are used to evaluate student knowledge are appropriate for the students' reading levels, tests will evaluate the objectives of the course rather than the students' reading abilities. The level of written communication should be adapted so it is appropriate to help the students attain standards appropriate to their capabilities.

Alteration of Texts and Other Resources

In addition to developing skill in writing materials, teachers should develop competency in altering materials that are valuable but are written above the reading levels of the students. For example, as a teacher you may find many interesting articles in current journals or magazines that are written far above the reading levels of your students. You may believe that the concepts in these articles are extremely important for the students, and you may want the students to have copies to keep. If you develop competency in altering materials, you will have more resources available for use with your classes. We are not suggesting that content area teachers rewrite all of the materials they intend to use. However, if at times you do find some materials written at a high readability level, and you want to alter them, you will have more resources available for use with your classes.

At times it may be necessary to alter the readability level of some of the textual materials, also. Since textbooks are usually written by more than one author, you have probably found that some parts of the textbooks are more difficult to read. We are not suggesting that you rewrite all of your textbooks at lower readability levels. Certainly this is impossible! We are saying, however, that until more authors and publishers begin to evaluate the readability of textbooks and make them more readable, teachers must be able to alter some of the textual materials if they desire to use them.

Letters to Parents

With more emphasis on parent involvement, teachers are frequently asked to write letters to parents. If you are aware of how to write materials at specified readability levels, you will do a better job in making the letters readable for parents. Sometimes there is a lack of communication between teachers and parents because of the use of educational jargon and/or technical language, which many parents do not understand. If you are aware of how to write materials at specified readability levels, you will be able to choose appropriate words for letters and notes to parents.

In summary, if you develop skill in writing at specified readability levels, you will be confident that your students can read the materials you prepare. If you develop skill in altering readability, more resources will be useful for your classes. Your use of these skills will result in more appropriate reading materials in your classroom, which will enable more of your students to accomplish the objectives of your content area.

Prerequisites for Preparing Materials for Specified Readability Levels

Before you can complete this module successfully, you will need to have developed competency in using Fry's Graph for Estimating Readability. We hope that you have completed Module 1 and passed the Posttest to demonstrate your skill in applying this competency. If you have not completed Module 1, you should go back to it now before attempting to complete this module.

If you experienced difficulty in learning how to use Fry's graph and were not able to develop this competency, we suggest that you consider another technique for determining readability. This technique was developed by Alton L. Raygor at the University of Minnesota in 1977. Raygor developed a graph for estimating readability that is similar to the Fry graph. However, the major difference is that word difficulty is estimated by

Teachers are writers when they prepare tests and handouts.

counting long words (words of six or more letters), rather than by counting syllables. Raygor's graph also takes into consideration sentence length. Thus, Raygor's graph is also based on the two major factors that influence readability: sentence length and word difficulty.

Raygor's Graph. According to our experiences in working with content area teachers, if you were unable to develop proficiency in using Fry's graph, chances are you had difficulty counting syllables. If you did have difficulty counting syllables, you will probably prefer using the Raygor graph. Rather than having to count syllables to determine word difficulty, you simply circle and count the words in the 100-word passage that have six or more letters. The other procedures for determining readability are exactly the same.

   If you will now refer to Raygor's graph (figure 2), you will notice many similarities between the Fry and Raygor graphs. First, the number of sentences is indicated on the left side of the graph, as it is on the Fry graph. The major difference is that the longer sentences (3.2 sentences in 100 words) are indicated at the top of the graph and the shorter sentences (28 sentences in 100 words) are indicated at the bottom of the graph. Now direct your attention to the bottom of the graph where the number of long (hard) words is indicated. Notice that the number of long words ranges from 6 to 44. As you look at the grade level bands in the center of the graph, you will notice that the Raygor graph can be used to estimate the readability of materials from third grade through professional or graduate-school level.

Figure 2

The Raygor readability estimate

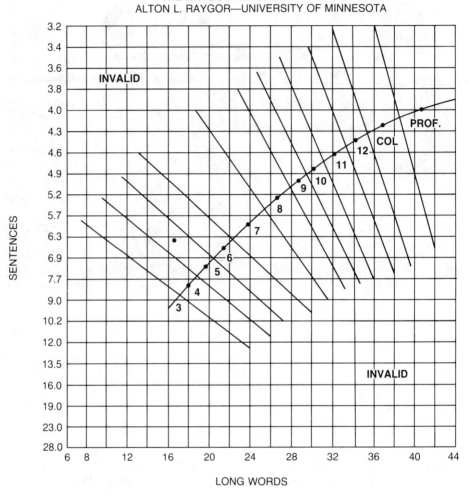

THE RAYGOR READABILITY ESTIMATE
ALTON L. RAYGOR—UNIVERSITY OF MINNESOTA

Directions: Count out three 100-word passages at the beginning, middle, and end of a selection or book. Count proper nouns, but not numerals.

1. Count sentences in each passage, estimating to nearest tenth.
2. Count words with six or more letters.
3. Average the sentence length and word length over the three samples and plot the average on the graph.

Example:		Sentences	6+ Words
	A	6.0	15
	B	6.8	19
	C	6.4	17
	Total	19.2	51
	Average	6.4	17

Note mark on graph. Grade level is about 5.

If you do decide to develop skill in using the Raygor graph, the directions are as follows:

1. Count out three 100-word passages at the beginning, middle, and end of a book. Be sure to include proper nouns in your word count, but do not count numerals.

2. Count the number of sentences in each passage, estimating to the nearest tenth.

3. Circle and count the words having six or more letters. Words having six or more letters are defined as *long* (hard) *words*.

4. Average the sentence length and the number of long (hard) words over the three samples, and plot the average on the graph.

The directions then for using the Raygor graph are exactly the same as for using the Fry graph except that (1) you skip the numerals when you count the 100-word passages; and (2) rather than having to count syllables, you simply determine word difficulty by circling and counting those words that have six or more letters.

Practicum Exercise

If you would like to use the Raygor graph, you can use it on the following selection, "A Positive Use of Fire." Follow these directions:

1. Count the first 100 words in the selection (skip numerals).

2. Count the number of sentences to the nearest tenth.

3. Circle and count those words that have six or more letters.

4. On Raygor's graph, plot a line across from the number of sentences and a line up from the number of hard or difficult words. The grade-level band in which the lines intersect is the estimate of readability.

A Positive Use of Fire

If you look around, signs of fires, long past or quite recent, will be evident. In the southeastern United States, pine forests are a product of fires. If they were not burned periodically by natural or artificial means, hardwoods would replace the pines. Here in the Sanctuary, fire is used carefully, under controlled conditions to maintain the pines and keep a proper balance between the pines and the undergrowth. If fire were kept out for a long time, the undergrowth would gain considerable height; then if wildfire swept through, even the fire-resistant pines would be in danger. All of the plants that grow here are "fireproof," coming back rapidly after a burn.

How many sentences are there in the 100-word sample?   _____

How many hard words are there in the 100 words?   _____

What is the readability of this sample?   _____

Answers to the Practicum Exercise

When you counted the number of sentences in this selection, you found that there were approximately 5.1 sentences. Words having six or more letters are defined as *difficult* or *long* words. You circled and counted the number of words having six or more letters, a total of 30 long words. When you plotted these points on the graph, you came across from approximately 5.2 and up from the line indicating 30 long words. You then found that the readability for the selection is ninth grade.

A Positive Use of Fire

If you look around, signs of fires, long past or quite recent, will be evident. In the southeastern United States, pine forests are a product of fires. If they were not burned periodically by natural or artificial means, hardwoods would replace the pines. Here in the Sanctuary, fire is used carefully under controlled conditions to maintain the pines and keep a proper balance between the pines and the undergrowth. If fire were kept out for a long time, the undergrowth would gain considerable height; then if wildfire swept through, even the fire-resistant pines would be in danger. All of the plants that grow here are "fireproof," coming back rapidly after a burn.

If you prefer using Raygor's graph to Fry's graph because you found counting words with six or more letters easier than determining the number of syllables in each word, you may wonder why we did not include this graph in Module 1, "Determining Readability Levels of Content Area Materials." We decided to use Fry's Graph for Estimating Readability, since there have been more research studies done comparing the results you get with Fry with the most respected readability formulas (Dale-Chall and Spache). There have been only a limited number of research studies done concerning the validity of Raygor's Graph for Estimating Readability. According to these preliminary studies, the results obtained using the Raygor graph are very similar to the results obtained when using the Fry graph. For example, Baldwin and Kaufman (1979) found the correlation between the Raygor and Fry readability estimates to be .87. In a comparison of the results obtained by using the Raygor and Fry methods for 100 different reading materials, they found that the estimates for 50 of the materials were exactly the same according to both graphs. For 25 of the books, the Raygor graph indicated estimates one grade above the results found on the Fry graph. Conversely, Raygor's graph was one grade below on 19 of the materials. The mean grade level of all the reading passages was ninth grade according to both Raygor and Fry graphs.

Baldwin and Kaufman also found it faster to determine the readability of materials by using the Raygor graph compared with the Fry graph. However, there was no significant difference between the Raygor and Fry groups in the errors made when using the graphs.

As more research studies are done, it may be that we will recommend Raygor's graph. However, at this time we feel more comfortable recommending Fry's graph, since it is based on more research. For the present, we encourage you to use the Fry graph, unless you have experienced much difficulty in counting syllables.

Now that you have the prerequisite skill for completing this module, go to Enabling Element 2 to find out how to alter reading levels of your subject area materials.

Enabling Element 2
Altering Reading Levels of Subject Area Materials

Specific Objective 2

You will take a specified passage at the twelfth-grade reading level and alter the passage for a student with a sixth-grade reading level.

Enabling Activities

*1. Read Study Guide 2 and identify the steps in the altering procedure.

*2. Do the Practicum Exercise, which asks you to rewrite the fourteenth-grade passage, "Florida," for a student with a ninth-grade reading level. Check your response with the one at the end of this Enabling Element.

3. Select a passage from a magazine or newspaper article in your subject area, and alter the passage for a student in your class who reads two years below the level of the material.

4. Select an editorial from the newspaper or a short selection from a magazine, and rewrite the selection to a lower or higher reading level.

5. Check the reading level of your essay test items. Alter them if necessary.

6. Try this if you have problems communicating with your students. Record one of your lectures. Select a 100-word unit and use Fry's or Raygor's graph to determine the listening level. Is it necessary to alter your oral communication?

7. You probably have a particularly good pamphlet that you have not shared with your students because you thought it was too difficult for them. Select some 100-word passages and rewrite them to lower reading levels. Ask your students to read the rewritten passages. If the material is now readable, you may want to rewrite the remainder of the pamphlet and some of the other materials you have been storing simply because they are too difficult for your students to read in their present form.

Study Guide 2

The readability level of material can be altered by increasing or decreasing the reading difficulty of the material. This Study Guide emphasizes lowering the readability level. It is the authors' experience that although many content area resource materials are

---

*Indicates core Enabling Activities.

available for students who are reading above grade level, the supply of lower-level material is very limited.

It is easy to rewrite materials to a lower reading level. This is accomplished by changing sentence length and word difficulty as necessary. Remember, sentence length and word difficulty are the two most important factors influencing the readability of materials.

Read the following selections. The first was written at the eighth-grade level, and the second was written at the fourth-grade level. As you read the two selections, you will notice that the content is the same. Try to determine what changes were made to lower the second selection to a fourth-grade reading level.

Selection 1: Eighth-Grade Reading Level

A glance at the advertisements in magazines leaves no doubt as to the interest of people in their weight. The dictators of fashion have made us weight conscious. And now the writers of advertisements are trying to convince the thin and fat alike that if they will only buy this exercising machine, this or that drug, or eat certain foods, a beautiful figure will result. They promise to make us look like, or at least desire to be like, the model who is pictured in the advertisement. They usually fail to point out that each person is different.

Selection 2: Fourth-Grade Reading Level

Do you ever read magazines? If so, you have probably noticed all the advertisements about weight. Most people are interested in their weight. The people who determine what is in style make us attach importance to weight. Now advertisers are doing the same thing. Some will tell you to buy an exercise machine. Others try to sell drugs to reduce or gain weight. Special food or liquid diets are often suggested, too. All of the advertisements try to make us want to be like the model in the picture. Yet each person is different. The advertisements do not say this.

What are the differences in the two selections?

1. _____

2. _____

If you look closely at the two selections, you will notice one difference is that more sentences were used in the last selection. The fourth-grade selection has eleven sentences as compared with the five sentences found in the eighth-grade selection. When you add more sentences and decrease the length of the existing sentences, you reduce the number of complex ideas per sentence that the student must comprehend. Understanding is facilitated because the ideas are offered in smaller doses.

Another difference in the two selections is that the fourth-grade selections includes fewer difficult words. The words *conscious*, *dictators*, *fashion*, and *pictured* have been replaced by shorter synonyms. This generally reduces the number of syllables and thereby lowers the reading level. The fourth-grade selection has 137 syllables, and the eighth-grade selection has 140 syllables.

How to Alter Readability of Written Materials

Revising the sentence structure of the selection is perhaps the easier of two ways to alter the readability level. Often good materials include long sentences with many details used to express the thought or idea. Consider the following descriptive sentence.

> In general, each flower consists of a floral axis upon which are borne the necessary organs of reproduction (stamen and pistils) and usually accessory organs (sepals and petals), which may serve both to attract pollinating insects and to protect the essential organs.

When reading this sentence, one must process and organize many different facts:

1. Each flower consists of a floral axis.
2. The necessary organs of reproduction are borne on the floral axis.
3. The necessary organs of reproduction are stamens and pistils.
4. Sepals and petals are also borne on the floral axis.
5. Sepals and petals are accessory organs.
6. Sepals and petals attract pollinating insects.
7. Sepals and petals protect the essential organs.

To lower the readability, it is necessary to introduce the facts in many sentences rather than in one long complex sentence. This aids the reader's organization of facts and usually improves comprehension because the facts are introduced in shorter doses. For example, the above sentence might be written as follows:

> In general, each flower consists of a floral axis. The necessary organs of reproduction, stamens and pistils, are borne upon the floral axis. The floral axis also contains sepals and petals. Sepals and petals are important because they attract pollinating insects and protect the essential organs.

Did you find this easier to understand? Probably so, because the thoughts concerning the parts of a flower were presented in four sentences rather than in one. As you read, you had an opportunity to process each fact in a separate sentence rather than having to separate the complex sentence to notice each fact. The need to "run that by again" does not occur.

The second method of lowering readability is to decrease the number of syllables by substituting shorter words for longer words. A dictionary or thesaurus is helpful when changing words in the selection; however, you will find it difficult to find synonyms for some basic words. For example, stamens and pistils do not have any easier synonyms.

The emphasis in such a case should be on changing the sentence length rather than on changing the vocabulary. This is not to say that it is not necessary to change some vocabulary words; but overall it is easier to lower the readability level by increasing the number of sentences.

Procedure for Altering Readability to a Lower Level

When changing a selection to a specified readability level, follow these directions.

1. **Look for difficult words in the selection.** Usually the longer the word is, the more difficult it is for students to read. Identify those words that are multisyllabic or those words that have six or more letters.

2. **Change some of the harder words to easier words.** See if you can substitute synonyms for the difficult words. If so, change some of the difficult words by substituting shorter and easier words.

3. **Reread the sentences to determine if you can divide some of them into two or three shorter sentences.** Remember that it is easier to change readability by increasing the number of sentences and, in doing so, you present the number of thoughts in shorter doses.

4. **Rewrite the selection using shorter sentences and easier words.**

5. **Determine the readability of the altered selection to see if you have lowered its reading level.**

A Special Note. When altering the readability of selections it is not essential that the word count be exactly the same. Often the word count is increased or decreased when changing vocabulary and sentence length. Remember that the goal is to alter the selection so your students can read and understand it, not to get an exact amount of words. If the word count in the altered selection is less than 100 words, simply follow the directions for using Fry's graph with selections containing fewer than 100 words (Enabling Element 3, Module 1).

**Illustrations of the Steps for Altering Materials to a
Lower Readability Level**

Now that you know the procedure for altering reading levels, let us try your skill on the following selection entitled "Florida." In its present form, we know that the selection is written at the fourteenth-grade level because it contains 7.2 sentences and 168 syllables. Let us see if we can reduce the selection so children with a sixth-grade reading level could learn more about Florida. Remember, it is not essential that the word count be kept exactly the same when a selection is altered to change its readability. Often the word count is increased or decreased when changing vocabulary and sentence length. Our goal is to alter the selection so students can read and understand it, not to get an exact number of words. If the word count in your altered selection is less than 100 words, simply follow the directions for using Fry's graph with selections containing fewer than 100 words (Enabling Element 3, module 1) to determine the new readability level.

Florida

In 1565 the Spanish founded St. Augustine, the oldest permanent European settlement on the North American mainland. Most of Florida is young even though the state contains the country's oldest city. Cape Canaveral, a symbol of the space age, is the launching site of space vehicles. Walt Disney World is changing the rolling, citrus-clad hills around Orlando and attracting tens of thousands of tourists. Miami Beach entertains thousands of visitors.

Annually the woodlands of northern Florida are a rich resource of pulpwood. The orange groves of central Florida produce much of the country's orange crop. The vegetable fields of southern Florida produce fresh vegetables—corn, beans, and tomatoes—which are sent to the colder parts of the country in the winter.

Rewrite "Florida."

Step 1: Look for difficult words in the selection. As you read "Florida," you will notice several difficult words such as *permanent, settlement, symbol, launching, vehicles, citrus, annually,* and *woodlands.*

Step 2: Change some of the harder words to easier words. It is not possible to change every difficult word in a selection, but you can make the selection easier to read by using synonyms for some of the more difficult words. For example, you can use the synonym *yearly* for *annually, lasting* for *permanent, sign* for *symbol, woods* for *woodlands,* and *blast-off* for *launching.*

Step 3: Reread the sentences to determine if you can divide some of them into two or three shorter sentences. You will notice that most of the sentences in the selection are about ten to fifteen words long. You can divide some of these sentences into two sentences. For example, the first sentence could be rewritten to say, "In 1565 the Spanish founded St. Augustine. This is the longest lasting European settlement on the mainland of North America." By dividing long sentences into shorter ones, we control the number of thoughts introduced to students at one time.

Step 4: Rewrite the selection using shorter sentences and easier words. A revised selection might look like the following:

Florida

In 1565 the Spanish founded St. Augustine. This is the longest lasting European settlement on the mainland of North America. Most of Florida is young, even though it has the country's oldest city. Cape Canaveral, a sign of the space age, is the blast-off site of space vehicles. Walt Disney World is changing the rolling, citrus-clad hills around Orlando. Disney World is getting tens of thousands of tourists now. Miami Beach entertains thousands of visitors.

Yearly the woods of northern Florida are a rich source of pulpwood. Orange groves of central Florida produce much of the country's orange crop. Vegetable fields of southern Florida produce fresh vegetables. Corn, beans, and tomatoes are sent to colder parts of the country in the winter season.

Step 5: Determine the readability of the altered selection to see if you have lowered its reading level. If you use Fry's Extended Graph, you will find the readability for this selection to be ninth-grade level because it now contains 9.1 sentences and 159 syllables.

Practicum Exercise

Now it is time for you to practice changing the readability level of some of your content material. You may want to choose the test items, letters to parents, study or listening guides that you have developed, or articles that you use frequently with your classes. Follow the five steps illustrated above. We believe that after doing this several times, you will be able to change a 100-word selection in approximately ten minutes. As we said earlier, we are not implying that you should rewrite all of your textbooks and supplemental materials. Certainly this is impossible! Yet, skill in altering reading levels is beneficial. After completing this Practicum Exercise successfully, go on to Enabling Element 3 to develop another skill that will prove to be extremely helpful—writing materials at specified readability levels.

Enabling Element 3
Writing Materials at Specified Readability Levels

Specific Objective 3

You will select a topic from your content area and write a 100-word passage at the fifth-grade reading level.

Enabling Activities

*1. Read Study Guide 3. It provides detailed directions and examples of how you can write materials at particular reading levels.

*2. Use Fry's or Raygor's graph to check a few of your test items. At what readability levels did you write them? If the readability level is too high, prepare new questions at a lower readability level. You may administer both forms of the test and compare the results.

 3. Work together with members of your content area to identify important concepts, ideas, or other knowledge. Have each member select a few topics and then prepare a

---

*Indicates core Enabling Activities.

handout at a low reading level. If the members of your department cooperate, you will have many low-level reading materials on your most important topics.

4. Check the readability levels of some of the items on a standardized test in your area. Should standardized test makers also be able to write at particular readability levels? Could the reading level be one reason some students do poorly on standardized tests?

5. The next time you prepare a course outline or assignment sheets, follow the directions for writing materials at specified readability levels. Observe and compare the reactions of your students.

*6. Do the Practicum Exercise to develop skill in writing materials.

Study Guide 3

Teachers have the responsibility of preparing for students specialized material, such as test items, assignments, and handouts with supplemental information. Since students must be able to read these prepared materials, it is essential that the reading levels of the materials be appropriate.

How to Write at Particular Readability Levels

Perhaps the easiest step in the procedure for writing materials at specified readability levels is to write as if you were talking to your students. After doing so, use Fry's graph to check the readability. If the readability level is appropriate, there will be no need to alter the material. If the reading level is too difficult, you can follow the procedure suggested in Study Guide 2 for altering materials. Let us examine the steps in this procedure in more depth.

Step 1: Write the materials as if you were talking to your students. When writing materials at specified readability levels, begin by writing down the information as if you were talking to your students. If you are trying to write low level materials, you will want to use shorter sentences and shorter words. At this point, be more concerned about expressing your ideas than about the reading level. After the ideas are well organized, you can go back to find the difficult words and the longer sentences that need to be changed. First say what you want to say.

Step 2: Check the reading level by using Fry's graph. Follow the directions provided in Module 1 to find out the readability level of materials that you have written. If you use Fry's graph several times, you will develop a sense of the reading difficulty of written materials and a sense for the necessary adjustments. If you are not proficient in using Fry's graph, use Raygor's graph.

Step 3: Alter the readability level if necessary. If adjustments are necessary, follow the procedures suggested in Study Guide 2 of this module for altering the readability level of materials: (1) look for difficult words in the selection; (2) find synonyms for these difficult words; (3) identify the longer and more complex sentences; (4) change the complex sentences into simple sentences; (5) determine the readability of your rewritten selection. Remember, it is not essential to have the same word count in your altered selections as in the original.

Illustrations of the Steps

Step 1. Suppose you teach social studies and must prepare an examination. Your first step is to write the questions as if you were talking to your students (as in giving an oral examination). Suppose your test items read as follows:

Sample Test Items

Essay Questions
1. What effects do you think Europe's great population growth in the nineteenth century had on the population growth of the United States during the same period?
2. What are the Soviet planners doing to overcome the hazards of the droughts that are so prevalent throughout the grassland areas of southern USSR?

True and False
1. Penetration of the interior of Africa was a relatively easy matter for the explorers because of the continent's many navigable rivers.

Short Answer
1. Name an area in northern Eurasia where farming is not an important occupation because there is no month that is free of frost, hence, where it is too cold for food crops to be grown except in sheltered places.

Step 2. Your next step is to use Fry's graph to determine the readability of the questions. In determing the readability levels of the test items, you find 110 words in all. Use the first 100 words to determine the number of syllables and sentences. You find 168 syllables and 3.7 sentences in the first 100 words. According to these facts, the readability level is at the fourteenth-grade level on Fry's graph.

Step 3. Suppose most of your students are reading at the ninth-grade level. This means you need to alter the readability level by changing some of the longer words and longer sentences. Your newly rewritten questions might read as follows:

Rewritten Test Items

Essay Questions
1. Europe had a great population growth in the nineteenth century. What effects do you think Europe's growth had on the population growth of the United States in the same period?
2. Droughts are common throughout the grassland areas of southern USSR. What are Soviet planners doing to overcome the hazards of the droughts?

True and False
1. Getting to the interior of Africa was pretty easy for the explorers because there are so many rivers the explorers were able to use to get there.

Short Answer

1. In some places the weather is too cold to grow food crops except in sheltered places. Name an area in northern Eurasia where farming is not an important occupation because there is no month that is free of frost.

The reading level of your newly revised questions is now at the ninth-grade level because there are seven sentences and 156 syllables. You changed the number of sentences from four to seven and also decreased the syllable count by 12 by changing words like *prevalent* and *penetration*.

Practicum Exercise

You learn by doing. Write some test items or directions for an assignment, or prepare a handout you need at this time. Try to write the material at the most appropriate grade level for most of your students. You may want to work with one of your colleagues to develop a series of handouts on topics that are extremely important to all students.

Final Comment

The new skills you have developed will enable your students to learn more in your content area. If you will use the suggestions for altering and writing materials several times, the procedures will become automatic. We believe you will find this competency most useful when preparing test questions, study guides, listening guides, articles that are ''too good for the students to miss,'' and handouts explaining assignments and requirements. After you have used the procedure several times, it will not be necessary to determine the readability levels of altered selections for you will have a sense for readability. Of course, if you do not apply the skills, chances are your students will continue to be frustrated by written materials in your content areas. The decision is yours.

Posttest

Directions: Read each of the following statements and complete each Posttest item. One hundred percent accuracy is expected.

1. State the two major reasons why teachers should be able to write and alter materials for specified readability levels.
2. Rewrite the following selection, ''The Comma,'' so it has sixth-grade readability. In its present form, ''The Comma'' contains 100 words, 6 sentences, 166 syllables; and it has twelfth-grade readability according to Fry's graph.

The Comma

When speaking to someone, you are communicating information or ideas from your mind to his. If you communicate effectively, you control the flow of information and ideas in such a way that the listener can follow you easily. You do this by using changes in stress and pitch and by using pauses. Likewise, you use punctuation to control the flow of information in writing. Punctuation separates one sentence or thought from another, thus keeping the relationships among parts of the sentence clear and distinct. The comma is especially useful for this purpose, so remember to use commas to separate thoughts.

3. Describe the three steps necessary to write materials at the fifth-grade readability level.

Posttest Answers

1. One of the responsibilities of teachers is that of preparing written materials such as tests, handouts, and directions to assignments. If the students are expected to read the materials, teachers must write them at appropriate reading levels so communication is possible. Teachers should be able to alter selections so they will have more resources available for teaching their classes.

2. If you have rewritten the "The Comma" on a sixth-grade reading level and can substantiate the reading level using Fry's or Raygor's graph, you have successfully completed Posttest item number 2. Remember that your selection need not contain exactly 100 words, but it must be at the sixth-grade level. The following is a sample revision of the selection on a sixth-grade level according to Fry's graph (9 sentences and 139 syllables).

The Comma

When speaking to someone, you are relaying ideas and information. The ideas go from your mind to his. If you are communicating well, you control the flow of thoughts in such a way that the listener can follow easily. You can do this by using changes in stress and pitch. Pauses can be used, too. When you write, you use commas to control the flow of thoughts. Commas are used to separate one thought from another in a sentence and thus make the sentence clear. The comma is really useful for this purpose. You can use commas to separate thought units.

3. Three steps necessary to write materials at the fifth-grade level are
   a. Write the selection as if you are talking to your students.
   b. Use Fry's or Raygor's graph to check the readability level.
   c. Alter the selection if necessary by changing the number of sentences and syllables. At the fifth-grade level you can have approximately five to twelve sentences (depending upon the number of syllables) and approximately 108 to 146 syllables (depending upon the sentence length).

Selected Bibliography

Baldwin, R. S., and Kaufman, R. K. "A Concurrent Validity Study of the Raygor Readability Estimate." *Journal of Reading* 23, no. 2 (1979): 148–53.

Craig, L. C. "If It's Too Difficult for the Kids to Read—Rewrite It!" *Journal of Reading* 21, no. 3 (1977): 212–14.

Endicott, A. L. "A Proposed Scale for Syntactic Complexity." *Research in the Teaching of English* 7 (1973): 5–12.

Flesch, R. *The Art of Readable Writing.* New York: Collier Books, 1951.

Jacobson, M. D. "Reading Difficulty of Physics and Chemistry Textbooks." *Educational and Psychological Measurement* 25 (1965): 449–57.

Klare, G. R. "The Role of Word Frequency in Readability." *Elementary English* 45 (1968): 12–22.

Koenke, K. "Another Practical Note on Readability Formulas." *Journal of Reading* 15 (1971): 203–8.

Kulm, G. "Sources of Reading Difficulty in Elementary Algebra Textbooks." *The Mathematics Teacher* 66 (1973): 649–52.

McCuaig, S. M., and Hutchings, B. "Using Fry's Graph to Describe the Variation of Readability." *Journal of Reading* 18 (1975): 298–300.

Raths, L. E. "What Is a Good Teacher?" *Childhood Education* 40 (1964): 451–56.

Raygor, A. L. "The Raygor Readability Estimate: A Quick and Easy Way to Determine Difficulty." *Reading: Theory, Research, and Practice.* Edited by P. David Pearson. Pp. 259–63.

Shepherd, J. W., and Dickerson, F. E. "A Fry Graph Wakes up Student Writers." *Journal of Reading* 20, no. 4 (1977): 292–94.

Spache, G. D. *Good Reading for Poor Readers.* 9th ed., rev. Champaign, Illinois: Garrard, 1974.

Determining Suitability of Materials

Contents

Prospectus
  Rationale
  Objectives
  Resources and Time Required
Pretest
Branching Program Alternatives for Pretest Responses
Enabling Element 1: *The Informal Suitability Survey*
Enabling Element 2: *Constructing an Informal Suitability Survey*
Enabling Element 3: *Administering and Scoring an Informal Suitability Survey*
Enabling Element 4: *Planning Differentiated Reading Assignments*
Posttest
  Posttest Answers
Selected Bibliography

Prospectus

Rationale

One factor that influences student achievement in content areas is the suitability of the textbooks or other commonly required written materials. Materials can be classified as suitable if the student can recognize 95 percent of the words and comprehend 75 percent of what he or she reads. Just as there is not one golf club suitable for all the various shots on the golf course, neither is there one textbook suitable for all the students in a typical class. One task of the content teacher is to determine the suitability of available materials so that pupils are capable of handling assignments.

We believe the easiest way to determine whether the books you are planning to use are suitable is to have the students attempt to read a sample selection from the book. Just as Goldilocks went from one chair to the next to find one that was "just right," your students can try reading sample selections from the various content area materials to find those reading materials that correspond to their capabilities. Some printed materials will be too difficult, some will be too easy, and others will be just right!

This module is designed to teach you how to construct, administer, score, and interpret an Informal Suitability Survey for your content classes. An Informal Suitability Survey is a device consisting of (1) a sample reading selection, (2) accompanying motivation statement to provide a purpose for reading, and (3) comprehension questions to check understanding. The Informal Suitability Survey can be used to determine the suitability or appropriateness of the materials you have available and help you match these to your students. The result should be that students can read their assignments and, therefore, succeed in content areas.

Objectives

Terminal Objective

You will use an Informal Suitability Survey to determine the suitability of content area materials.

Specific Objectives

1. You will describe an Informal Suitability Survey and state the major purpose for using one with your class.
2. You will construct an Informal Suitability Survey by selecting a representative passage of 200 words, writing a motivation statement, and preparing five appropriate comprehension questions.
3. You will administer and score an Informal Suitability Survey following the procedures described in this module.
4. After scoring an Informal Suitability Survey, you will state the specific implications of the findings for planning differentiated reading assignments.

Resources and Time Required

You will need textbooks or other commonly required reading materials used in your subject area to complete this module. Paper is needed for developing an Informal Suitability Survey. If you have completed Module 1 on readability, you may want to refer to it for determining the reading difficulty level of your subject area material. However, it is not essential to have completed Module 1 on readability before this module. The estimated time to complete the starred core Enabling Activities is four to five hours.

Pretest

Directions: For each question, determine the word that indicates your belief regarding your competency. If you are in doubt, choose NO.

1. Before you can develop an Informal Suitability Survey, you must   YES   NO
   realize what it contains and why you might use it. Can you describe an

Informal Suitability Survey and state the reasons for using one in subject area classes?

2. The materials needed to construct an Informal Suitability Survey are commonly available. Do you have a collection of selections and accompanying motivation statements and comprehension questions? Have you developed an Informal Suitability Survey using these materials?   YES   NO

3. If you want to implement the concept of an Informal Suitability Survey in your classes, you must learn how to administer and score one. Can you administer and score an Informal Suitability Survey to determine the suitability of required reading material?   YES   NO

4. The results of any evaluative procedure are useless if they are not interpreted. Do you know how to interpret and use the results from an Informal Suitability Survey to plan differentiated reading assignments?   YES   NO

Branching Program Alternatives for Pretest Responses

1. If you cannot describe an Informal Suitability Survey and state the purpose for applying the concept of one in your classroom, Enabling Element 1 will help you acquire this information. If you can describe an Informal Suitability Survey and state its major purpose, you are ready for Enabling Element 2.

2. You are well prepared if you have a selection with accompanying motivation statement and comprehension questions to be used in determining the suitability of your textbooks. Enabling Element 2 is designed to help you develop these materials into an Informal Suitability Survey if you have not done so.

3. If you have already administered and scored an Informal Suitability Survey to determine the suitability of materials for your students, you need not do Enabling Element 3. This element is designed for those who have never administered and scored such a device. Procedures for both individual and group administration are presented.

4. Your answer to this question is very important. The implications from an Informal Suitability Survey are essential for increasing your effectiveness as a teacher. Do Enabling Element 4 if you have any doubts. If you already know the implications, you are ready for the Posttest.

Enabling Element 1
The Informal Suitability Survey

Specific Objective 1

You will describe an Informal Suitability Survey and state the major purpose for using one with your class.

Enabling Activities

*1. Read Study Guide 1. Determine what an Informal Suitability Survey is and the value of using such surveys.

2. Teaching is both satisfying and frustrating. Think of those things that frustrate you most. Does the fact that some students cannot read the textbook or other required material frustrate you? If so, are you committed to doing something about it?

3. Consider the students who cannot read your textbook or other commonly required reading materials. How do they feel when you make an assignment? How do they feel when others are sharing information gleaned from the reading assignments? How do they respond?

4. Discuss why there is such a wide range of reading achievement among secondary students. Make a list of possible reasons. Module 10, "Identifying and Helping Problem Readers," can be used to verify your ideas.

5. Look at the students in your classes to notice the range in their heights. If a standard size of clothing were required, it would be inappropriate for many students. Is there any reason to believe that mental abilities will not vary as do physical characteristics?

6. Collect the written materials you commonly use in teaching your classes. You will be using these reading resources as you complete the other enabling activities in this module.

Study Guide 1

The first task in bowling is to find a ball that fits. Bowlers move from one rack of balls to another to find a suitable ball. Others go to the expense of having the holes drilled to fit their own fingers, thumb, and span. It is a fact that one bowling ball is simply not suitable for all bowlers.

---

*Indicates a core Enabling Activity.

Such is the case with textbooks or other commonly required reading materials used in content area classes. Materials that are too difficult for some students are suitable for others. This is true because one-third of the students within a classroom read below their current grade level, one-third read at the grade level, and one-third read above their current grade level. The range of reading levels of a typical seventh-grade class is between third and eleventh grade, and this range increases as students advance in grade level.

The wide range in reading achievement is to be expected because of the heterogeneous nature of school populations. Students vary in height, weight, attitudes, and mental ability, to mention just a few factors. Textbooks, on the other hand, vary in readability less than the group of students served in any subject area classroom. The difference between the students' reading levels and the book reading level produces an instructional problem for subject area teachers. One text is simply not suitable for every student.

Description of an Informal Suitability Survey

For each student in their classes, content teachers must determine the suitability of textbooks or other required reading material. A useful technique to identify the suitability of a textbook and/or other written material is the Informal Suitability Survey. *An Informal Suitability Survey is an informal device that can be used to determine if students can handle selected content area reading material.*

An Informal Suitability Survey consists of a representative selection from some commonly required content area material. In addition, a motivation statement and comprehension questions accompany the selection. To develop the Informal Suitability Survey, the teacher (1) selects a representative selection from commonly required reading materials, (2) writes the motivation statement to provide a purpose for reading the selection, and (3) prepares comprehension questions covering vocabulary, facts, and inferences in order to check the students' understanding of the selection. The teacher then administers the Informal Suitability Survey to students to determine if the textbook is appropriate in terms of their reading capabilities. For example, the speech or language arts teacher might use the following Informal Suitability Survey, which was constructed from a language arts textbook.

Sample Informal Suitability Survey

Name _____   Date _____
                                     Source _____
                                     Circle One: Suitable Unsuitable

Motivation Statement: Many students like to find jobs, and of course, all of you will probably be employed some day. Read the following selection to answer the question, "How do I prepare for a job interview?"

Selection:

Preparing for the Job Interview

An interview is a meeting between two or more parties to exchange information. The purpose of a job interview is to provide opportunities for the employer and prospective employee to exchange information. The employer desires to know if the applicant possesses the necessary capabilities and qualities to handle certain responsibilities. The candidate wants to know if the responsibilities, working conditions, and salary are suitable for his or her needs.

There are two different ways employers interview prospective candidates. In the *open-ended* interview the employer generally begins by saying, "Tell me a little bit about yourself." The prospective employee then has the responsibility of informing the employer of his or her strengths and capabilities as a person. The *closed* interview technique is different in that the employer asks many specific questions. For example, the employer may ask questions about your grades in school, family background, previous responsibilities and interests.

In preparing for a job interview, you should try to learn about the job so you have questions to ask. You may want to discuss the type and responsibilities of the work with your family, friends, or people who have similar jobs. Make a list of the important questions you have.

Another step in preparing for an interview is simply "know yourself." Be prepared to give the interviewer a concise picture of your interests and capabilities. Evaluate yourself to determine those things you do well and the characteristics you have that others seem to like.

Make the appointment for the interview and then plan to arrive a few minutes early. Promptness is generally considered very important by most employers. Evaluate your personal appearance to see if you are creating the image you desire. Usually, simple, conservative clothing is just right for an interview. Be ready to greet the employer with a ‌*300th word* smile and simply be yourself!

Comprehension Questions:
(V = Vocabulary; F = Factual; I = Inference)
1. *(V)* What does *prospective* mean?
2. *(F)* What is the main purpose of a job interview?
3. *(F)* What three things should you do in preparing for a job interview?
4. *(F)* What information does an employer usually like to have about an applicant?
5. *(I)* Why do you suppose some employers like to use the open-ended interview technique?

As you can see, an Informal Suitablity Survey is a sampling technique to determine if the materials you are considering for use with the students are appropriate. The above selection consists of a 300-word passage; however, you may want to use 200-, 400-, or even 500-word selections. If you have many materials available, you can construct a series of Informal Suitability Surveys and then match the materials to the students. If only one textbook is available, you may need to determine the students who are capable of reading the text and then make adaptations for other students.

You may be wondering how many Informal Suitability Surveys you will need. The answer to this question depends upon the availability of textbooks and other commonly

An individually administered Informal Suitability Survey requires time, but yields so much information.

used printed materials related to your content area. If you plan to use one textbook with all of the students, you will need to develop only one Informal Suitability Survey. Of course, you must be aware that the book is going to be unsuitable for some of the students. You may want to give each student a copy of the textbook and adapt the reading assignments to the capabilities of the students. For example, if only one textbook is available, you know that some students will be able to read the textual materials to obtain ideas and information. Other students may be able to gain information and ideas from the pictures, diagrams, or other illustrations in the text. Of course some parts of a textbook are easier to read than other parts because of the nature of the concepts. If the textbook was written by several different authors, some parts may be easier to read. If you use only one textbook, you must realize from the onset that some students will be unable to complete the reading assignments. Please do not put the blame on the students for not doing their assignment, but rather realize you are promoting failure by expecting the impossible. Going back to our analogy at the beginning of this Study Guide, in essence you are asking a child to roll a bowling ball that has holes too small for the child's fingers. You cannot jump up and down in frustration when the student continues to roll gutter balls.

We recommend that you attempt to find many different reading resources for your content area classes. If you are able to obtain books related to your objectives and yet written at different readability levels, you will more effectively help students accomplish the objectives of your content area. Of course, using more reading sources requires making more than one Informal Suitability Survey. The general guideline is to identify those reading resources you *commonly* use and to develop one Informal Suitability Survey for each one of these materials.

As mentioned in Module 1, you can also match materials to students by comparing readability levels of the materials to the students' reading levels. To do so, you must have the reading scores for all your students. Often these scores are either unavailable or invalid. Students have many different reading levels, depending upon their interests and the background information they possess on any specific topic. For example, a student who is very interested in math may be able to read higher level books because he or she knows the specialized vocabulary and symbols and is highly motivated. This same student may read social studies books at a level two or three years lower because of a lack of interest and/or a good background in social studies. Using the Informal Suitability Survey, then, is a more valid technique than using readability formulas for matching specific materials to your students. Enabling Element 2 will help you construct an Informal Suitability Survey.

Enabling Element 2
Constructing an Informal Suitability Survey

Specific Objective 2

You will construct an Informal Suitability Survey by selecting a representative passage of 200 words, writing a motivation statement, and preparing five comprehension questions consisting of three factual questions, one vocabulary question, and one inference question.

Enabling Activities

*1. Read Study Guide 2. This Study Guide provides the necessary directions to help you make your own Informal Suitability Surveys.

*2. Do Practicum Exercise 1 to practice constructing an Informal Suitability Survey. Compare your efforts to the answers to Practicum Exercise 1 found at the end of this Enabling Element.

*3. Select a 200-word passage representative of the textbook used most often in one of your classes, and write a motivation statement and five comprehension questions as directed in Practicum Exercise 2.

*4. Evaluate your questions. When writing the factual questions, did you select significant facts? What about your question concerning vocabulary? Is the vocabulary word essential to the meaning of the selection? Does your inference question require knowledge from the selection as well as information from the reader's experiences?

5. What are the advantages of having ten questions as compared to five? Try checking comprehension with ten questions as compared to five. Are there differences in your findings?

---

*Indicates core Enabling Activities.

*6. Discuss why it is important to provide a statement to motivate the reader. What are the advantages of presenting questions before asking students to read the selection? Are there implications for introducing all reading assignments?

Study Guide 2

When developing an Informal Suitability Survey, remember the final product consists of (1) a representative reading selection from any textual material commonly used in the class, (2) a motivation statement giving the student a purpose for reading the selection, and (3) comprehension questions to determine if the students understand the reading selection. Specific instructions for constructing an Informal Suitability Survey follow.

Step 1: Select a Representative Passage

Select a representative passage from your textbook or other frequently assigned reading materials. The length of the passage will vary with the grade level and nature of the materials. Generally a 200-word passage is preferred. However, if it is difficult to find 200 consecutive words (as in some math books), you can use a 100-word selection. For longer textbooks, you may want to develop a 300- or 400-word selection, or two 200-word passages. The selections need not contain exactly 200, 300, or 400 words, but it is necessary to mark the 200th, 300th, or 400th word for scoring purposes. The important fact to remember is that it is essential to choose a selection that is a *representative*, self-contained sample of the material being considered for use.

Select two or three passages of 200 words if you are surveying the suitability of a major textbook. The extra passages can be used as alternate forms of the Informal Suitability Survey for students whose scores you doubt.

Skip all proper nouns (capitalized name of a particular person, place, or thing) and numerals when counting words for your passages. Proper nouns are not counted because they are usually introduced to students when regular reading assignments are made. Numerals are not counted because they are not words. Mark the 200th, 300th, or 400th word by making a slash after it.

To illustrate Step 1, suppose you are a social studies teacher and you chose the following selection. This selection is representative of materials in the major text you would like to use with your students. Your word count (skipping proper nouns and numerals) reveals approximately 200 words.

Sample Selection from a Social Studies Textbook:
Becoming a Naturalized Citizen

People who desire to become naturalized citizens of the United States must be at least eighteen years old. The applicant must be able to sign a petition in his or her own handwriting. They must demonstrate skill in reading, writing, and speaking the English

---

*Indicates core Enabling Activities.

language unless physically unable to do so. Those applicants who have been residing in the United States for 20 years are exempted from the English proficiency examination.

A person who desires to become a naturalized citizen must be of good moral character and well-disposed to the good order and prosperity of the United States. There are residence requirements that must be met before filing a petition to become a citizen. The petition must have two credible citizen witnesses who have personal knowledge of the applicant's character, residence, and loyalty. The applicant must demonstrate knowledge and under- standing of the fundamentals of United States history and form of government.

Naturalization is denied to any person who within 10 years has been subversive, including Communists or others who favor totalitarian government and who were members of a proscribed organization (unless the petitioner was under 16 or forced under duress).

As with other federal statutes, there are exceptions to the guidelines stated above. Of course, the guidelines are subject to change by the /200th word/ Congress of the United States.

Step 2: Write a Motivation Statement

Write a motivation statement for each passage to provide the students with a purpose for reading. The motivation statement usually consists of two sentences. The first sentence is a general statement concerning the topic of the representative passage. This sentence provides the reader with a frame of reference for reading the selection. The second statement is a question or command stating what the reader should be trying to learn. For example, a motivation statement for the above passage on becoming a naturalized citizen might read as follows:

> People who desire to become United States citizens, but were not born in the United States, can become naturalized citizens. Read this selection to determine the requirements for becoming a naturalized citizen.

The motivation statement provides the student with a frame of reference and purpose for reading and thus ensures his attention and concentration on the selection.

Step 3: Prepare Five Comprehension Questions

Once you have selected the passage and your motivation statement is prepared, you will need to write questions for checking comprehension. You will need five questions for this purpose. Specifically, you should write one vocabulary question, three factual questions, and one inferential question. If you have long selections of 400 words or more, it may be desirable to write ten comprehension questions (two vocabulary, six factual, and two inferential).

Factual Questions. The factual questions require answers that are *directly stated* in the passage. These questions should be concerned with the most important facts in the selection rather than interesting but picayune details that are not important to remember. Perhaps the easiest way to prepare your factual questions is to read the selection and then list the three most important facts that are contained in it. After having identified the significant facts, you can write questions for each one of them.

Vocabulary Questions. Vocabulary questions are designed to test the student's understanding of a word used in the selection. The vocabulary questions generally include words that are used in the selection but whose meanings are not necessarily obvious in the selection. When writing vocabulary questions, do not choose words that have been set aside in italics and precisely defined for the reader. Rather, select words essential to the understanding of the selection that are not italicized. Vocabulary questions should be related to the most important concepts in the selection.

Inferential Questions. Inferential questions require of the reader some knowledge from the selection as well as some thinking as the reader relates the selection to his or her experiences. A good inferential question requires the reader to combine the information presented in the passage with his or her experiences in order to answer the question. The answer to an inference question cannot be stated directly in the selection. Because each student's experiences are different, there may be more than one correct answer to any inference question.

You can determine the format you would like to use for writing your questions. Essay and short-answer questions usually require more memory; however, multiple choice items might be more feasible when you need to administer and grade the selections for large groups of students. Samples of the three types of questions are given below. The questions are over a 200-word selection typical of selections found in social studies textbooks. Notice the different types of questions and the possible formats (essay or multiple choice).

Sample Questions

Essay or Short Answer
(F = Factual; V = Vocabulary; I = Inference.)
1. *(F)* How old must a person be before he can apply to become a naturalized citizen? (18)
2. *(F)* Name two proficiencies a person must have to become a naturalized citizen. (Skill in using the English language and knowledge of United States history and government)
3. *(F)* Which applicants do *not* have to take a test to demonstrate proficiency in reading, writing, and speaking English? (Those who have been residing in the United States for 20 years and those who are physically unable to do so)
4. *(V)* What does *subversive* mean? (Tendency to destroy or overthrow)
5. *(I)* Why is it necessary for the applicant to have certain proficiencies? (The applicant must know the form of government because he or she will be under its rules and regulations. The applicant must know English so he or she can communicate with others in the country).

Sample Multiple-Choice Questions
(F = Factual; V = Vocabulary; I = Inference.)
1. *(F)* Circle the letter that indicates how old a person must be to be eligible to become a naturalized citizen.
   a. Seventeen   c. Twenty
   b. Eighteen   d. Twenty-one

2. *(F)* Circle the letter that indicates the two proficiencies a person must have to become a naturalized citizen.
   a. Knowledge of English and science
   b. Knowledge of the government of the United States and communistic government
   c. Knowledge of English and the history and government of the United States
   d. Knowledge of English and mental health

3. *(F)* Applicants who want to become naturalized citizens do not have to demonstrate proficiency in using English if
   a. They are proficient in using some other language.
   b. They are physically unable to do so.
   c. They have resided in the U.S. for 20 years.
   d. Both *b* and *c*.
   e. All of the above.

4. *(V)* Circle the letter that indicates the meaning of *subversive*.
   a. communist   c. tendency to disagree
   b. tendency to overthrow   d. tendency not to believe

5. *(I)* An applicant must have certain proficiencies in order to become a naturalized citizen because
   a. The applicant should know the forms of government under which he or she will be living. The applicant needs to know the language to communicate most effectively so that he or she can be a productive citizen.
   b. United States citizens are at a higher intellectual level than citizens in other countries; therefore, all citizens must have certain proficiencies to maintain the high standards found in the United States.
   c. Knowledge of English and history is important so that the person will not feel like a foreigner in his or her own country.
   d. Good moral character and knowledge of English and government are important because the United States already has a high rate of crime and illiteracy.

Applying the Concept of an Informal Suitability Survey

We recommend making an Informal Suitability Survey for each one of the textual materials you commonly use. In addition to these materials, many content area teachers use supplemental books from the library, newspaper articles, magazine or journal articles, pamphlets, or other printed materials. It is unnecessary to make Informal Suitability Surveys for all of the materials you use with your students. You can apply the *concept* of an Informal Suitability Survey without preparing one for each of the materials. When you are trying to match supplemental materials to students, remember to listen as students read to see if they are missing more than one out of 20 words (95 percent correct). This will help you know whether or not the material is too difficult. Likewise, after the student reads the selection, if you ask four questions and the student gets three of them correct (75 percent), you will know that the material is suitable. Continual observation is your best technique for determining suitability of content area materials.

Let us suppose you are working with your students in the library. The students are attempting to locate materials concerning some unit theme. As you move around to give individual help to students, you informally help them find suitable materials. For example, you find a book you would like to suggest to Josephine; you survey the book to find a representative passage. Rather than counting 200 words, you simply count the words in the first two lines, divide by two to get the average, and then use this figure to determine approximately how many lines will contain 200 words. You then give Josephine a purpose for reading and listen to see if she is able to recognize the words. If you do not want to ask her to read aloud, you simply direct her to begin reading silently after you give her a purpose for reading. While she is reading, you look at the material and think of questions to ask to see if she is able to comprehend the selection.

In summary then, the most useful purpose of an Informal Suitability Survey is to match students with reading materials. It is not necessary to construct a paper and pencil Informal Suitability Survey for every material you use in teaching, but rather only for the major textbooks you desire to use. You will be applying the concept of an Informal Suitability Survey informally as you help students find materials they are capable of reading. You will be applying this concept every time you take your students to the library or share materials with them from your own resources.

Now that you know how to develop an Informal Suitability Survey for the major material you hope to use with your students, go on to the Practicum Exercises, which provide an opportunity to apply this knowledge.

Practicum Exercise 1

Let us suppose you are a science teacher and you want to determine the suitability of a textbook that you really like and want to use with your students. You have looked through the textbook and selected a passage representative of the textual materials. You have counted the number of words and indicated the 300th word. You have skipped all proper nouns and numerals in your word count.

Now it is time to write a motivation statement and five comprehension questions. Read the following selection; then write a motivation statement and five short-answer or essay comprehension questions, consisting of three factual questions, one vocabulary question, and one inference question. After doing so, check your response with ours at the end of this Enabling Element.

Sample Science Selection

A cloud is a mass of small water droplets or tiny ice crystals that float in the air. Some clouds have rounded bumps and appear to be piled up. Other clouds appear in layers or sheets.

Seeing clouds does not always mean it is going to rain. Rain clouds only form when so much water vapor gathers that the water droplets become large and heavy. When the water droplets become too heavy, precipitation will occur, usually in the form of rain or snow.

You may wonder where this water vapor comes from. Water vapor comes from water that has evaporated from lakes, oceans, rivers, or from moist soil and plants. When this water evaporates it is called water vapor. Of course, the air can only hold a certain amount of water vapor at any given temperature; when the temperature drops, some of the water vapor begins to condense. *Condense* means to change into a liquid form, or in our case, to change into tiny droplets of water.

Water vapor can rise to form clouds in many different ways. First, some clouds are formed by *evaporation*. When the sun warms the ground, the air next to the ground is heated. Since the warm air is lighter than the same volume of cooler air, the warm air rises. As the air rises, it expands and becomes cooler. If enough water vapor is in the expanding air, the vapor will condense and form clouds.

Second, some clouds are formed by *lifting*. When warm, moist air moves up the side of a hill or over a range of mountains, it is lifted and cooled by expansion. This cooling causes the water vapor to condense and form clouds that seem to hang over the mountains.

Finally, weather fronts where masses of warm and cool air meet each other, produce *300th word* clouds by what is called *frontal activity*. The water vapor in the rising air becomes cooler and condenses, thus creating the water droplets that form clouds.

Motivation Statement:

Essay or Short-Answer Questions to Check Comprehension
1. *(F)*

2. *(F)*

3. *(F)*

4. *(V)*

5. *(I)*

Answers to Practicum Exercise 1

When you check your responses with ours, you may find that they do not exactly match our motivation statement and/or questions. There is more than one way to provide a purpose for reading this selection, and there are many different questions that may be asked to determine if the student actually comprehended the selection. As you compare your responses to ours, keep in mind that the motivation statement should consist of two sentences. The first sentence gives the reader an indication of what the selection is about; the second provides a command or question directing the student to read the selection. When evaluating your questions, you should see if:

1. The factual questions concern details important to the comprehension of the selection.
2. The vocabulary question concerns a word from the selection that is not obviously defined in the selection.
3. The inferential question requires the student to combine knowledge from the selection with information from his or her background of experiences.

Sample Answers to Practicum Exercise

Motivation Statement: Did you ever wonder how clouds are formed? Read this selection to find out what clouds are and how they are formed.

Sample Essay Questions
1. *(F)* What are clouds made of? (Small water droplets or ice crystals.)
2. *(F)* When do rain clouds form? (When enough water droplets become large and heavy.)
3. *(F)* Name two ways that clouds are formed. (When moist air moves up the side of a hill, it is lifted and cooled. This cooling causes the water vapor to condense and form clouds. Second, sometimes weather fronts are formed because warm and cool air meet each other. Thus, the water vapor in the warm air rises and becomes cooler and condenses.)
4. *(V)* What is precipitation? (Rain or snow, which is made up of water droplets or ice crystals.)
5. *(I)* Why do some areas get more rain than other areas? (It all depends upon the direction of the wind, temperature, and closeness to bodies of water and mountain ranges.)

Practicum Exercise 2

Are you ready to prepare an Informal Suitability Survey for your students? You can do so by following these steps:

1. Select a representative 200-word passage. Make sure the passage is self-contained (does not refer to pictures or illustrations). Skip all proper nouns and numerals as you count the 200 words. If the selection does not end with the 200th word, mark the 200th word by making a slash after it.
2. Write a motivation statement to provide a specific purpose for reading.
3. Prepare five questions to check comprehension: one vocabulary, one inferential, and three factual.

After you have developed an Informal Suitability Survey, go on to Enabling Element 3, which explains how to administer and score this device.

Enabling Element 3
Administering and Scoring an Informal Suitability Survey

Specific Objective 3

You will administer and score an Informal Suitability Survey following the procedures described in this module.

Enabling Activities

*1. Read Study Guide 3. It provides directions for administering and scoring an Informal Suitability Survey. Do the Practicum Exercise to apply your new knowledge.

*2. Administer an Informal Suitability Survey to an individual and to a small group of students. Which procedures seem better suited to your purpose? What are the advantages and limitations of administering the Informal Suitability Survey to an individual? Group?

3. Give examples of the ways in which comprehension is affected by (a) insertions, (b) substitutions, and (c) omissions.

4. If your instructor has a tape of a student reading a selection, practice recording the word recognition errors.

*5. If a student reads a 300-word selection, makes fourteen word recognition errors, and misses one of the five comprehension questions, is the material suitable? Check your response with the Summary Scoring Guide in figure 3.

*6. If you administer a selection individually and find that the student can recognize the words perfectly but fails to answer three of the five comprehension questions, can you consider the material suitable? Check your response with the Summary Scoring Guide.

7. Make a chart to record the results of the Informal Suitability Survey.

Study Guide 3

An Informal Suitability Survey can be administered to individuals or groups of students. Content area teachers are advised to administer the survey to the entire class initially, and then administer the survey individually to students who had extremely poor or doubtful results.

Before administering an Informal Suitability Survey, you must prepare a master, or

---

*Indicates core Enabling Activities.

ditto, with the selection. Begin by placing the motivation statement on the top of the master and follow with the selection. Dittoed copies of the questions will also be needed. When all the materials are available, the survey can be administered as follows:

Group Administration

1. Be sure to have at least fifteen to thirty minutes available for the test. In addition, suggest work for those who might finish early so they do not disturb others.
2. Explain to the students that you want to determine how well they can read the textual material used in your course. Indicate that grades will not be given, but rather the results will be used to help you determine useful material for teaching the course.
3. Distribute the selection and questions to the students, and ask them to keep the materials face down on their desks. When all the students have a copy of the selection, read the motivation statement to them and tell them they can have as much time as they need to read the selection. When they have finished reading the selection, tell them to answer the comprehension questions. If you do not want them to refer to the selection when answering the questions, collect the selections before you distribute the questions. Since students will be able to refer to the text when studying, they should probably be permitted to refer to the selection when answering the questions. The decision is yours.
4. Your main responsibility for step 4 is observing the students to make sure they are taking the test seriously and not simply marking the answers randomly without reading the selection. You can also observe (a) the rates at which different students finish, (b) the attitudes of the students toward the task, and (c) reading habits such as head movements and finger pointing.
5. Check the papers to find how many of the questions were answered correctly, and refer to the scoring guide to determine for whom the selection is suitable or unsuitable.

Individual Administration

The individually administered Informal Suitability Survey requires more time than group administration; but it is also more informative because, in addition to the silent reading, you listen to the students read orally. You may want this opportunity to listen to and talk with some students who puzzle you. If so, follow these directions:

1. Make sure you can spend seven to ten minutes with the student in a quiet place.
2. Tell the student you want to determine how well he or she can read the textbook and/or other required reading material used in your class.
3. Read the motivation statement to the student, and ask the student to read the selection silently. Tell the student you are going to ask questions after he or she has read the selection.
4. When the student has completed the silent reading of the selection, ask the five comprehension questions you have prepared. Put a check mark after the question if

the student's response is incorrect, and leave it blank if the correct response is given. If there is more than one part to the answer, you may give partial credit.

5. After checking comprehension, tell the student to read the selection aloud. As the student is reading the selection, follow along on your copy. Your task is to notice word recognition errors within the 200-, 300-, or 400-word selection. Specifically, look for four major types of word recognition errors:

   a. *Substitution*—If the students says or substitutes one word for another word, cross out the word the student should have said, and write in the word the student did say. Do not mark errors on proper nouns or numerals because proper nouns or numerals were not counted in the passage. An example follows:

   A subpoena *is a legal notice to appear as a witness in court.*

   (*subject* written above *subpoena*)

   b. *Omission*—If a student omits a word or an entire sentence, circle the omitted word or sentence. Again, do not count errors in proper nouns or numerals. If the student omits proper nouns or numerals, simply pronounce them. Count single or multi-word omissions (entire sentence) as one error.

   A subpoena is a (legal) notice to appear as a witness in court.

   c. *Pronunciation*—If the student hesitates when attempting to pronounce a certain word (other than a proper noun or numeral), ask the student to try, allowing at least five seconds. If the student does not say the word, pronounce it and write a capital *P* above the word that you pronounced. Also write a capital *P* above a word if the student requests you to pronounce it.

   A subpoena *is a legal notice to appear as a witness in court.*

   (*P* written above *subpoena*)

   d. *Insertion*—If a student inserts a word, write in a caret where the word was inserted and write the word above the caret.

   A subpoena *is a legal notice to appear as a* expert *witness in court.*

6. As you administer the Informal Suitability Survey to a student, observe his or her reading habits and obtain a feeling for the student's attitude toward reading. Specifically, consider the following questions:

   a. Is the student relaxed and comfortable when reading? Some students will display many signs of anxiety or even refuse to read out loud to you because they are so far behind in reading.

   b. Is it necessary for the student to point or use some marker to keep his or her place?

   c. Does the student read word by word, or in phrases?

   d. How much confidence and enthusiasm are displayed?

7. Refer to the scoring guide to determine the suitability of the selection.

Criteria for Scoring an Informal Suitability Survey

One criterion for classifying materials as suitable is that the student should comprehend at least 75 percent of the information. This is not to say that you expect students to comprehend *only* 75 percent of what they read. But if the students are able to comprehend 75 percent of what they read, you can increase their comprehension by doing the following: introduce specialized vocabulary words (Module 5); help with comprehension (Module 6); teach a study strategy (Module 7); and provide specific purposes for reading (Module 9). The other criterion for classifying materials is that students recognize 95 percent of the words. Again, you want the student to recognize all of the words, but if he is able to read 95 percent independently, you will be able to help him with the others by applying the word pronunciation strategy introduced in Module 8.

Scoring Surveys Administered to Groups

Informal Suitability Surveys typically have five questions; thus a student who misses one question scores 80 percent for comprehension. Two questions would be 60 percent, and so forth. A selection then can be considered unsuitable if the student misses two or more of the five questions. If the student misses only one, or one and a half, the material can be designated as suitable. The authors realize that missing one and a half questions out of five is equal to 70 percent; however, they have found no significant difference between 70 percent and 75 percent when determining suitability, especially when only five questions are used.

If ten questions are used in checking comprehension, the selection can be considered as unsuitable if a student missed *more than* three of the ten questions. If the student misses three questions or less, the material can be considered suitable.

Scoring Surveys Administered Individually

When an Informal Suitability Survey is administered individually, each student gets a score for comprehension and a score for word recognition. The word recognition errors (omissions, insertions, substitutions, and words the teacher must pronounce) are recorded. The general guideline for scoring the word recognition errors is that students should be able to recognize 95 percent of the words for the selection to be considered suitable. This does not mean teachers want students to recognize only 95 percent of the words, but this is a base from which the teacher builds. The teacher will introduce vocabulary (Module 5) and help needful students pronounce multisyllable words (Module 8) before asking the students to read the selection.

You probably realize now why proper nouns and numerals were not marked as word recognition errors. In selecting the passage for the Informal Suitability Survey you did not count proper nouns because these are usually introduced by the teacher in making reading assignments. Likewise, numerals were not counted because they are not words. Since the criterion for word recognition is that the student must recognize 95 percent of the words, only errors on words that were included in the word count can be considered. You should now also understand why you were directed to mark the 200th, 300th, or 400th word in the selection. When marking word recognition errors you only mark errors up to these lengths. If the selection is longer, do not mark errors past these word limits.

If a 200-word selection is used, the students can make as many as ten word recognition errors and the material is still classified as suitable. If a 100-word selection is used, the student can make only five word recognition errors for the material to be classified as suitable. A student may make as many as fifteen word recognition errors on a 300-word selection, twenty on a 400-word selection, and so forth. Of course the same criterion for comprehension that was described earlier is used to determine the suitability of an individually administered Informal Suitability Survey.

If the survey was administered individually, both scores probably indicate either that the selection is suitable or that it is unsuitable. However, a score on word recognition may indicate suitability while the score on comprehension indicates unsuitability, or vice versa. Keep in mind that comprehension is the most important criterion because reading is the meaningful interpretation of printed symbols. However, if the student scores below the suggested criteria (75 percent comprehension and 95 percent word recognition) for *either* word recognition or comprehension, the selection should be considered unsuitable. The following Summary Scoring Guide (figure 3) can be used as you determine suitability of materials.

Figure 3

Summary scoring guides for informal suitability surveys

Group Administration (Comprehension Only)

Suitable	Unsuitable
5 Questions: 3½–5 correct 10 Questions: 7–10 correct	5 Questions: 0–3 correct 10 Questions: 0–6 correct

Individual Administration
(Word Recognition and Comprehension)

Suitable		Unsuitable	
Comprehension		Comprehension	
5 Questions: 3½–5 correct 10 Questions: 7–10 correct		5 Questions: 0–3 correct 10 Questions: 0–6 correct	
Word Recognition		Word Recognition	
Number of words	Errors	Number of words	Errors
100	0– 5	100	6 or more
200	0–10	200	11 or more
300	0–15	300	16 or more
400	0–20	400	21 or more
500	0–25	500	26 or more

Reminder: Errors made when pronouncing proper nouns and numerals are not counted as word recognition errors. If the survey was administered individually, the scores for *both* comprehension and word recognition must meet the criteria for suitability for the material to be classified as suitable.

It may be that a student is on the borderline of the scoring guide presented in figure 3. For example, a student who made six errors in 100 words is on the border.(The limit for word recognition errors for 100 words is five.) It is necessary for you to analyze the types of errors the student made in word recognition. Some errors are more important than others. For example, if the student read the sentence, "A subpoena is a legal notice to appear as a witness in court," and substituted the word *subject* for *subpoena*, the meaning of the sentence was lost. But if the student had simply substituted the word *an* for *a*, the word recognition error would not have been as important. Likewise, if the student inserted the word *the* in front of the word *court* in the above sentence, the meaning was not drastically changed. On the other hand, if the reader had inserted the word *supreme* before the word *court*, the meaning would have been drastically changed. If a student is on the borderline in terms of the number of allowable errors, analyze the errors to determine whether or not the meaning was drastically changed. You can make a decision as to the suitability or unsuitability based upon your analysis.

Practicum Exercise

Let us suppose that you have administered a group Informal Suitability Survey, which you constructed from the major textbook that you desire to use in the course. Of the five comprehension questions you asked, Alfredo missed four. You now decide to individually administer an Informal Suitability Survey from a book with a lower readability level.

You call Alfredo aside during your planning period and tell him you want to find materials he will be able to read. You mention that you have a sample selection from another textbook and would like him to read it. You read the motivation statement to him and observe as he reads silently. After the silent reading, you check his comprehension. (Alfredo's responses are presented after the selection.) You then ask him to read the selection aloud and he makes the following errors. Is the selection suitable?

Venezuela

Venezuela is located on the north coast of South America. Venezuela's neighbors are Brazil, Colombia, and Guyana. Venezuela was (originally) a part of the Spanish vice royalty of New Granada. It was freed from Spanish rule by Simon Bolivar in 1818. It is now an independent republic.

The population of Venezuela is approximately twelve million five hundred thousand people. All citizens over eighteen are allowed to vote in the elections that take place every five years.

Many of the big oil companies—Exxon, Shell, and Gulf—have operations in Venezuela. As a result, the per capita income conceals many disparities in the actual income among the different groups in the population. Some people live in beautiful castles on the hillsides, whereas others live in shanty huts. About 3 percent of the population own 90 percent of the land.

The comprehension questions that you asked along with Alfredo's answers are as follows:

1. *(F)* In what continent is Venezuela located? (South America)
2. *(F)* What country originally ruled Venezuela? (Spain)
3. *(F)* Do the people in Venezuela get to elect their own rulers? (Yes. You must be eighteen years old to vote.)

4. (*V*) What does the term *per capita income* mean? (I don't know.)

5. (*I*) Would you like to live in Venezuela? Why or why not? (Yes. If I worked for the oil companies and owned lots of land I would like to live there.)

Answers to the Practicum Exercise

Yes, this material is suitable for Alfredo. He answered four of the five questions correctly and only made four word-recognition errors in 100 words. You could use this material in teaching Alfredo.

Figure 4

Material suitability chart

Suitability of Materials

Names of Students	Names of Materials			
1.				
2.				
3.				
4.				
5.				
6.				
7.				
8.				
9.				
10.				
11.				
12.				
13.				
14.				
15.				
16.				
17.				
18.				
19.				
20.				
21.				
22.				
23.				
24.				
Total				

Code: U = Unsuitable
　　　S = Suitable

**Keeping Records of Results from
Informal Suitability Surveys**

You may want to keep a record of the results from your Informal Suitability Survey. You can use the chart on page 81 or make a chart that includes the names of your students and lists the materials you surveyed. You can mark a U on the same line as the student's name under each type of material you found to be unsuitable. You can write an S under the material you found to be suitable. A chart like this is especially helpful if you administer a series of Informal Suitability Surveys to determine the appropriateness of the different materials that you have available for use. As mentioned earlier, it is very unlikely that you will find one type of material suitable for all students. Your chart will guide you as you select suitable materials for different students.

Enabling Element 4
Planning Differentiated Reading Assignments

Specific Objective 4

After scoring the Informal Suitability Survey, you will state the specific implications of the findings for planning differentiated reading assignments.

Enabling Activities

*1. Read Study Guide 4. Determine specific classroom practices that are desirable as you use the results of suitability surveys.

*2. Do Practicum Exercise 1, which asks you to develop a differentiated reading assignment. Share your plan with other colleagues to give them ideas for providing for individual differences. Perhaps they will like the idea and work with you and the media specialist to develop differentiated reading assignments concerning many units.

*3. Talk with your students about the fact that they do have different achievement levels in reading. You may begin your discussion by pointing out differences in height, talents, interests, and/or color of hair. Lead your students to realize that these differences make life interesting and exciting. Help them understand that you are happy about their differences and simply hope to help each one become better in your content area.

4. The next time you visit a materials display or talk with sales representatives from various publishing companies, ask what low-level reading materials they have available for your content area. Publishers generally try to market the kinds of

---

*Indicates core Enabling Activities.

materials teachers demand. If many teachers begin to request materials at different reading levels, publishers will make more materials available.

5. Are you beginning to see how the modules in this textbook are interrelated? You can review Module 1 on determining readability levels as you evaluate textbooks and materials for their potential use. Module 2 provides suggestions for preparing teacher-made materials appropriate for your classes. This module helps you determine the suitability of selected materials. As you progress through the modules, correlate the competencies you are developing.

Study Guide 4

In considering the implications of an Informal Suitability Survey we must remember the purpose of the instrument. As stated in Study Guide 1 of this module, such a survey is an informal device that can be used to determine if students can handle selected content area reading material. After administering the survey you know which textual materials are suitable or unsuitable for the different students. This Study Guide will help you develop skill in using results obtained from your efforts to plan differentiated reading assignments.

Planning Differentiated Reading Assignments

As mentioned earlier, it is impossible to find one textbook suitable for all students. Therefore, content area teachers need to plan differentiated reading assignments. A differentiated reading assignment is a teaching plan for individualizing reading assignments in science, social studies, and like content areas. It is a procedure commonly used by content area teachers when they have students reading from different sources but for the same purpose. The differentiated reading assignment permits the classroom teacher to use the unit approach with its common objectives, but to vary (differentiate) the reading assignments according to each student's reading capabilities.

The first part of a differentiated reading assignment is the *unit theme*. This section of the plan deals with a brief statement revealing the focus of the unit. In the following sample differentiated reading assignment, the unit is focusing upon the skin; thus the theme might be ''Caring for Your Skin.''

The second part of a differentiated reading assignment contains the *directions* for the students. The directions tell the students what they are to do to complete the assignment. Generally the directions tell students to read the recommended resources and answer the questions. At other times the directions indicate projects or other activities in which the students might want to become involved.

The *reading questions* make up the third part of the differentiated reading assignment. Usually these questions are developed via teacher-student discussions. The teacher might begin the unit by sharing some background information and then ask students what questions they would like to explore. Some teachers like to list major questions and then have the students add others.

The fourth part of a differentiated reading assignment contains a list of the *reading sources*. These are the recommended sources to be used by the students to gather information needed to answer the questions. Teachers generally use their knowledge of the difficulty of the materials and the reading capabilities of the students to assign specific sources to specific students. Or they may have students select sources they would like to use and with which they feel comfortable.

The last part of the differentiated reading plan contains the actual *reading assignments*. This section can include both the students' names and the appropriate references for each student to read. Although the reading assignments are differentiated according to the teacher's knowledge of the student's reading achievements, the materials are not designated as "more difficult" or "easy reading." Some teachers make the reading assignments by informally telling each student which resources he or she may want to use, rather than writing out a list of reading assignments and distributing copies to students. We recommend that you jot down possibilities and then orally suggest these to individual students or groups of students. Take time to examine the sample differentiated reading assignment now.

Sample Differentiated Reading Assignment

I. *Unit Theme:* Caring for Your Skin

II. *Directions:* You will soon be discussing the following questions. These questions will help you understand more about caring for your skin. To prepare yourself for the discussion, you will need to do some reading. Each one of you will find a reading assignment and recommended resources at the end of this plan. Read and prepare to answer the following questions.

III. *Reading Questions*
   1. What are the causes of acne?
   2. What is the best way to treat acne?
   3. What is the easiest and safest way to get a tan?
   4. What causes warts and moles?
   5. How are face-lifts done?
   6. What are some of the best ways to treat impetigo?
   7. Why do some people have birthmarks?
   8. What causes freckles?
   9. How can you best treat athlete's foot and jungle rot?
   10. Why do some people have dry skin and other people have oily skin?
   11. What can you do about caring for oily skin or dry skin?
   12. How is skin grafted?
   13. Why are there different colors of skin?
   14. What is the function of skin?

IV. *Reading Sources*
   1. *World Book Encyclopedia*—Articles about skin, acne, athlete's foot and warts.
   2. *First Aid*, by the American Red Cross
   3. Film—*Care of the Skin*, by Encyclopaedia Britannica Films

4. Film—*Healthy Skin*, by Coronet

5. *The Skin*, by Patrick Hare

6. *Question and Answer Book About the Human Body*, by Ann McGovern

7. *Cosmetic Surgery*, by William Brown

8. *Plastic Surgery: Beauty You Can Buy*, by Harriett LeBarre

9. Filmstrip—*Caring for Acne*

10. *Encyclopaedia Britannica*

11. Pamphlets by The American Medical Association and Dermatology Foundation

12. Selected articles in *Glamour* and *Today's Health*

13. *Medical and Health Encyclopedia*, edited by Morris Fishbein, M.D.

14. *Structure and Function of the Skin*, by W. Montagna

15. *Fungus Diseases and Their Treatment*, by Ivan Sarkang

16. Textbook—*You and Your Body*, chapter 7, "Care of Your Hair and Skin"

17. *You and Your Skin*, by Norman Goldsmith

18. Filmstrip—*Acne: Cause and Care*

V. *Reading Assignments: Plan 1*

Students	Reading Sources
Group A: Nathaniel, Josephine Harvy, Lara Rocky, Alfredo	1, 6, 7, 16
Group B: Ruth, Don O. J., Susan Holly, Jorge, Billie	3, 12, 17, 18
Group C: Mary, Paul, Martha Rex, Ed, Dalia, Tina	2, 4, 9, 11
Group D: Jeff, Jackie, Sharon Nikki, Angie, David Diane, Bill	10, 13, 14
Group E: Patricia, Melita Bob, Dick, Barbara Ann, Jeff	5, 8, 15

Did you notice that the last part of the differentiated reading assignment—the actual assignment list—was presented as Plan 1? As you examine Plan 1 for the reading assignments, you probably noticed the students in Group B are the students who are reading far below grade level. As you peruse the list of reading sources, you will notice that Group B will be using filmstrips, a low readability level book, and articles from magazines to answer the questions. The best readers in your class, those in Group D, will be using some of the more difficult reading sources. Regardless of reading level, however, all students will be able to find information that will help answer some of the questions that you planned with them about the care of the skin. In this way, each person can make some contribution.

Another way of differentiating reading assignments is to divide your students into teams. Please refer to Plan 2, which follows. On each team you would have excellent readers as well as those who read far below grade level. You would then ask each team to find answers by using a variety of sources. You can designate particular sources for the teams or simply discuss with them all the available sources and ask them to choose sources to answer the questions. If you decide to divide the reading sources among the teams, the reading assignments for your differentiated reading plan may be as follows:

V. *Reading Assignments: Plan 2*

Students	Reading Sources
Group A: Nathaniel, Ruth Mary, Jeff Patricia, Josephine, Don	1, 3, 7, 14
Group B: Paul, Jackie, Melita Maria, O.J., Martha Sharon	2, 5, 10, 15
Group C: Bob, Harvy, Holly Rex, Nikki, Dick Lara	4, 8, 13, 17
Group D: Jorge, Ed, Angie Barbara, Rocky Billie, Dalia	6, 9, 11
Group E: Diane, Anne, Alfredo, Tina Bill, Jeff	12, 16, 18

The advantage of using Plan 2 is the fact that the groups of students now include students with many different reading levels. Rather than competing with each other, the students compete as teams. Team A will want to find as many good answers to the questions as the other teams, and frequently, teammates help each other learn. Another advantage of this plan is that students who are poor readers are not categorized as such and given "easy" materials. When students work together as a team, the students within each group will naturally choose the reading resources that were provided for them. Students who have reading difficulties will prefer watching filmstrips or reading some of the materials that have a lower readability level.

We recommend that you use Plan 2, to allow students of many different achievement levels to work together and compete as teams. We have found that students do learn from each other and can work together well if there are many information sources. We also believe that students' self-concepts will be enhanced if a team approach is used rather than simply grouping students by reading ability. The decision is yours.

We are sure that you will readily see the advantages of a differentiated reading plan. If you realize that one textbook is not suitable for all and yet want all of your students to accomplish the objectives of your content area, the advantages of a differentiated reading assignment are apparent. The method helps each student use his or her capabilities to accomplish the objectives you have set.

Practicum Exercise

Now it is time for you to try your skill in planning a differentiated reading assignment. Choose a unit topic you are about to study with your students. Talk with the students to see what questions they have about the central theme of the unit. You may want to list additional questions. Next, talk with the media specialist or librarian to determine what available reading sources relate to the unit topic and the listed questions. Compile a list of these sources. Finally, consider the reading capabilities of your students, and suggest differentiated reading assignments (following either Plan 1 or Plan 2).

After having developed a differentiated reading assignment, plan how you will share it with your students. As mentioned earlier, it is not necessary to write out your plan and provide every student with a copy of it, but rather explain the directions contained in the reading plan to the students and specify the sources the different teams or individuals should use to answer the questions. You may want to suggest projects the students can do in addition to the reading assignments.

You may believe that making a differentiated reading assignment requires too many hours. Although we realize that extra hours are necessary when you are using more than one textbook with students, we believe you will be more effective if you use a variety of resources. If you continue to develop a repertoire of reading resources for the various topics in your content area, you will soon have quite a nice collection of reading materials appropriate for your students. We ask you to take steps in this direction rather than being overwhelmed by the work that is involved. If you can begin by simply suggesting a few sources to your students, you are on the right track!

Other Ways to Help Students Read Textual Materials

In addition to making differential reading assignments, what else can you do to help the students read the textual materials in your content area? Listed below are four responsibilities we hope all content teachers will accept—even when the reading materials are suitable.

1. If the textbook or other required material is suitable, you have a responsibility to introduce the specialized vocabulary words (especially the proper nouns) that may cause difficulty. Module 5 on word meanings has specific suggestions for helping students develop the meanings of words. See Module 8 for ways of helping students pronounce long words.

2. When introducing assignments, be sure to provide students with purposes for reading. When you prepared a motivation statement in constructing your Informal Suitability Survey, you were actually providing the students with a purpose for reading. Module 9, ''Motivating Reluctant Readers,'' has detailed examples for providing purposes as you introduce reading assignments.

3. Another way in which you can help the students get more from their textual materials is to continually remind them to use appropriate study strategies. Module 7 includes suggested study strategies and ways that you can demonstrate these to your students.

4. If the textbooks you are using include material that requires new or infrequently used reading skills, such as interpreting cartoons or graphs, discuss these materials in class. Also point out any special aids available in the textbook: index, appendices, or glossary.

Additional Techniques for Helping Students Who Cannot Read Available Materials

Suitable content area reading materials will not always be available. Rather than just leaving these students to "sit back" in your class, we hope you will consider the following suggestions:

1. If suitable reading materials are not available for all your students, you may want to talk with the department chairperson or librarian to see if new books are being ordered which cover the same concepts but are written at a lower readability level. Many publishing companies are beginning to publish books that include the same information, but are written at different reading levels. Write query letters to some of your favorite publishers to see what materials are available. Of course, if the textbook is unsuitable for most of your students, you will want to consider selecting new textbooks. Remember to determine the readability of textual materials which you are considering.

2. If you do not have any suitable materials for some of the students, perhaps you can have some of the better readers read the most important parts of the text on a tape to which other students can listen. Many times students are able to understand better through listening than reading.

3. There are many ways of gathering information rather than reading. If you use audiovisual materials in your class you can help the students develop concepts by seeing and hearing. In addition to using many audiovisual aids, you can provide more involvement activities during class sessions. Students generally enjoy role playing, simulation activities, and group discussions.

4. Feel free to read some of the most difficult parts of the textual materials to your students. This will provide an opportunity for the students to listen and learn, and at the same time be able to notice your model of reading. If you use expression by varying your rate, volume, and pitch, you can make the textbook come alive. Also, remember to use the illustrations, charts, and tables that are in the textbook.

5. You may want to develop some handouts which are appropriate for the students. The suggestions in Module 2 will be valuable for this purpose. Some teachers like to develop the handouts with their classes and then put them on a ditto. The latter procedure can be especially valuable when concluding a unit of study. The title of the handout might concern "big ideas" or "things to remember" about the topic being studied.

Perhaps the most important fact to keep in mind is that students who are having difficulty reading can survive in the content areas if you make these adaptations. Many times poor readers are labeled as lazy, uninterested, turned off, and slow. If you read the article, "Teachers Don't Want to Be Labeled," which was used as a sample in Module 1, you will realize that everyone is slow, average, gifted, interested, and uninterested, depending on the task at hand. Students and adults generally avoid those tasks that are difficult or frustrating. Just because you have students who are reluctant to read does not mean they are reluctant to learn. Module 10, "Identifying and Helping Problem Readers," has even more suggestions for you. Commit yourself to this challenge rather than "writing off" those who cannot read.

If you are now aware of the importance of finding suitable materials in light of the students' reading capabilities and have the procedures for developing, administering, and using results from an Informal Suitability Survey, you are ready for the Posttest. Remember, the final evaluation of your accomplishment of this competency rests solely in what you do as you conduct your classes. We have demonstrated the importance of finding suitable materials to help your students accomplish the objectives of your classes. Now our hope is that you will not just take the Posttest, but actually implement these ideas with your students.

Posttest

Directions: The following questions are designed to test your accomplishment of the objectives in this module. Check your responses with the answers on the following pages to determine if you have met the objectives of this module. You can recycle as necessary after checking your responses.

1. Describe an Informal Suitability Survey and state the major purpose for using one in your classes.

2. Outline and explain the three major procedures involved in constructing such a survey.

3. What information can you get from an individually administered survey that cannot be obtained when you administer one to a group?

4. Let us suppose you are a math teacher and you individually administered the following 200-word Informal Suitability Survey to John who was absent the day you administered the survey to the group. Is the selection suitable?

Solving Math Problems
Stated in Paragraph Form

The first step in solving mathematical problems written in paragraph form is to read the problems carefully to determine what you are supposed to find. After knowing this, reread the problem to find the relevant or irrelevant facts. For example, sometimes problems include facts that are not necessary to find the answer to the problem. The fact that Mrs. Jones waited in line for 12 minutes may be interesting, but it does not help you determine how much change she should receive, considering her purchase.

The next step is to decide what process you must use to find the answer. Remember that sometimes it is necessary to use two or three processes in order to answer the question. For example, if the problem says that Mrs. Jones bought three cans of milk at 19 cents a can, you must multiply the cost of the milk and then add this to the other groceries. Of course it would be necessary then to subtract the total cost from the amount given to find how much change she should receive. *back*

After you have done the ~~computation~~ *complete*, you should ask yourself if the answer makes sense. If it does not, check your arithmetic and *and* question the process that you used. */200 words*

Comprehension Questions
(V = Vocabulary; F = Factual; I = Inference.)
1. *(F)* What is the first step in doing math problems that are stated in paragraph form?
2. *(V)* What does *process* mean?
3. *(F)* What are ways of checking your answer?
4. *(F)* After you determine the question that is asked and the relevant facts, what is the next step to solve the math problem?
5. *(I)* Why do math problems stated in paragraph form sometimes include irrelevant facts?

John's Answers to the Comprehension Questions:
1. The first step in doing a math problem that appears in paragraph form is to determine what you are supposed to find.

2. Process means add, subtract, multiply, or divide.

3. You can check your answers by questioning the process you used or by redoing the computation.

4. Decide what process you should use to find the answer.

5. The book tries to get you mixed up. The teacher is trying to fool you.

5. Given the above information concerning John, state two ways you should help him read textual materials.

6. Describe the components of a differentiated reading assignment and the major purpose of the plan.

Posttest Answers

1. An Informal Suitability Survey consists of a representative selection from textual material you are planning to use, accompanying motivation statement, and questions to check comprehension. It is designed to determine if students can handle selected textual material.

2. The major procedures involved in constructing a survey are as follows:
   a. Select a 200-word passage representative of the reading material in a commonly used textbook or other written material. Skip all proper nouns and numerals when counting the 200 words, and then mark the 200th word with a slash. (The selection may be more than 200 words.)
   b. Write a motivation statement to give the students a purpose for reading.

   c. Write three factual questions, one vocabulary question, and one inferential question.

3. Information concerning the student's skill in recognizing words while reading orally is obtained when a survey is administered individually.

4. John's word recognition and comprehension errors for this selection indicate that the selection is suitable. He made seven word recognition errors in this 200-word selection and missed only one of the five questions.

5. You would still have to introduce new vocabulary words and provide John with a purpose for reading. You could also remind him of appropriate study strategies and help him read specialized materials, such as graphs.

6. The major components of a differentiated reading assignment are (a) unit theme, (b) directions, (c) reading questions, (d) reading sources, and (e) reading assignments. The major purpose of the plan is to provide suitable reading assignments for all students.

Final Comment

The use of the Informal Suitability Survey technique will help you determine the appropriateness of instructional materials for your students and thus lessen the likelihood of frustrated readers in your classes. The results should yield a higher number of completed reading assignments. Now that you understand the concept of an Informal Suitability Survey, you should be able to administer one without extensive preparation. For example, you can take a book off a shelf, read a selection rapidly, mentally note a motivation statement and comprehensive questions, and administer the survey. Duplication of materials may not always be necessary.

    If you have accurately completed all the Posttest items, you are ready for another module. If not, refer to the appropriate Enabling Element for clarification of your difficulty. If you cannot clarify the difficulty, contact your instructor.

Selected Bibliography

Campbell, A. ''How Readability Formulae Fall Short in Matching Student to Text in the Content Areas.'' *Journal of Reading* 22, no. 8 (1979): 683–89.

Cushenbery, D. C. *Remedial Reading in the Secondary School.* West Nyack, New York: Parker, 1972.

Graves, M. F.; Boettcher, J. A.; and Ryder, R. A. *Easy Reading: Book Series and Periodicals for Less Able Readers.* Newark, Delaware: International Reading Association, 1979.

Harker, W. J. ''Selecting Instructional Materials for Content Area Reading.'' *Journal of Reading* 21, no. 2 (1977): 126–30.

Johnson, M. S., and Kress, R. A. "Informal Reading Inventories." *Reading Aids Series*. Newark, Delaware: International Reading Association, 1965.

Karlin, R. *Teaching Reading in High School*. 2nd ed. Indianapolis: Bobbs-Merrill, 1972.

Kealey, R. J. "Helping Students Read the Content Area Textbook." *Reading Improvement* 17, no. 1, (Spring 1980): 36–39.

Lamberg, W. J., and Lamb, C. E. *Reading Instruction in the Content Areas*. Chicago: Rand McNally College Publishing Company, 1980.

Mavrogenes, N. A.; Winkley, C. K.; Hanson, E.; and Vacca, R. J. "Concise Guide to Standardized Secondary and College Reading Tests." *Journal of Reading* 18 (1974): 12–22.

Rakes, T. A. "A Group Instructional Inventory." *Journal of Reading* 18 (1975): 595-98.

Shepherd, D. L. *Comprehensive High School Reading Methods*. 2nd ed. Columbus, Ohio: Charles E. Merrill Publishing Co., 1978.

Smith, E. D.; Guice, B. M.; and Cheek, M.C. "Informal Reading Inventories for the Content Areas: Science and Mathematics." *Elementary English* 49 (1972).

Stine, D. E. "Tenth Grade Content—Fourth Grade Reading Level." *Journal of Reading* 14 (1971): 559–61.

Strang, R.; McCullough, C. M.; and Traxler, A. E. *The Improvement of Reading*. 4th ed. New York: McGraw-Hill, 1967.

Vaughan, J. L., and Gaus, P. J. "Secondary Reading Inventory: A Modest Proposal." *Journal of Reading* 21, no. 8 (1978): 716–20.

Diagnosing
Reading Skill Needs

Contents

Prospectus
   Rationale
   Objectives
   Resources and Time Required
Pretest
Branching Program Alternatives for Pretest Responses
Enabling Element 1: *Skills Necessary to Read Content Area Materials*
Enabling Element 2: *Constructing Reading Skills Tests*
Enabling Element 3: *Administering, Scoring and Using the Results of Reading
   Skills Tests*
Posttest
   Posttest Answers
Selected Bibliography

Prospectus

Rationale

Even when textual material is at the appropriate readability levels for your students, they can still have difficulty understanding the material if they do not possess all of the specialized reading skills required of your subject area. If teachers are aware of the specialized reading skills needed for effective reading in their content areas, they can help students master these skills and thereby increase the likelihood of success in their subject areas.

To help students become effective readers, it is necessary for you to diagnose their specialized reading skill needs. This module will help you to understand the specialized reading skills in your subject area. The module is not designed to make content area teachers into reading teachers. Content teachers are not responsible for teaching beginning reading skills. However, content teachers can and should help students develop the specialized vocabulary, comprehension, study skills, and higher level word pronunciation skills necessary in their subject areas. Detailed descriptions of the specialized reading skills for the various content areas are presented in this module along with practical suggestions for constructing, administering, scoring, and using the results of reading skills tests.

Objectives

Terminal Objective

You will use reading skills tests to determine if students have acquired the reading skills related to your content area.

Specific Objectives

1. You will state the four categories of reading skills and identify the major reading skills necessary to read materials in your content area.

2. You will construct reading skills tests to determine the reading skill needs of students in your content area classes.

3. You will administer, score, and use the results from reading skills tests in your content area.

Resources and Time Required

To complete this module, you will need textbooks and other reading materials commonly used in your subject area. You will need paper for developing the reading skills tests. If you have completed Modules 1 and 2 concerning readability, you may want to have the Fry or Raygor graph available to check and perhaps alter the readability level of your test items. However, it is not essential to have completed Modules 1 and 2 before doing this module. The estimated time to complete the starred core Enabling Activities is four to six hours.

Pretest

Directions: For each question, determine the word that indicates your belief regarding your competency. If you are in doubt, choose NO.

1. All content areas require some special reading skills due to the nature of the material. Can you (a) identify the major categories of reading skills and (b) state the reading skills necessary to read materials in your subject area classes?   YES   NO

2. Content area teachers are responsible for teaching the specialized reading skills necessary to read subject area materials. The first step in teaching is to determine the needs of students. Have you constructed a battery of reading skills tests to determine the reading skill needs of students in your content area?   YES   NO

3. After you develop or obtain reading skills tests, you must use them with your students. Can you administer, score, and use the results from reading skills tests in your content area?   YES   NO

Branching Program Alternatives for Pretest Responses

1. You are ready for Enabling Element 2 if you already know the categories of reading skills and major reading skills needed for reading materials in your content areas. If you are uncertain of the reading skills required for your content area, you will find Enabling Element 1 very valuable.

2. Enabling Element 2 is designed to help you construct reading skills tests to determine which students have or have not acquired the skills needed for reading your content area materials. If you have a battery of reading skills tests, go on to Enabling Element 3. If not, Enabling Element 2 will be valuable because it includes specific instructions and many model tests.

3. Suggestions for administering, scoring and using the results of reading skills tests are presented in Enabling Element 3. Do this Enabling Element if you need practical ideas for actually using the reading skills tests to provide for the individual needs of your students. If you can already do so, you are ready for the Posttest.

Enabling Element 1
Skills Necessary to Read Content Area Materials

Specific Objective 1

You will state the four categories of reading skills and identify the major reading skills necessary to read materials in your content area.

Enabling Activities

*1. Read Study Guide 1. Determine the reading skills that students need in order to read successfully in your content area.

2. Read the separate skill lists for the different content areas in Study Guide 1. Are there similar skills that are needed to read in all content areas? What are the differences?

3. State some examples of reading skills needed for success in content areas. After doing so, state why it is impossible for children to develop all the reading skills during the elementary school years (grades one through six).

---

*Indicates core Enabling Activities.

4. Evaluate your own reading. Do you continue to develop more skill in reading? Discuss the implications with your colleagues.

*5. Look through various textbooks and written materials that you commonly use with your students. Find specific examples of the reading skills needed for success in your content area. For example, look for specialized vocabulary and symbols. Note any tables, diagrams, charts, or illustrations. Consider the skills and knowledge that are necessary to use specialized reference materials in your content area. You will be able to use some of these materials and ideas as you actually construct skill tests.

Study Guide 1

In addition to determining whether or not students can read textbooks and other commonly required reading materials, many content area teachers want to know if their students have developed the specific reading skills necessary to succeed in their content areas. For example, many content area teachers have the following reading-related questions about their students:

Do they understand the meaning of the generic words used by the authors of the textual materials in my subject area? Teachers who ask this are concerned about the prerequisite vocabulary demands of the textual materials they are using. They understand that they need to introduce the technical vocabulary of their subject areas but want some assurance that students can handle the generic vocabulary. Teachers unsure about students' understanding of the generic vocabulary prepare tests to assess the students' readiness for the generic vocabulary demands of the textual material.

Can my students answer the types of comprehension questions I will ask them over the textual assignments I give them? Teachers who ask this question are concerned about how well their students can answer questions requiring them to recognize or recall information, translate information into their own words, apply what they have read to a new situation or problem, analyze what they have read, synthesize information to form a new communication, and evaluate what they have read. Comprehension questions are important in all subject areas, and students must have definite question-answering strategies to answer them. To be sure their students have the appropriate comprehension skills to read the textual materials, teachers prepare tests of comprehension skills.

Do my students have the necessary study skills and strategies to independently approach the reading of the assigned textual materials? Teachers who ask this question are concerned that their students may not know how to use basic study skills to locate information or material, to read graphic material, and adjust their reading rate. Similarly, they are concerned that their students may not be aware of and know how to apply study strategies for reading in social science, physical science, and mathematics textual materials. When teachers are concerned about what study skills and strategies their students have acquired, they prepare study skills and study-strategy tests.

---

*Indicates core Enabling Activities.

Do my students know how to pronounce the multisyllable, generic, and technical words in the textual materials I will assign them? Teachers who ask this question are concerned that their students may not be aware of the higher level word pronunciation skills and may not have a strategy for applying those skills to the multisyllable words that appear in the assigned textual material. These teachers know there are many two-, three-, and four-syllable words in their students' listening vocabularies that the students may not immediately recognize when they read. To help students who lack these skills gain independence in reading the textual materials, content area teachers must review some basic word recognition skills and show students how to incorporate these into a strategy for pronouncing words.

The wise content area teacher asks questions similar to these about each student at the beginning of each semester, term, quinmester, and the like. The teacher prepares the necessary skills tests to identify specific needs of those students the teacher believes will have difficulty with generic word meanings, answering comprehension questions, applying study skills and strategies, and/or pronouncing multisyllable words. Since we believe you want to be the best content area teacher you can be, in this module we will show you how to identify the major reading skills in your subject area and prepare appropriate skills tests. In subsequent modules, we will show you how to teach word meanings (Module 5), how to help your students comprehend (Module 6), how to teach your students to use study skills and strategies (Module 7), and how to teach your students to pronounce multisyllable words (Module 8).

Let us begin by examining a general list of reading skills required to read materials in different content areas. Locate and read the list of skills required to read materials in your content area.

Content Area Reading Skills

Art
Generally, students in art classes must be able to do the following:

Word Meaning
1. Develop a technical vocabulary, which includes such words as *acetone, asymmetric, batik, bisque, burnish, grog, lithography,* and *vermiculite.*
2. Analyze prefixes, suffixes, and stems of technical terms to determine the specific word meaning.

Comprehension
3. Answer various types of questions.
4. Follow directions exactly, such as for firing ceramic products.
5. Read critically to note viewpoints and see relationships between various aspects of different cultures.

Study Skills and Strategies
6. Locate and use reference materials with information about art criticism and the history of art.
7. Read diagrams, such as an illustration of how to make a leather project.
8. Adjust reading technique to fit the purpose and nature of the material.
9. Use a study strategy such as SQ3R.

Word Pronunciation
10. Pronounce such multisyllable words as *engrave, frontage, abstract,* and *expressionism.*

Business Education

Students in business education classes, such as accounting, bookkeeping, business mathematics, and typing, must be able to:

Word Meaning

1. Understand the meaning of such technical terms as *division of labor, synthetic, profit, technology, consignment,* and *proprietorship.*

Comprehension

2. Answer various types of questions.
3. Accurately follow written directions, such as those for using different models of machinery (typewriters, copy machines, calculators) or keeping detailed records (payroll register, etc.).
4. Critically read application forms, invoices, tax forms, and legal papers.

Study Skills and Strategies.

5. Read graphs, charts, and diagrams, such as those in cash receipts journals, eight-column worksheets, and balance sheets.
6. Use the different parts of reference books, such as handbooks for secretaries or accountants.
7. Rapidly alphabetize materials, as is required in filing or locating reports.
8. Apply a study strategy such as SQ3R.

Word Pronunciation

9. Pronounce such multisyllable words as *typewriter, calculator, computer, journalizing, duplicating, stenciling, tabulation,* and *transactions.*

English Language Arts and Literature

Reading is extensively required for success in the English language arts area. In most schools, English teachers have the major responsibility for teaching word meaning skills, comprehension, study skills and those techniques necessary to pronounce multisyllable words. Specifically, students in English classes must be able to:

Word Meaning

1. Understand specialized vocabulary such as *adjective, figurative language, infinitive phrase, inside address,* and *collective noun.*
2. Develop scope and depth of vocabulary by studying word origins, slang, idioms, denotations and connotations of words, multiple meanings, and word relationships such as synonyms, antonyms, and homonyms.

Comprehension

3. Answer various types of questions to identify significant details, central ideas, mood, sensory images, sequence of ideas, and relationships among ideas, and make inferences about characters, settings, and events.
4. Critically evaluate what is read by determining the authors' purpose, distinguishing facts from opinions, identifying propaganda techniques, and identifying characteristics of good writing.
5. Read creatively to respond to the authors' ideas.

Study Skills and Strategies

6. Use the card catalogue, the *Reader's Guide to Periodical Literature,* and other reference materials to locate information.
7. Develop a flexible style and rate of reading appropriate for different types of literature (poetry, drama, fiction, nonfiction, and so forth). Use study strategies as necessary.
8. Organize ideas into an outline, summarize, take notes from a book.

9. Develop skill in using reference materials such as dictionaries, encyclopedias, and a thesaurus.
10. Use a study strategy, such as SQ3R.

Word Pronunciation

11. Pronounce words using context clues, structural analysis, phonics, and the dictionary.

Foreign Language

Students in foreign language classes must be able to:

Word Meaning

1. Understand specialized vocabulary words, such as *cognates, tense, stem-changing verbs, subjunctive,* and *auxiliary verbs.*
2. Associate foreign words with their English counterparts.
3. Use dictionaries to locate words and phrases and their associated multiple meanings.
4. Learn the etymology of words from different languages.

Comprehension

5. Answer various types of questions.
6. Recognize differences and likenesses in sentence structure and grammar.
7. Comprehend idiomatic expressions.

Study Skills and Strategies

8. Use resource books to learn more about the culture and customs of a foreign country.
9. Use textual aids such as glossaries, vocabulary lists, practice exercises, and suggestions for
   studying.
10. Use a study strategy, such as SQ3R.

Word Pronunciation

11. Distinguish between similar sounds.
12. Read orally using correct pronunciation and appropriate phrasing and expression.
13. Use dictionaries to locate words and phrases and use the pronunciation guides to pronounce
    the words and phrases.

Health

To be successful in health, students must be able to:

Word Meaning

1. Understand such technical vocabulary as *respiratory, ductless glands,* and *personality.*

Comprehension

2. Answer various types of questions.
3. Read and follow specific directions as required in using first aid.

Study Skills and Strategies

4. Read graphs (life expectancy in the United States, etc.)
5. Read diagrams, such as those showing the parts of the body.
6. Read charts, such as those showing the characteristics of commonly used drugs.
7. Outline and take notes while reading.
8. Use a study strategy, such as SQ3R or PQRST.

Word Pronunciation

9. Pronounce such multisyllable words as *convulsion, tissue,* and *endocrine.*

Homemaking

Homemaking includes such courses as home economics, clothing, bachelor living, child development, and interior decorating. In these courses, students must be able to:

Word Meaning

1. Learn the specialized vocabulary, such as *sauté*, *marinate*, *gel*, *burnet*, and *dice*.

Comprehension

2. Answer various types of questions.
3. Read and follow directions, such as those for recipes.
4. Read carefully to understand instructions for operating various appliances, etc.
5. Critically read newspapers, catalogues, and magazine articles, including advertisements.

Study Skills and Strategies

6. Read labels to find ingredients, directions, and cautions.
7. Interpret charts, graphs, diagrams, patterns, drawings, and cutaways.
8. Use an appropriate study method such as SQ3R or PQRST to read textbooks, articles, and pamphlets.

Word Pronunciation

9. Read specialized abbreviations, signs, and symbols, such as those found in recipes and labels.
10. Read bills and statements accurately, including the various codes used on them.
11. Read such specialized materials as thermometers, meters, invoices, and legal forms.
12. Pronounce multisyllable words, such as *decorating*, *economics*, and *draperies*.

Industrial Arts

To be successful in industrial arts, students must be able to read using specific reading skills. Students must be able to:

Word Meaning

1. Understand such technical vocabulary as *abrasive materials*, *arc welding*, *chamfer*, *bevel*, *compression ratio of engines*, *cotter pin*, and *pumice stone*.

Comprehension

2. Answer various types of questions.
3. Read and follow safety rules and instructions for care of equipment.
4. Read detailed instructions to produce or repair particular products, such as carburetors.
5. Understand explanations and instructions as found in technical books or journals.

Study Skills and Strategies

6. Use the aids available in various manuals (indexes, glossaries, manufacturer listings, and so forth).
7. Read and interpret drawings, blueprints, charts.
8. Read detailed diagrams (such as for a cross section of a water faucet, an expanded view of a valve-stem assembly, or a blueprint for making a portable classroom).
9. Read tables, such as for the uses, colors, and strengths of different plastics.
10. Use a study strategy such as SQ3R or PQRST or SQRQCQ.

Word Pronunciation

11. Pronounce such multisyllable words as *ripsaw*, *tannin*, and *whipstitch*.
12. Read the specialized symbols and abbreviations that are used in many illustrations and directions.

Mathematics

In order to succeed in mathematics, students must be able to:

Word Meaning

1. Understand such specialized vocabulary terms as *transitive property*, *integer*, *vector*, and *quadratic*.
2. Understand common stems, prefixes, and suffixes.

Comprehension

3. Answer various types of questions.
4. Read detailed material slowly to determine the significant and insignificant facts.
5. Follow directions precisely, as in detailed explanations of various processes requiring step-by-step operations.
6. Critically analyze such statistical records as tax data and financial reports.

Study Skills and Strategies

7. Locate and read reference materials on such topics as famous mathematicians or the application of a specific mathematical theory.
8. Interpret materials used to express relationships, such as principles, axioms, formulas, and equations.
9. Read tables, such as those listing square roots or common logarithms of numbers.
10. Read various types of graphs, such as bar graphs, line graphs, pictographs, and flowcharts.
11. Read such visual materials as diagrams and geometric forms.
12. Use an index, table of contents, or other aids to locate information.
13. Remember the meanings of symbols and abbreviations.
14. Use an appropriate study strategy, such as SQRQCQ, for reasoning problems requiring reading.

Word Pronunciation

15. Pronounce such multisyllable words as *function* and *tangent*.
16. Recognize common prefixes and suffixes.

Music

It is no surprise that many reading skills are required in music. The students must be able to:

Word Meaning

1. Understand the meanings of technical music terms, such as *adagio*, *cantata*, *impressionism*, *recapitulation*, *vibrato*, and *timbre*.
2. Understand the foreign derivation of many of the specialized music terms.

Comprehension

3. Read to answer various types of questions.
4. Read different types of literature to appreciate the setting in which the music was written.
5. Notice the author's bias when evaluating critical reviews of music.

Study Skills and Strategies

8. Use a study strategy, such as SQ3R, when appropriate.
6. Use such special reference books as a dictionary of musical terms and indexes of literature in music.
7. Use such textbook aids as an index of songs and classified indexes.

Word Pronunciation

9. Learn the specialized symbols and notations required to read music.

Take time to determine what reading skills your students have.

10. Read the words of songs using the syllable divisions.
11. Pronounce such multisyllable words as *exposition* and *prelude*.

Physical Education

Several reading skills are important for understanding information gained through reading in physical education classes. In order to read and understand physical education materials, students must be able to:

Word Meaning

1. Learn such technical vocabulary as *fault, love, dead ball, anchor, seeded,* and *bootleg play*.
2. Read signals used by referees in various games.

Comprehension

3. Read to answer various types of questions.
4. Read and accurately follow directions, as in the rules for playing various games.
5. Read books and articles about different sporting events and characters to find major ideas, significant details, sequence of events, and conclusions.

Study Skills and Strategies

6. Locate reference materials with information about sports, such as the *World Almanac* and football guides.
7. Read such charts as those listing records of World Series games and various champions.
8. Read illustrations, such as diagrams of a squash court, a lacrosse field, or a basketball court.
9. Read diagrams of plays used in different sports.
10. Remember details, such as the measurements of courts, various positions of the body, and ways of scoring.

11. Use a study strategy such as SQ3R, PQRST, or SQRQCQ.

Word Pronunciation
12. Identify specialized symbols.
13. Pronounce such multisyllable words as *armdrag* and *hammerlock*.

Science

An efficient reader of science materials knows how to use the related skills. The science reader must be able to:

Word Meaning
1. Understand the technical vocabulary of science, such as *angle of reflection, cumulus, electrode, inertia, isotope,* and *ion.*
2. Analyze stems, prefixes, and suffixes to determine the meaning of technical words.

Comprehension
3. Read to answer various types of questions.
4. Differentiate facts from opinions.
5. Read and follow directions as required for doing experiments.
6. Read to test, prove or predict outcomes.
7. Organize ideas from reading and understand the relationships between the ideas in order to draw conclusions or make inferences or evaluations.

Study Skills and Strategies
8. Use library skills to locate and research a topic in various journals, U.S. Government publications, and other reference materials.
9. Interpret such graphic and visual materials as weather maps or diagrams of such things as the operation of a refrigerator.
10. Use a study technique such as PQRST.

Word Pronunciation
11. Quickly identify symbols, formulas, and abbreviations.
12. Recognize common prefixes, suffixes, and stems as an aid to word pronunciation.
13. Pronounce such multisyllable words such *fulcrum* and *conduction.*

Social Studies

Social studies teachers need to be aware of the many reading skills required for reading in their content area. Specifically, students must be able to:

Word Meaning
1. Use such technical vocabulary words as *alliance, autonomy, butte, coniferous, equinox,* and *sovereign.*
2. Recognize the meaning of common prefixes and suffixes, which can be used as aids to word meaning.

Comprehension
3. Answer various types of questions.
4. Find the main idea and supporting details in reading selections.
5. Recognize cause and effect relationships.
6. Read critically to identify propaganda techniques.
7. Read to compare and contrast information and situations.
8. Read to distinguish fact from opinion.

Study Skills and Strategies

9. Be able to use the different parts of a book, such as summaries, chapter intro⌐ vocabulary lists, glossaries, preface, and footnotes.

10. Use such libarary resources as *Reader's Guide to Periodical Literature,* the card catalog, and others as may be appropriate.

11. Effectively and efficiently locate information in such reference materials as encyclopedias and almanacs.

12. Read maps (population, rainfall, physical, political, soil, etc.), tables, charts, graphs, and cartoons.

13. Understand time and space relationships.

14. Take notes in outline form from a book or other assigned reading.

15. Use a study strategy such as SQ3R.

Word Pronunciation

16. Pronounce such multisyllable words as *ingot* and *typhoon.*

17. Use common prefixes and suffixes to aid in the pronunciation of technical words.

Speech and Drama

Many of the reading skills previously mentioned are also required for students to succeed in speech and drama classes. Specifically, a student must be able to:

Word Meaning

1. Use such technical vocabulary words as *pitch, tone, power, fluff, accent, affirmative, connotation, denasal quality,* and *melodrama.*

2. Recognize the meaning of specialized symbols and abbreviations.

Comprehension

3. Read to answer various types of questions.

4. Read for specific directions, such as in guides to good listening, guides for making nominations speeches, and ways of organizing materials.

5. Identify the mood and tone of various characters.

6. Determine the nature of the setting in which something is to occur.

7. Critically evaluate what is read and creatively respond to the ideas (as would be necessary for a debate).

8. Determine the author's purpose for writing.

9. Notice the author's organization of ideas.

Study Skills and Strategies

10. Locate and efficiently use reference materials that may be needed for preparing speeches or plans.

11. Read to outline and take notes that will be useful for preparing speeches and debates.

12. Use a study strategy such as SQ3R.

Word Pronunciation

13. Read orally with appropriate expression, phrasing, and rate.

14. Pronounce such multisyllable words as *articulation* and *filibuster.*

You now have reviewed the major reading skills for your subject area under the categories of word meaning, comprehension, study skills and strategies, and word pronunciation. You should remember your content area reading skills and the four categories under which they are classified. If you can, you are ready for Enabling

Element 2, which will show you how to construct skills tests. After you have constructed these tests, you will be ready to determine if your students have the specific word meaning, comprehension, study skills and strategies, and word pronunciation requirements of your subject area.

Enabling Element 2
Constructing Reading Skills Tests

Specific Objective 2

You will construct reading skills tests to determine the reading skill needs of students in your content area classes.

Enabling Activities

*1. Read Study Guide 2. Identify the procedures and suggestions for making reading skills tests for your content area.

*2. Complete the Practicum Exercise. Select a reading skill needed in your content area from those listed in Study Guide 1 and prepare a reading skills test. Use sample selections from your textbooks (tables, charts, maps, diagrams, symbols) or other appropriate materials you expect students to read. Perhaps some of your old quizzes can be revised to serve as reading skills tests.

3. Look at some of the standardized achievement tests in your content area. Could the tests be scored in such a way that you would learn which reading skills different students need? If so, can you use these as supplements to the teacher-made test in order to identify the specific reading skill needs of your students?

4. Many of the newer textbooks include reading skills tests or review tests. You may want to use the presence of these tests as one of your criteria as you evaluate textbooks for possible adoption. If your present books contain these skills tests, you will not have to spend as much time constructing them.

5. See Enabling Element 2 in Module 8 for a specific example of a word pronunciation test. After completing Module 8, you will be able to add this test to your battery of reading skills tests.

Study Guide 2

Most content area teachers construct achievement tests as a routine part of the teaching process. Actually, the construction of reading skills tests differs very little from regular achievement tests or quizzes. Read the four steps; then do the Practicum Exercise.

---

*Indicates core Enabling Activities.

Step 1: Determine the Reading Skills in Your Content Area

As in developing other tests, the teacher's first task is to determine the *objectives* that must be tested or evaluated. In constructing skills tests in reading, you must consider the reading skills students should have accomplished or need to develop in order to read your content area material. Refer to the appropriate list in Study Guide 1 of this module to determine what skills you need to test. For example, if reading a graph is a necessary skill in your content area, you may want to construct a skill test to see which students can correctly read and interpret a graph.

Step 2: Selecting the Specific Content for Your Reading Skills Test

Now that you have determined the specific reading skills needed for your content area, it is necessary for you to select the textual material you will use to prepare your skills tests. To do so, you must have a clear understanding of each reading skill and then examine your textual materials for their reading skill requirements. Here are some common reading skills and sources of test items. Examine the sources of test items to get ideas on where you can get the materials you need for your content area reading skills tests.

Reading Skill	Sources of Test Items
Word Meaning (See also Module 5, ''Teaching Word Meanings,'' for more ideas.)	
1. Understand general and technical words	1. Look through the assigned textbook chapters or glossaries.
2. Understand special prefixes, suffixes, and stems.	2. Look in assigned magazines, your course syllabus, various handouts you distribute, various visual aids you use, and other supplemental materials.
Comprehension (See also Module 6, ''Helping Students Comprehend,'' for more ideas.)	
1. Answer recognition and recall questions, which require recognizing or recalling details, main ideas, conclusions, and directions.	1. Look in textual materials for passages about which you can ask questions requiring students to recognize or recall details, main ideas, conclusions, and directions.
2. Answer translation questions, which call for restating details, main ideas, conclusions, and directions.	2. Look in textual materials for passages about which you can ask questions requiring students to state in their own words details, main ideas, conclusions, and directions.
3. Answer application questions, which require students to first recognize, recall or translate information and then use it to explain a situation or solve a problem.	3. Look in textual materials for passages about which you can ask questions that require students to apply what they have learned to explain a situation or solve a problem.

4. Answer analysis questions, which require students to identify the details that contribute to a main idea, conclusion, or inference.

4. Look in textual materials for passages about which you can ask questions that require students to identify the details that support a main idea, conclusion, or inference.

5. Answer synthesis questions, which require students to combine information to form main ideas, conclusions, and inferences.

5. Locate textual material from which students must combine information to form main ideas, conclusions, or inferences. Or locate passages from which students must select information and combine it with experience to answer a question.

6. Answer evaluation questions, which require students to identify criteria, gather facts, make judgments, and form evaluation statements.

6. Locate passages in textual materials that deal with controversial issues to ask questions requiring students to establish criteria, gather facts, make judgments, and form evaluations.

Study Skills and Strategies (For more ideas, see Module 7, ''Helping Students Use Study Skills and Strategies.'')

1. Read graphs, tables, diagrams, and other visual or graphic aids.

1. Find examples in your textbooks and supplementary materials. Have the students use the textbook or supplementary material to answer questions about the specific textual aid.

2. Use reference materials

2. List the references available in your content area, and develop questions to see if students know what is in the different reference materials and how to use them.

3. Correctly use textbooks

3. Notice the aids in your textbooks, such as preface, index, vocabulary lists, and appendices. Design questions that will help you determine whether or not the students know how to use these aids.

4. Outline and take notes

4. Select a passage that can be outlined or from which notes can be taken. Direct the students to outline the material, and then evaluate the forms they use.

5. Use the appropriate rate of reading

5. Select different passages from textual materials you commonly use. Provide the students with a purpose for reading each selection, and then ask them to indicate the appropriate rate at which the selection should be read: slow, normal, or rapid.

6. Use proper study strategies (SQ3R in Social Science materials, PQRST in physical sci-

6. Give each student a selection from a suitable technical material. Ask the student to de-

ence materials, SQRQCQ in mathematics materials)

scribe his or her strategy for study reading. Compare the answer to the appropriate study strategy to determine if the student's study strategy is adequate.

Word Pronunciation (For more ideas, see Module 8, "Helping Students Pronounce Multisyllable Words.")

1. Accurately read symbols, abbreviations, and formulas

1. Survey your most commonly used materials to see what symbols and abbreviations appear frequently. Find formulas that can be used to see if students can determine relationships.

2. Quickly recognize symbols—visual perception

2. Prepare a list of symbols. Flash them on an overhead projector, and ask the students to write the symbols as quickly as possible.

3. Correctly pronounce prefixes, suffixes and technical stems

3. Make a list of affixes and stems commonly found in your content area, and ask the students to read them.

4. Correctly pronounce multisyllable words

4. Make a list of typical words found in your text. Type them on 5x7 index cards. Show them to one student at a time to determine if they know the basic word pronunciation skills.

5. Use proper word pronunciation strategy

5. Ask the students to write their answer to this question, "When I come to a word in my reading that I do not recognize, how do I go about pronouncing the word?"

After your examination of the common reading skills and sources of test items, you should have some idea of what materials to look in for the content of your reading skills test. For example, if you have decided to test for technical vocabulary words, you need to skim through the chapters of your textbook or use the glossary to make your word selection. For comprehension skills, you may have decided that you need to select passages and questions from magazines, newspapers, and similar publications. For study skills, you may want to use your textbook to test your students' understanding of basic textual aids such as preface, table of contents, list of tables, index, vocabulary lists, appendices, and so forth. For word pronunciation, you may have decided to survey various textual materials to identify a list of representative multisyllable words you can ask your students to pronounce. By the end of the second step, you should have identified the major reading skills you want to test and selected the actual material you will use for the test.

Step 3: Prepare the Test

Your third step is to actually prepare the tests you will use for testing the reading skills. Each test will need a title, a statement of its objective, a statement identifying the materials to be included in the test, or the actual materials themselves, and finally an indication of the acceptable level for mastery. Now examine the following sample skills test for Symbols in Mathematics.

The first thing you should notice about the sample skills test is that it begins with a title. In a general way, its title indicates what is tested. When you prepare a sample skills test, be sure to write a title that in a general sense explains what is being tested.

Sample Skills Test
Symbols in Mathematics

Objective: Given sets of math symbols and their definitions, the student will match each symbol with its definition.

Material: Test

Directions to the Student: Match the definition with the symbol by placing the appropriate letter in the blanks provided.

_____ 1. +	a. since; because
_____ 2. −	b. is greater than
_____ 3. =	c. degrees
_____ 4. <	d. difference between
_____ 5. >	e. plus; positive
_____ 6. ≧	f. pi; equal to 3.14159+
_____ 7. ≠	g. is equal to
_____ 8. ○	h. is less than
_____ 9. ∩	i. minus; negative
_____10. ∴	j. intersection
_____11. π	k. is equal to, or greater than
_____12. − :	l. not equal to

Acceptable Level for Mastery: 100 percent

Next you should notice that there is an *objective*. The objective spells out precisely what is given to the student and what the student is expected to do. For this sample skills test, the student is "Given sets of math symbols and their definitions." And what is a student to do with these? "The student will match each symbol with its definition." When you prepare your sample skills test, you will want to write an objective that begins with "Given. . . ." and ends with "the student will. . . ."

The third section of the sample skills test either specifies where to locate the *materials* that will be used in the test or contains the actual test materials. If actual materials from a textbook or similar source are going to be used, then the title of the textbook, page number, and precise beginning and ending points would be identified. Reproduced material should be contained within the test.

The fourth section is *Directions to the Student*. This section contains the precise directions the student must read and follow to complete the test. The more direct and precise the directions are, the more accurate will be the results you obtain from your students. When you write directions for your skills tests, you will want to make them as clear as the directions provided in the sample skills test. To check their clarity, you may want to share them with your colleagues before you use them with students.

The fifth section contains the *test* and/or questions, task, etc. that go with it. If a source such as a textbook is used for the skills test, then only the questions need to appear here. This sample includes the test, but others you see later will include only test questions.

The sixth section contains the *Acceptable Level for Mastery*. This is the percentage of items a student must have correct to be considered to have achieved mastery. More will be said about this later.

Here are some sample skills tests for you to examine and study. Notice that each has a title, objective, statement of material, directions to the student, and acceptable level for mastery. Sample skills tests are provided for each of the four major areas of word meaning, comprehension, study skills and strategies, and word pronunciation. From studying these skills tests, you should learn how to prepare reading skills tests of your own.

Sample Skills Test (Vocabulary)
Science

Objective: Given a set of words and their meanings, both arranged in separate columns and random order, the student will match each word with its specific definition.

Material: Tests containing a list of words and a second list of definitions, both in random order.

Directions to the Student: Match the words with the definitions by writing the letters from the right-hand column in front of the words that match in the left-hand column.

Test:

1. _____ style	a.	The pollen-bearing portion of the male reproduction organ of flowering plants
2. _____ amino acids		
3. _____ mitosis	b.	A spherically shaped bacterium
4. _____ cell	c.	Automatic, unlearned behavior
5. _____ anther	d.	Organic compounds that are the building blocks of proteins
6. _____ hormone	e.	The basic structural unit of life
7. _____ muscle	f.	The female portion of a flower, usually consisting of ovary, style and stigma
8. _____ coccus		
9. _____ instinct	g.	A secretion of the endocrine gland that controls and coordinates cell and organ functions
10. _____ pistil		
	h.	The process by which the nucleus duplicates before cell division
	i.	An organ or tissue that can contract to produce motion
	j.	The slender stalk of the pistil of a flower

Acceptable Level for Mastery: 80 percent

Sample Skills Test (Vocabulary)
Business

Objective: Given a set of words, the student will write their definitions.

Materials: Tests.

Directions to the Student: Define the following terms with concise responses.

Test:
1. Assets–
2. Balance sheet–

3. Certified check–
4. Collator–
5. I.T.W.–
6. Excise tax–
7. F.I.C.A.–
8. Liabilities–
9. Net pay–
10. Promissory notes–
11. Voucher–
12. Requisition–

Acceptable Level for Mastery: 80 percent

Sample Skills Test (Comprehension)
Answering Application and
Analysis Questions in Music

Objective: Given an article from a magazine on music, the student will read the article and answer questions that require him or her to apply and analyze.

Material: Magazine, *Musical Fun,* article on "Vocal Music," pp. 25–28.

Directions to the Student: Locate the article, "Vocal Music" in *Music Fun* Magazine. Read the article. When you are through, answer the following questions on a separate sheet of paper.

Test:
1. How are the terms *soprano, mezzo-soprano,* and *alto* related to the terms *tenor, baritone,* and *bass*?
2. What facts support the author's conclusion that choral music interest is on the rise throughout the world?
3. What possible effects will the rise in popularity of choral music have on sales of instrumental records?
4. How do Ralph Allen's ideas differ from those of Adele Redford's on the value of music as therapy?
5. How are music symbols like a code?

Acceptable Level of Mastery: 80 percent

Sample Skills Test (Comprehension)
Answering Recognition and
Recall Questions in Art

Objective: Given a selection from the textbook *Great American Art,* the student will answer questions requiring recognition and recall of specific information.

Material: Textbook, *Great American Art,* section on "What Made Art Flourish," pp. 137–41.

Directions to the Student: In your textbook, *Great American Art,* read the section on "What Made Art Flourish in America." (It begins on page 137 and ends on page 141.) Then answer the following questions on a separate sheet of paper.

Test:

1. To what does the author attribute human beings' interest in art?
2. How is the word *commemorative* defined in this selection?
3. What are some *formal* reasons for our interest in art?
4. What is a *commemorative* reason for our interest in art?
5. What is *nonverbal art*?
6. How does the author relate *beauty* and *significance* to art?
7. What are some of the examples given of *useful arts*?
8. Where are the art centers of America?
9. Who are some of the early American artists?
10. Which art form is most popular in America?

Acceptable Level of Mastery: 80 percent

Sample Skills Test
Using Reference Books in Geography

Objective: Given a commonly used reference and questions designed to show how well the reference can be used, the student will use the reference and answer the questions.

Material: Test.

Directions to the Student: Answer the following questions using the current *World Almanac.*

Test:
1. What kinds of information are presented in an almanac?
2. Why are almanacs valuable?
3. Where is the index in an almanac?
4. On what page would you find information about New Jersey?
5. What kind of information is presented about New Jersey?
6. On what page would you find information about the Catholic religion?
7. What page tells you about telephones in the United States?

Acceptable Level for Mastery: 100 percent.

Sample Skills Test
Using a Textbook

Objective: Given a textbook, the student can explain and use the different parts.

Material: Student's textbook and test questions.

Directions to the Student: Use your textbook to answer the following questions.

Test:
1. Who is the author? What are her qualifications?
2. When was the book copyrighted?
3. What is the purpose of each part of the book?
4. Is there a list of tables? Figures?
5. Does the book have an index? When will you use this?
6. Are there pictures and diagrams to help you learn?
7. How are the chapters organized?
8. How are definitions of new words presented?
9. What aids are included at the end of each chapter?

10. Are there any appendices? What information is included in the appendices? How can this information help you?

Acceptable Level for Mastery: 80 percent

Sample Skills Test
Study Skills and Strategies
Reading Tables and Graphs

Objective: Given tables, graphs and questions requiring the student to interpret them, the student will answer the questions to demonstrate an understanding of tables and graphs.

Material: Tables, graphs, and questions

Directions to the Student: Examine this table and answer these questions:

Test:
1. What is the title of the table?
2. What is the unit of measurement?
3. What are the column (vertical) and row (horizontal) headings?
4. What is the significance of the table?
5. How can you use the information from the table?

   In addition, write five questions requiring the student to read the table.

Sample questions for graphs:
1. What type of graph is used?
2. What is the unit of measurement?
3. What information is presented?
4. How is the information arranged?
5. What symbols are used? What do these symbols mean?
6. What is the significance of the information presented in the graph?

Acceptable Level for Mastery: 80 percent

Sample Skills Test
(Word Pronunciation)
Recognizing Prefixes and Suffixes

Objective: Given a list of words separated into prefixes, suffixes and base words, the student will pronounce the words to demonstrate recognition of the prefixes and suffixes.

Material: List of words formed with prefixes and suffixes.

Directions to the Student: Read aloud each of the following words.

Test:
ab strac *tion*
ante date
bi focal
de form *ity*
dis honest ly
ir respons *ible*
non conform *ist*
trans port *able*
ultra modern
un event *ful*

Acceptable Level for Mastery: 80 percent

Sample Skills Test
(Word Pronunciation)
Pronouncing Words

Objective: Given a list of multisyllable words typical of those found in a science textbook, the student will examine and pronounce each word.

Material: Ten multisyllable words

Directions to the Student: Examine each of these words carefully. Using what you know about pronouncing multisyllables, pronounce each word aloud.

Test:
1. motion
2. carbon
3. station
4. shelter
5. planet
6. sensation
7. relation
8. exercise
9. contemplate
10. universe

Acceptable Level of Mastery: 80 percent

Step 4: Determine the Acceptable Level of Mastery

When a test is given to a group of students, it sometimes contains information over which the student should have total mastery. When this is the case, the acceptable level of performance is 100 percent. That means that the student must get all the items correct on the test before moving to new material. An analysis of the test results reveals the specific items each student needs to be taught before being moved into new material.

If a test is merely a sample of the knowledge the student must have, the student need not correctly answer every question in order to demonstrate mastery of a certain skill. Usually 80 percent correct is considered mastery for such a test. As a teacher, you are in the best position to determine the sufficient level of mastery your students must achieve. The mastery level should be no lower than 80 percent on your tests, and sometimes as high as 100 percent. But the determination of the exact percentage for mastery required is up to you.

Practicum Exercise

It is your turn to prepare a skills test for any reading skill important for your content area. You have already identified some of the important reading skills and selected some of the material you will use for testing the skill. Now you need to prepare the test and set the acceptable level of mastery. Use the following outline of the six major areas of the skills test to prepare your own test.

TITLE

Objective: Given _____

_____, the student will _____

_____.

Material:

Directions to the Student:

Test:

Acceptable Level of Mastery: _____

Answers to the Practicum Exercise

Check your skills test to see if its title explains in a general way what is being tested. Check your objective to see if it *specifically* states what is given to the student and what the student is expected to do. Check to see if you included a statement identifying all the materials necessary for the student to complete the test. Did you then provide the student with clear and precise directions? The directions should explain what is to be done to complete the test. Did you remember to have one of your colleagues check your directions to see if they are as explicit as you believe them to be? Finally, you should have included a percentage for the acceptable level of mastery. If it is necessary for the student to have total mastery, then you should have indicated 100 percent; but if your test is only a sample of the knowledge the student must have, then 80 percent of the answers would be an acceptable level of mastery.

You are now familiar with the basic reading skills in your subject area and know how to construct reading skills test. You are ready to learn how to administer, score, and use the results from the reading skills tests to help your students improve their reading skills in your content area.

Enabling Element 3
Administering, Scoring, and
Using the Results of Reading Skills Tests

Specific Objective 3

You will administer, score, and use the results from reading skills tests in your content area.

Enabling Activities

*1. Read Study Guide 3, which gives suggestions concerning when to administer reading skills tests, how to score and record the results, and the implications for using the results.

*2. Prepare a reading skills test for one skill in your content area. Administer the test to a student.

*3. Make a skill chart to record the reading needs of your students in your content area, and use this completed record chart to list skill groups. Modules 5, 6, 7, and 8 will provide many valuable suggestions for teaching some of the reading skills.

4. Establish a skill center that includes materials and activities designed to help students develop a specific reading skill. Obtain the cooperation of the librarian and perhaps other teachers in planning a series of skill centers to be located in the library or media center.

5. Share your skills tests with colleagues in your content area. Encourage them to try the tests and then to make tests of their own.

---

*Indicates core Enabling Activities.

Study Guide 3

Administering Reading Skills Tests

Now that you have constructed reading skills tests pertinent to your content area, it is necessary to try them with the students. Some teachers like to administer the tests at the beginning of the course so they can immediately determine their students' reading needs. This information then can be used in helping the students throughout the semester, quarter, or quinmester. Other teachers use the skills tests as pretests, before the unit in which the skills are most likely to be used.

Remember that the purpose of reading skills tests is to determine if the students have the prerequisite reading skills to get the most out of their textbooks and supplemental materials. The general guideline then should be to administer the tests early in the semester or immediately before the skills are needed so you can provide the necessary instruction. Of course, diagnosis is most useful when it is continuous. Certainly one of your most important diagnostic devices is observation of students as they read different types of material and respond to your questions. The task of diagnosis is never completed—you are continually evaluating students to determine their instructional needs.

When administering the skills tests, simply tell the students you want to see what they have learned in other classes. Indicate that grades will not be given, but rather the results will be used to help you teach the skills that will help them get more out of their reading. After the tests, informally talk with the students to discuss what they have learned about various reading skills.

Scoring Reading Skills Tests

Grades are not given for performance on reading skills tests. The purpose of the reading tests is to help you become aware of the students' reading skills needs. Use the Acceptable Level of Mastery for a test to determine if a student's performance was acceptable or unacceptable. Students performing acceptably should move to other skills tests or other tasks. Students whose performance is unacceptable should be taught those reading skills necessary to help them achieve the acceptable level of mastery. They should be taught these skills with the day-to-day reading materials used in your classroom.

Using Results from Reading Skills Tests

A *skills chart* is one method of recording the results from reading skills tests that is economical in terms of time and yet very valuable for noticing the instructional needs of the students. Skills charts include a list of skills at the top and the names of each student on the left column. If you place a check mark under the skills by each student's name to indicate successful accomplishment of the skill, you can glance at the skills chart (see

Related Reading Skills in Social Studies

Names of Students	Word Meanings	Comprehension		Study Skills & Strategies		Word Pronunciation	
		Analysis	Evaluation	Interpret Tables	Use SQ3R	Prefixes & Suffixes	Strategy
1. Jimmy		✓	✓	✓	✓	✓	✓
2. Alfonso	✓	✓	✓	✓✓			✓✓
3. Joseph	✓	✓		✓	✓		✓✓
4. Jennifer		✓			✓✓	✓	✓✓
5. Mykel	✓	✓	✓	✓✓	✓✓	✓✓	✓✓
6. Mark	✓	✓					
7. Carlos	✓	✓					
8. Alice	✓		✓				
9. May	✓	✓		✓	✓	✓	✓✓
10. Sally	✓	✓	✓	✓✓			✓✓
11. Zody	✓	✓		✓✓			✓✓
12. Jesus	✓						
13. Odelfa	✓	✓✓					
14. Tina	✓	✓✓	✓		✓		
15. Susan		✓		✓✓	✓✓	✓	✓✓
16. Chris	✓			✓✓	✓✓		✓✓
17. David							
18. Grant		✓✓	✓	✓			
19. Sandy	✓	✓		✓	✓	✓	✓
20. Karen	✓	✓✓		✓	✓✓		
21. Andrea	✓	✓✓					✓
22. Miguel		✓			✓		
23. Tony	✓	✓		✓✓	✓	✓	✓
24. Andy	✓	✓✓	✓	✓✓			
25. Lynette	✓	✓✓		✓	✓	✓	✓
26. Beth	✓	✓✓					
27. Bobby				✓✓	✓✓		
28. Tasha	✓			✓	✓✓		✓
29. Tonya	✓						
30. Liska	✓	✓					

Figure 5
Sample skills chart

figure 5) to determine the students who need special help in developing the required reading skills.

After you have identified the needs of your students, it is time for instruction. If certain reading skills are needed by most of the students, you can have total group instruction. For example, if you want your students to know how to read tables and the skills test results show that most of the students are unable to do so, you can develop some lessons that will help them learn to read tables through a group presentation.

Perhaps half of the students demonstrated accomplishment of a skill, and the other students did not. In this case, you can design a *skill group* to help students accomplish this skill. Skill groups are temporary groups that are dissolved when most of the students have accomplished the skill. The scheduling of skill groups is flexible, depending upon the other demands for the teacher's time.

Since teaching time is limited, you may want to plan some *skill centers*. A skill center is a place in the classroom, study hall, or library where you store the materials, equipment, and supplies concerning some particular skill. For example, a skill center on how to read tables would include many practice activities and examples designed to help students read tables. Keep in mind that a skill center does not have to be an entire corner of a room or require a special table for display. A skill center might be located in a cardboard box to which the students come and take materials to help them accomplish the skill. The purpose of the skill center is to provide instruction and practice activities to help students independently develop skills. Although some students may need additional teacher or peer instruction, once you have set up the skill center, many students will be able to use the activities independently.

Skill centers are especially valuable when only a few students need to develop the skill. Providing for all the individual needs of your students is impossible; thus, you need materials to which you can refer students. As you plan skill centers, try to include self-correcting activities. Also, provide opportunities for students to help each other. These techniques help you save valuable time.

There are other suggestions in the following modules that can be used to help you meet the needs of your students. Module 8 will provide ideas for helping students pronounce words, and Module 5 suggests many activities to help students develop the specialized vocabulary in your area. Module 6 provides ideas for helping students comprehend what they read, and Module 7 will help you teach some study strategies that will help your students. Even with all of these ideas, you will have students who are so far behind that help is needed. You are not expected to teach beginning skills to your students; simply help them develop the reading skills related to your area. Module 10, "Identifying and Helping Problem Readers," provides suggestions for helping problem readers learn in the content classes. In addition, it suggests the resource persons to whom problem readers should be referred.

Final Note

You now know how to determine the reading needs of students in your content area classes. This skill is not valuable unless you are committed to doing something with the results. Make a commitment to actually meet the individual needs of your students by setting up skill centers, meeting with skill groups, and teaching the reading skills as a part of your normal instructional activities.

Posttest

1. State the four major categories of reading skills, and write one reading skill for each from your subject area.
2. List the four steps you should follow when constructing a reading skills test in your content area. Write a statement describing each of the steps.
3. Write a brief paragraph describing how you plan to administer, score, and use the results from the reading skills test in your content area.

Posttest Answers

1. The four major categories into which reading skills are divided are word meaning, comprehension, study skills and strategies, and word pronunciation. If you correctly identified these categories and specified for each of them one major reading skill from your content area, you have accomplished this objective.
2. The four steps in constructing reading skills tests are
   a. Determine the reading skills required in your content area.
   b. Select the specific content for your reading skills test.
   c. Prepare the actual test.
   d. Determine the acceptable level of mastery.
3. Your paragraph should describe how you will administer, score, and use the results from your reading skills tests. You need to administer the test to one or more students, score the test to determine what reading skills your students need to be taught, and then you will need to prepare a skills chart to summarize the reading skill needs of your students. Finally, you must decide how you will go about organizing your students and commence instruction.

Selected Bibliography

Allington, R. L. "Improving Content Area Instruction in the Middle School." *Journal of Reading* 18 (1975): 455–61.
Bormuth, J. "The Cloze Readability Procedure." *Elementary English* 45 (1968): 429–36.

Burmeister, L. E. *Reading Strategies for Middle and Secondary School Teachers*. Reading, Massachusetts: Addison-Wesley Publishing Company, 1978.

Chance, L. L. "Using a Learning Stations Approach to Vocabulary Practice." *Journal of Reading* 18 (1974): 244–46.

Derby, T. L. "Informal Testing in Vo-Ed Reading." *Journal of Reading* 18 (1975): 541–43.

Frankel, J. C. "Reading Skills through Social Studies Content and Student Involvement." *Journal of Reading* 18 (1974): 23–26.

Kratzner, R. R. and Mannies, N. "Building Responsibility and Reading Skills in the Social Studies Classroom." *Journal of Reading* 22 (1979): 501–5.

Lamberg, W. J. and Lamb, C. E. *Reading Instruction in the Content Areas*. Chicago: Rand McNally, 1980.

LaRocque, G. E. Developing Special Skills for Reading Genres. *Reading Improvement* 14, no. 4 (Fall, 1977): 182–86.

Maxwell, M. J. "Developing a Learning Center: Plans, Problems, and Progress." *Journal of Reading* 18 (1975): 462–69.

Palmatier, R., and Bennett, J. M. "Note Taking Habits of College Students." *Journal of Reading* 18 (1974): 215–18.

Pyrczak, F., and Rasmussen, M. "Skills Measured by Selected Reading Tests Designed for High School Use." *Reading Improvement* 13, no. 3 (Winter 1974): 5–8.

Roe, B. D.; Stoodt, B. D.; and Burns, P. C. *Reading Instruction in the Secondary School*. Rev. ed. Chicago: Rand McNally, 1978.

Sanacore, J. "Locating Information: The Process Method." *Journal of Reading* 18 (1974): 231–33.

Viox, R. G. "Evaluating Reading and Study Skills in the Secondary Classroom: A Guide for Content Teachers." *Reading Aids Series*. Newark, Delaware: International Reading Association, 1968.

Teaching Word Meanings

Contents

Prospectus
   Rationale
   Objectives
   Resources and Time Required
Pretest
Branching Program Alternatives for Pretest Responses
Enabling Element 1: *Levels of Word Meaning*
Enabling Element 2: *Guidelines for Teaching Word Meanings*
Enabling Element 3: *Activities for Teaching Word Meanings*
Posttest
   Posttest Answers
Selected Bibliography

Prospectus

Rationale

No one needs to convince you that teaching word meaning is an important part of your subject area teaching responsibility. You know that without the specific technical vocabulary students will not be able to read assignments or understand your lectures.

You know word meaning is important, but do you know how important? Do you realize that approximately 60 percent of comprehension is accounted for by vocabulary? In other words, comprehension is 60 percent word meaning. Are you aware that subject area word knowledge correlates highly with overall knowledge, success, and grades in the subject area? As a subject area teacher, you will need to systematically expand the vocabulary of your students. This module will help you effectively teach word meanings.

Objectives

Terminal Objective

You will be able to introduce and expand word meanings in your subject area.

Specific Objectives

1. You will list three levels of word meaning and write a definition for a word at each of the three levels of word meaning.
2. You will list the six major guidelines for teaching word meaning in your subject area.
3. You will categorize a list of instructional activities into three levels of word meaning, and you will select activities to develop the fullest meaning of words in your subject area.

Resources and Time Required

All the resources required are provided to complete the starred core Enabling Activities. For the extension Enabling Activities, you will need to refer to a dictionary, thesaurus, textbooks, workbooks, or charts from your teaching area. The estimated time to complete starred core activities is three to four hours.

Pretest

Directions: For each question, determine the word that indicates your belief regarding your competency. If you are in doubt, choose NO.

1. Words have many meanings, and each meaning has many denotations   YES   NO
   and connotations. The more one knows about a word, the more one will
   understand about what he or she reads. Can you list three levels of word
   meaning and define a word at each of the three levels?

2. Teaching is both a science and an art. To be an effective teacher, you   YES   NO
   must be aware of what researchers and practitioners have learned about
   teaching your subject area. This must be combined with your creative
   ability to develop the best possible instruction. Can you list six major
   guidelines for teaching word meanings in your subject area?

3. Word meaning is one of the real stumbling blocks to understanding   YES   NO
   written material. This stumbling block can be removed by the teacher
   who chooses appropriate activities to introduce and teach word meanings in his or her subject area. Can you categorize a list of instructional
   activities into the three levels of word meaning, and select activities
   that are best for developing the fullest meaning of words in your subject
   area?

Branching Program Alternatives
for Pretest Responses

1. Words can be defined at three different levels of word meaning. If you can list three
   levels of word meaning and define a word at each level, you are ready for Enabling
   Element 2. If not, Enabling Element 1 will help you acquire the information needed
   to do so.

2. As teachers, we need to be aware of the guidelines for teaching word meanings suggested by research and experience. If you can list six major guidelines for teaching word meaning, you are ready for Enabling Element 3. If not, Enabling Element 2 will present these guidelines to you.

3. The activities you choose to teach word meanings will dictate the level of understanding acquired by your students. If you are aware of many activities for introducing new words at each of the three levels of word meaning and can select activities to develop the fullest meaning of words in your subject area, you are ready for the Posttest. If not, Enabling Element 3 will help you accomplish this task.

Enabling Element 1
Levels of Word Meaning

Specific Objective 1

You will list three levels of word meaning and write a definition for a word at each of the three levels of word meaning.

Enabling Activities

*1. Read Study Guide 1 to identify four types of vocabulary. Give examples of words in your listening, speaking, and reading vocabularies that are not in your writing vocabulary.

*2. Write a statement describing each of the three levels of word meaning. Write a definition of the word *barrier* at all three levels of word meaning.

*3. Identify five words from your subject area, and define them at each of the three levels of word meaning.

4. Ask your students to define the word *democracy*. Listen to their responses to see at which of the three levels of word meaning they can define *democracy*.

5. Write a statement describing how understanding of what a student hears and reads is improved as words move through the three levels of word meaning in the student's vocabulary.

6. Teach the five words from Enabling Activity 3 to students at each of the three levels of word meaning. Before teaching, ask the students to define the words; then determine and expand their present levels of understanding.

Study Guide 1

Every person has four vocabularies which develop from birth in approximately this order: listening, speaking, reading, and writing. The infant listens to family members

---

*Indicates core Enabling Activities.

and friends as they use words with him. Soon the young child begins to say these words. For example, many parents teach their child to say the word *ball* by saying the word *ball* as they show the child a ball and place it in the child's hand. The parents repeat this procedure many times. To the amazement of the parents, most children begin to say the word *ball* by the time they are eleven to twelve months old. Usually when the child enters school, he or she begins to learn to read the word *ball* when it is presented in written form, and finally learns to write the word *ball*.

Some words in your listening and speaking vocabularies may not be in your reading and writing vocabularies. For example, you may be able to listen to someone use the word *phlegm*, and you can use it as you describe mucus in your throat, but perhaps it looked strange to you as you just read it. Likewise, we have found that many people know the word *phlegm* as a part of their listening, speaking, and reading vocabularies, but cannot correctly write the word.

One of the continual tasks of every teacher is to help students increase these four vocabularies. You will want to make sure children can listen to and understand many words, use them in conversation, recognize them in print, and (if the words are used frequently when writing) learn to spell them. Our concern in this module is helping students develop a *reading* vocabulary, which will in turn help them comprehend.

There is no precise agreement on the size of vocabularies at various age levels. For example, research findings for twelfth graders vary on their estimates of vocabulary size between 15,000 and 45,000 words. The lack of agreement seems to be due to the manner in which "word" is defined. Some educators consider *walk, walking,* and *walked* as one word; others consider these to be three words. Other educators count each definition of a word as a new instance of a word. In the latter case, the word *run*, which has at least 130 definitions, would be considered as 130 separate words.

High school students, like all of us, are constantly adding new words to their vocabularies. Although the period of vocabulary growth is most rapid between 2½ and 7 years of age, growth remains considerable as long as schooling is continued. When schooling is discontinued, most adults add only about twenty-five new words a year to their vocabulary. In the middle to latter years of life, there is some evidence of overall decline in vocabulary size.

As a word comes into our vocabulary, it generally passes through at least three distinct stages of specific understanding. At first we have only a very specific understanding or association with the word. This means that the learner associates only a single definition, instance, event, or object with the word. For example, the word *sofa* at this level is perceived as a specific object of a precise size, shape, or color; the object is probably located in the living room of the learner's home. The learner is not aware that there are other sofas located in other homes, stores, and offices.

At the second stage, the learner has more than a specific understanding of the word; he or she begins to develop a functional understanding. Now the learner can answer the question, "What is the function of a *sofa*?" At this level *sofa* becomes something we sit or recline upon, and *sofa* can be used in a sentence to demonstrate understanding.

At the third and most abstract level of understanding, the learner develops a concept of *sofa*. For our purposes, a concept can be thought of as a cluster of impressions or perceptions for which words are used as labels. At the third level, the learner understands that *sofas* come in a variety of shapes, sizes, and colors, to mention a few things, and that they are part of a larger category called furniture. Sofas are not the only type of furniture;

many other things, such as tables and chairs, are also classified as furniture. At this level of understanding, the learner has a more complete understanding of the word *sofa*. Since word meanings are constantly changing, it is probably safe to say that the complete understanding of a word is never acquired.

Words, as they come into our vocabularies, do not automatically or naturally rise through the three stages of this hierarchy. Many words are transfixed at the specific or functional levels and never reach the general or conceptual level. Students whose vocabularies contain words principally at the specific or functional levels will have serious problems understanding their reading assignments, since authors communicate at the general or conceptual vocabulary level.

It is our responsibility as teachers to encourage and foster vocabulary growth in number of words as well as depth of meaning. Students need to know many words and need to have the fullest meaning possible of the words they know.

Today's secondary school students take a variety of courses during their years in school. The variety of courses contain many new words students must learn in order to master the subject areas. While most subject area teachers are aware of the importance of vocabulary to the understanding of their subject area, many teachers fail to teach for conceptual understandings of words. Instead, their strategy is to cover as many words as possible, briefly defining each as they go along. Research does not demonstrate that mere incidental exposure to large numbers of words expands vocabulary or develops conceptual understandings of words. For the most part, teachers who rush through vocabulary lessons, briefly and only verbally defining words, are wasting both their time and that of the students.

Words are understood at three levels of understanding. A word becomes transfixed in the hierarchy of understanding at the specific, functional, or general level depending on how it is experienced or learned. Asking students to look up a list of words in a dictionary generally transfixes those words at the specific level in the hierarchy. Asking students to define words as used in sentences, to obtain suitable synonyms, and to write a single sentence using each word generally transfixes words at the functional level of understanding. Providing direct experiences with new words and asking students to incorporate the new words into their written and oral assignments, as well as their daily discussions, generally tranfixes the new words at the conceptual level of understanding.

As a general rule, the more direct experiences a student has with a word, the more likely is the word to become transfixed at the conceptual level of understanding. The more vicarious and incidental the experience, the more likely the word is to become transfixed at the specific or functional level.

As a content area teacher, it is imperative for you to listen to your students to find out the levels at which they understand the words that belong to your specialized area. When you ask students if they have ever heard of a particular word, many students may nod their heads, indicating yes. If you take a few minutes to ask for the students' definitions of a particular word, you will be able to determine the level at which they understand the word and then plan activities to expand their meanings of the word. For example, if a music teacher asks students whether they have ever heard of the word *rhythm*, most of the students will readily say yes. However, when asked to define it, one student may only be able to say, "She has rhythm." After hearing this specific definition, the teacher can expand the students' level of understanding by explaining the functions of rhythm in music. Listen to your students! Then clarify and expand their definitions of words.

Defining Words

To be sure you understand the various levels of word meaning, we will take you through the process of defining three words. The following words are common and known to all of us.

> telephone
> jump
> vote

Before we define these words, let us review each of the three levels of word meaning. At each level we will give you an explanation as well as sample sentence using the word *book*.

Specific Level of Word Meaning. At the specific level, the student has a word associated with a single idea, event, definition, or object. A student asked to define the word *book* might respond, "A book is something found in schools."

Functional Level of Word Meaning. At the functional level, the student understands one of the major uses or functions of a word. A student asked to define the word *book* may respond, "A book is something you read." Or the student may demonstrate an understanding by using the word in a sentence, "I like to read books."

Conceptual Level of Word Meaning. At the conceptual level, the student recognizes that a word has more than one meaning or function. The student recognizes that there are many ideas associated with the word and clusters these ideas by some common element. When asked to define the word *book*, he or she responds, "Since books can be used for storing, obtaining, or transmitting information, they are a way of sharing information or a means of communication."

You now should have the levels of meaning in mind and a fair understanding of their distinctiveness. A detailed look at the words *telephone, jump,* and *vote* should further clarify these distinctions for you.

Telephone. At the specific level of word meaning, a student recognizes that a telephone is a colored object that hangs on a wall, sits on a desk, or the like. At the specific level, the student would define *telephone* as, "It hangs on the wall," or "There is one in the office," or a similar statement. At the functional level of word meaning, the student recognizes a major use of a telephone. When asked to define *telephone*, this student responds with something like "I use it to call my friends," or "You talk on it." At the conceptual level of word meaning, the student recognizes that a telephone is one of many different means for communicating with people and there are telephones located in many places throughout the student's community, nation, or world.

Jump. At the specific level of word meaning, *jump* is what a student does when he moves his or her body up and down. It is not uncommon at this level of understanding for a student to actually demonstrate by jumping. At the functional level of word meaning, a student defines *jump* as the thing he or she does when jumping rope or making high jumps, pole vaults, and other similar things. At the functional level the student defines *jump* in terms of some accomplishment, "I like to jump up and down." At the conceptual level, *jump* is defined as a method of exercise or a method of moving quickly. The student will give examples of prices *jumping, jumping* an opponent in checkers, or even *jumping* a dead battery as in starting a car.

Vote. At the specific level of word meaning, the most common specific association with the word *vote* is "something done during elections." Remember, at this level a student has only a single association with the word. That association may be an event, a definition, or an instance (to mention just three possibilities of associations). At the functional level of word meaning, probably the most common function heard is "a way of getting someone elected." In any event, at this level the student describes the word in terms of its major function or use. At the conceptual level, the student realizes that *vote* is just one part of a complex government process called democracy in which decisions or choices are made by the people.

It should be clear from these three examples that a student has only a single something associated with a word at the specific level of word meaning. At the functional level of word meaning, the student is able to describe a major use of a word or use the word in a sentence that demonstrates his or her understanding. At the conceptual level, the student has many facts and ideas associated with the word and recognizes and uses the word in many different sentences and contexts.

Practicum Exercise

Now let us see if you can define a word at the three levels of word meaning. We will use a word that we are sure everyone knows—the word is *noun*. For each of the following levels of word meaning, formulate an explanation of how the word *noun* would be defined. Write your definitions here:

Specific Level of Word Meaning—

Functional Level of Word Meaning—

Conceptual Level of Word Meaning—

Answers to Practicum Exercise

Compare your explanations with ours.

Specific Level of Word Meaning.   At this level, the word *noun* can be defined as a word, or some specific noun such as *John* or *dog*. Only a single observation or definition is associated with the word.

Functional Level of Word Meaning.   At this level, the word can be defined in terms of a major use or function, or used in a sentence that demonstrates understanding, that is, "a word used in talking or writing about some person, place, or thing."

Conceptual Level of Word Meaning.   At this level, you have many facts and ideas associated with the word. You may see the noun as one of the major form classes or parts of speech denoting person, place, or thing. You can use and recognize the word *noun* in different sentences, and you are able to identify nouns in written and oral language. At this level, you demonstrate a more complete understanding of the word as you differentiate proper nouns and common nouns and as you contrast nouns to pronouns.

If you think you can now define words at the three levels of word meaning, you are ready to move to Enabling Element 2. If not, you may want to obtain a dictionary, thesaurus, or a book containing synonyms and get together with someone using these modules to further clarify this concept of vocabulary development.

Enabling Element 2
Guidelines for Teaching Word Meaning

Specific Objective 2

You will list the six major guidelines for teaching word meanings in your content area.

Enabling Activities

*1. Read Study Guide 2, and prepare a written list of generalizations to guide you while teaching word meanings.

*2. From your list of prepared generalizations, prepare a second list of six key phrases. Examine your list of key phrases and prepare an acronym that will assist you in recalling them as you teach word meanings.

3. With students and teachers, discuss the list of guidelines for teaching word meaning. Determine if their experiences agree with findings from research and practice.

---

*Indicates core Enabling Activities.

4. Using the guidelines presented in this Study Guide, evaluate some of the popular vocabulary development books on the market. For example, one guideline suggests that the study of Latin stems has questionable value for vocabulary development. Look at some of the popular books to see how much stress is placed upon the study of Latin stems. Which books would you recommend to your students?

*5. List five words used in your content area that have both a general meaning and a technical meaning. Write the technical meaning of these words as they are used in your content area. For example, the general meaning of *rich* is having wealth; however, the word *rich* is used by the home economics teacher to mean full of choice ingredients.

Study Guide 2

One of the authors once overheard two teachers discussing whether teaching was a science or an art. One teacher maintained that teaching was a science and therefore required only the application of basic principles and guidelines developed through research. The second teacher maintained that it was really an art, the talents for which were most likely transmitted from one person to another genetically. After considerable discussion, the two teachers concluded that teaching was both a science and an art. As scientists, teachers read research on teaching and examine carefully their own practices to arrive at generalizations and guidelines to become more effective and efficient teachers. As artists, teachers use their creative genius and talents to make the subject of their teaching interesting and relevant to their students' needs.

Manzo and Sherk, in ''Some Generalizations and Strategies for Guiding Vocabulary Learning,'' presented an excellent list of guidelines for vocabulary improvement. Their list was developed after a systematic examination of research on vocabulary acquisition. Teachers who follow these guidelines will improve the efficiency and effectiveness of their vocabulary instruction. Selected guidelines taken directly from their list (modified for our purposes) follow: **

Guidelines for Teaching Word Meaning
1. New words are learned best when taught as labels for direct experiences.

2. Vocabulary development must have the continued and systematic attention of all classroom teachers.

3. Many encounters with a word in like and differing contexts are necessary before it can be learned.

4. The teacher's attitude toward vocabulary improvement and the superiority of his or her own vocabulary are contagious and vital factors in improving student vocabulary.

5. Study of a limited number of words in depth is more productive than superficial acquaintance with lists of words.

6. It is possible, but may be practically foolish, to teach words that are not part of the

---

*Indicates core Enabling Activities.

**Reprinted with permission from the *Journal of Reading Behavior* 4, no. 1 (Winter 1971–72): 81–82.

verbal community in which students live. The lack of opportunity for use must result in eventual atrophy.

7. Introducing vocabulary consistently with only one or two activities does not encourage word learning.

8. The wide-reading method of acquiring vocabulary, which stresses little more than wide, free reading with no other attention paid to words, is usually not very effective for influencing rapid and marked improvement.

9. The study of Latin positively influences knowledge of morphemes, but does not seem to influence knowledge of vocabulary.

A review of these guidelines suggests that word meaning instruction must be intensive, systematic, and regularly provided in an enthusiastic manner by every subject area teacher. Preferably, words should be introduced with direct and real experiences in a variety of contexts and gamelike situations. Words should be selected for daily assignments based upon students' needs, and the continued use of these words should be stressed in all assignments. Keeping these guidelines in mind as you teach will improve the effectiveness of your vocabulary instruction.

Guidelines 1 through 6 are probably the most important for increasing the effectiveness of your vocabulary instruction. These guidelines suggest things that you must do in order to increase your effectiveness, while Guidelines 7 through 9 deal with questionable practices for improving the vocabulary of your students.

Go back and read Guidelines 1 through 6 again. This time, decide which are the key words in each guideline statement. Make notes to help you remember the guidelines. When you are through, return to and continue reading with the next paragraph.

In Guideline 1, did you choose *direct experiences?* Students develop the fullest understanding of words when they learn them from real experiences rather than vicarious ones. A teacher can create situations that allow words to be taught through direct experiences. In such situations, students must use new words to communicate with each other and with the teacher.

In Guideline 2 the key words are "*continued* and *systematic* attention of all classroom teachers." Vocabulary development cannot be left up to a few teachers—it is every teacher's responsibility. We have found that content area teachers who do have specialized knowledge are the most effective teachers in helping students understand technical words in particular subject areas. In teaching specialized vocabulary from different content areas, the language arts teacher is not as effective as are the content area teachers themselves. Vocabulary instruction is most effective if it occurs daily in all classes and is systematic in nature. Please keep in mind that typical beginning readers need at least thirty-eight repetitions to learn one basic sight word. Likewise, middle- and secondary-school students must hear and see a word used frequently in order to make it a part of their listening, speaking, reading, and writing vocabularies.

The key words in Guideline 3 are *many encounters . . . in like and differing contexts*. Numerous encounters with words in varying types of oral discussions, reading materials, and writing assignments are necessary for students to develop the fullest understanding of the words you want them to learn. Many encounters are also needed to provide the necessary *mass* and *distributed* practice students need in order to get the word and its definition from immediate to long-term memory. Unless a word is acquired and stored in long-term memory, it will soon be forgotten and surely not used by the student as a building block for further knowledge.

In Guideline 4 the two most important words are *teacher's attitude*. Most of the research completed on teaching demonstrates that the teacher is the most important school-related variable in students' success or failure. When teachers approach vocabulary instruction with enthusiasm and positive attitudes, the vocabulary growth among students is considerable. On the other hand, when teachers approach vocabulary instruction with a casual or negative attitude, vocabulary growth is minimal.

A limited number of words in depth is the heart of Guideline 5. Many teachers believe they have too much course content to cover and too little time to cover the material. These teachers do not develop in-depth word meanings. Often, many words are assigned to students for study at one time, and the burden falls upon the students to develop the in-depth understanding. The best vocabulary instruction focuses upon a few words, their varied meanings, uses, and application in reading, writing, listening, and speaking. One of your major responsibilities as a content area teacher is to decide which words are most important for all students to understand. It is better to select 10 words for in-depth study than to select 100 words, which the students will simply define and forget.

Guideline 6 contains two important ideas, which are separate although related. The first idea deals with teaching words that . . . *are not part of the verbal community in which the student lives*. The second is *the lack of opportunity for use must result in eventual atrophy*. This guideline does not suggest that teachers teach *only* those words and meanings common to the verbal community in which the students live. However, it suggests that teachers select those words for vocabulary instruction that will help students in their daily communication of information. Try to avoid teaching words that will not be used either in the verbal community in which the student lives or the education community in which he or she is educated, since the lack of opportunity to use words would cause the words to be quickly forgotten.

One of the ways to help yourself remember the six major guidelines is by using an acronym. Acronyms are words made from beginning parts or beginning letters of other words. Sometimes these are real words, and sometimes they are nonsense words. Use the key words you have selected to build an acronym to help you remember the six major guidelines for making your vocabulary instruction more effective.

Our acronym is below. If you like your acronym better than ours, use your own.

Guideline	Acronym	Key Words
6	V	Verbal community
3	O	Opportunities for use
2	C	Classroom teacher
4	A	Attitude
1	B	Build meanings through direct experience
5	S	Study in depth

The Necessity for Applying the "VOCABS" Guidelines

One reason the English language is difficult to master is that many of our words have multiple meanings. Many words have both a general and a technical meaning. According to the *Guinness Book of World Records*, the word *set* has the most meanings of any word in the English language.* The word *set* has at least 194 definitions! In a general sense, *set* means to place. However, the word *set* also has many technical meanings. Consider the following definitions of *set* as it is used in different content areas.

Content Area	Use or Definition of *Set*
Art	Describes the process in making a color fast, as in dying. In jewelry making, means to cover and encrust with gems.
Business Education	To put down on paper, or in a record book. Also used to describe putting a seal on a document.
Language Arts	May refer to a collection of books.
Health	The teacher refers to ''setting'' a broken leg or finger.
Homemaking	The students learn proper ways to ''set'' the table or to let the Jell-o ''set.''
Industrial Arts	To put a moveable part of a machine in place. For example, you are going to ''set'' the gears into motion.
Math	A group of things.
Music	The teacher encourages students to ''set'' down, or write, words to music.
Physical Education	Prepare to begin, ''Get set.'' Also, in square dancing ''sets'' are formed, and in tennis you can play a ''set.''
Psychology	A mind ''set.''
Science	In botany, *set* means to develop after pollination, or to form fruit in the plant's blossom. Science teachers talk about the sun ''setting'' as it appears to descend below the horizon.
Social Studies	To fix a bond or fine at a certain amount of money; to appoint; or to fix limits or boundaries.
Speech and Drama	The scenery, or to make up scenery.

It is essential that content area teachers assume the responsibilities for vocabulary development. You know the technical definitions of words used in your content area better than any other teacher in the school; thus, you are the best person for helping students learn these technical definitions. If every teacher in your building has a

---

*N. McWhirter, *Guinness Book of World Records* (New York: Bantam Books, Inc., 1980), p. 211.

favorable attitude toward vocabulary development, builds meanings through direct experiences, helps the students study a limited number of words in depth, provides opportunities for students to use the words, and uses a variety of activities to help students learn the meanings of words, the students will be able to get more meaning from their reading assignments.

As you apply the guidelines suggested in this Study Guide, you may want to encourage your students to use a strategy for building their reading vocabulary. The strategy might be as follows:

1. Be alert for new words when you are reading.
2. Ask me to explain the word to you and/or look the word up in a dictionary. Make sure you find the definition that goes along with the way the word was used in context.
3. Keep a vocabulary notebook. In your notebook, make a separate entry for each word. Include the pronunciation of the word, the general meaning of the word, and the technical meaning of the word as it applies to our class. For each definition, write a sample sentence using the word.
4. Try to use the new word, and listen to discover how others use the word.

Enabling Element 3 provides various instructional activities you can use to help students develop technical meanings of words as they apply to your content area. If you do encourage students to ask you the meanings of words, you will need a variety of activities to increase the students' levels of understanding. You will find more than twenty-five such activities in Enabling Element 3.

Enabling Element 3
Activities for Teaching Word Meaning

Specific Objective 3

You will categorize a list of instructional activities into three levels of word meaning, and you will indicate which activities develop the fullest meaning of words in your subject area.

Enabling Activities

1. Prepare a list of all the activities you can think of that can be used to teach word meanings to your students. Place a plus (+) in front of those you feel are the best activities for developing the most complete understanding of a word. Place a minus (−) in front of those you feel develop the least complete understanding of a word.

*2. Read Study Guide 3 to become familiar with a number of activities that can be used to teach word meanings and to determine with which of the three levels of word meaning each activity is associated.

3. Compare the list of activities you prepared in Enabling Activity 1 above with those presented in Study Guide 3. Did you learn some new ways to teach word meaning?

*4. Do the Practicum Exercise. Choose a word for which you want all students to know the meaning as used in your content area. Now define the word at each of the levels of word meaning — specific, functional, and conceptual. Finally, think of activities for teaching the word to your students at levels appropriate for their understanding.

5. Teachers are learners! Many teachers say they always learn more than their students. Make it a habit to continue to increase your vocabulary by looking for new words and/or expanding your level of word meanings. If you are able to analyze how you learn word meanings, you can pass these techniques on to your students.

Study Guide 3

This Study Guide provides a number of activities that can be used as models for developing instructional activities for word meaning. These activities are arranged according to the three levels of word meaning presented in Study Guide 2. To review, the three levels of word meaning are:

1. **Specific level of understanding.** At this level the student has one object, event, instance, definition, or the like associated with a word. The student usually can only recognize and/or recall the single association. He or she may associate the word *democracy* with a type of government or the United States, but have no further understanding or other associations with the word.

2. **Functional level of understanding.** At this level the student states a major use of the word or can use the word in a sentence that demonstrates understanding. At this level the student not only understands that a democracy is a type of government, but understands that in a democracy people vote to select representatives who pass laws and administer the government. "In a democracy, people select their representatives."

3. **Conceptual level of understanding.** At this level the student has many facts and ideas associated with the word. He or she recognizes and can use the word in a variety of sentences or contexts. The student recognizes that a democracy is government by many people. It is based on the beliefs that all people have the same rights, freedoms, and responsibilities. He or she may further understand that we have a representative democracy in the United States whereby the people elect public officials who act according to the people's wishes.

---

*Indicates core Enabling Activities.

Through classifying activities by levels of word meaning, we hope to help you evaluate the activities you have been using for developing word meaning. We also hope to provide you with ideas for selecting future activities. One word of caution before we begin. Activities at the specific level are not inherently bad. When coupled with higher level activites, they sometimes form a learning chain from the simple to the complex. They become undesirable when they are overemphasized and are the only activities used to develop word meanings.

Read each of the following sets of activities for developing word meaning. The activities are classified by level of word meaning. Determine where the activities you listed and rated are classified.

Activities at the Specific Level

The following activities develop primarily, but not exclusively, the specific level of word meaning. These activities usually lead to a single association between word and object, event, instance, or definition.

1. *Write definitions.* Locate isolated words in a glossary and write a definition and sentence.

2. *Write sentences.* Locate isolated words in a dictionary and write a definition and sentence.

3. *Study affixes.* Match prefixes, suffixes, and stems with their most common meanings.

pre	to pile up
struct	before
ment	action or resulting state

4. *Play word games. Scrabble, Probe, Boggle, Spill and Spell,* and such games are generally useful for word identification. Rarely do such games bring about a discussion of word meaning. When they do, usually only one definition or synonym is mentioned.

5. *Use vocabulary exercise books.* Programmed vocabulary enrichment books introduce a single word at a time, define the word, and then use it in a number of sentences. The programmed teaching technique often works for words related to the student's academic or social needs. What is wrong with most of the programmed texts is that the words are not matched to the student's academic or social needs; therefore atrophy results soon after the lesson is completed. If you don't use it, you soon lose it!

6. *Memorize and associate.* Memorize Latin or Greek stems, prefixes, and suffixes and associate them with single meanings. For example:

   The prefix *in* means not.
   The stem *cred* means believe.
   The suffix *ible* means can be.
   Incredible means cannot be believed, or unbelievable.

7. *Give a simple definition* when a student asks the meaning of a word. For example, if a student asks what *picayune* means, and you respond by saying, ''Petty,'' the student will have one specific definition.

8. *Show a picture of an object,* or present the object itself, without much discussion. For example, if you show a picture of a conch shell, or bring a shell to class, and simply tell the students, ''This is a conch shell. It is spiral,'' they will have a specific level of understanding.

Activities at the Functional Level

The following activities develop primarily, but not exclusively, the functional understandings of words. Examples of directions to the student are included with each sample activity. These activities develop and expand a major use or function of a word.

1. *Suggest synonyms.* When defining a word, you can usually suggest many synonyms. For example, you can define *ludicrous* by saying its meaning is similar to those of *comical, ridiculous, laughable,* or *funny.*

2. *Give antonyms.* Frequently, you can tell students words that mean the opposite of the word they are learning. The antonyms of *ludicrous* are *serious, sorrowful,* or *tragic.*

3. *Classify words.* Telling the students the group in which a word belongs helps them understand its function. If you tell them *ludicrous* is an adjective that describes situations or ideas, they can suggest some situations that are ludicrous or absurd.

4. *Make analogies.* Sometimes you can make comparisons to help students learn words. For example, if a student wants to know what *potable* means, you may say *potable* is to beverages as *edible* is to foods. You would then carry on the explanation by giving examples of beverages that are potable as compared with nonpotable beverages.

5. *Explain, give examples, and discuss.* Before reading new material, the teacher selects words that need explanation. These words are usually presented in phrases or sentences so that *context clues* are used. Then the teacher explains or checks the students' knowledge of the meaning of these words, shows illustrative material if available, and gives additional examples of their use. Students should also give additional examples of use. Teachers and students may explain meanings by using different types of sentences or contextual clues.

    a. *Definition clues.* The unknown word is defined in the descriptive content. For example, if you are teaching the word *peruse*, you might say, ''I want you to peruse chapter 2 so you will know the material thoroughly.''

    b. *Synonym clues.* A synonym clue uses a familiar word with the same meaning to define an unfamiliar word. For example, ''I want you to peruse, or study, chapter 2.''

    c. *Familiar expression clues.* A common expression is used to relay an idea or offer clarity. ''I want you to peruse chapter 2 until you know it forwards and backwards.''

    d. *Comparison or contrast clues.* The unknown word is compared to or contrasted with something known. "I want you to peruse, not survey, chapter 2."

8. *Pictures, graphs, charts, and other visuals.* A collection of visuals associated with an object or event a word represents is very useful for developing word meaning if you provide opportunities for discussion of similarities, uses, and other explanations. If you show a picture of a conch shell and then explain the uses of the shell, talk about where conch shells are found, and have students note the similarities and differences of conch shells as compared to other shells, you will help students understand at the functional level.

9. *Studying functions* of prefixes, suffixes, and stems. Research suggests that this method of vocabulary study may be more beneficial for more able students. The major part of this study should occur after the fourth grade.

10. *Demonstration.* At times it may be necessary for you to become an actor or actress as you demonstrate the meaning of a word. Verbs are especially appropriate for demonstration. For example, you could pretend to be *perambulating* (strolling), *perusing* (examining something thoroughly), or *dartling* (to dart again and again). Have fun and then continue your discussion and clarification!

Activities at the Conceptual Level

The following activities develop primarily, but not exclusively, the conceptual understandings of words. Please keep in mind that to understand a word at the conceptual level, many different activities are necessary rather than just one activity.

1. *Provide real and direct experiences.* If you are trying to help the students understand what a democracy is, it would be most valuable if you could have your students visit a capitol building to see *democracy* in action. One real limitation that teachers must face is that frequently it is not possible to provide real and direct experiences. Some students are fortunate in that they get to visit several places with their parents and have many experiences; whereas others stay in the same neighborhood during their childhood years. If you have opportunities to take students on field trips, we encourage you to do so.

2. *Use simulation.* Since it is difficult to provide real and direct experiences, teachers attempt to provide many simulation experiences for students. For example, you can set up a mock legislature in your classroom. Although such a simulation requires many hours of work and preparation, the result will be that the students will have a better understanding of a democracy. The science teacher who wants to teach students about the digestive system may dissect a frog or chicken and then compare the digestive systems of the animal to the digestive system of human beings. Use as many simulation activities as possible.

3. *Compare meaning.* Comparison of the geographical, historical, social, or psychological significance of words is a good way to develop higher level word meaning. If you are trying to help the students understand the word *tree* at the conceptual level, you can teach them about the different regions of the world and the fact that different

types of trees grow in different temperate regions. You might also talk with them about the historical significance of trees. Of course you can also discuss conservation and how products from trees affect the economy. The more comparisons you and your students can make, the higher the level of word meaning.

4. *Use audio-visual aids.* When it is not possible to provide first-hand experiences, movies, slides, filmstrips, or recordings will help students understand a word at the conceptual level. A science teacher may be able to find a filmstrip that defines *chlorophyll* better than any definition the teacher could provide. A history teacher could use the voice recordings of historical events to help the students better understand the meanings of words such as *war* and *catastrophe*.

5. *Discuss connotations.* Connotations are implied emotional meanings attached to words through stress, gesture, or past experience. Connotations may be positive or negative feelings transmitted with words. Our language is replete with them. Discussions of connotative word meanings should start with denotative (dictionary) meanings. For example, to define the word *yellow*, you would begin with the dictionary definition of color. You would continue your discussion to explain the meaning of *yellow* as it is used in a sentence to imply fear or cowardice. Of course you would have to combine this activity with several other activities to develop the understanding of the word *yellow* at the conceptual level.

6. *Study changes in word meaning.* Studying the changes in word meaning over a period of time can develop an interest in word study. Most desk dictionaries have a code indicating the (obs) obsolete word meaning, the (OE) Old English meaning, and the like. Study of word changes expands students' associations with a word. Expanding associations through varied experiences is what moves a word to the conceptual level of understanding.

7. *Use many reference materials.* After students have developed an understanding of a word at the functional level, they may be able to get into different reference materials to understand the word at the conceptual level. For example, students learning about the word *glass* can look in the encyclopedia and in some specialized books for more information about glass. Frequently, pictures as well as other aids are found in reference materials to help students expand the level of understanding.

Putting It All Together to Expand Word Meanings

As mentioned in Study Guide 2, teachers should use a variety of activities to introduce new words. Rather than selecting one or two of the activities you just read, try to use several different activities to help students learn the meanings of words. Read the lesson plan below for an example of using a variety of activities for teaching the meaning of a particular word.

Demonstration Lesson Plan
Objective: The students will be able to define the word *potable* at a higher level of understanding.

Instructional Procedures:

Write the word *potable* on the chalkboard and pronounce it (po-tə-b'l). Ask the students if any of them have heard of the word or seen it written before. Listen to their definitions to determine their present level of understanding. Remember, your task is to help the students understand the word at a higher level. For some students this higher level will be the specific level of understanding; for others it may be the functional; and for some it may be the conceptual level of understanding.

At the *specific* level, the word *potable* simply means drinkable. At the *functional* level, *potable* is a term used to describe beverages, especially water. A student who understands *potable* at the functional level will realize that this word is used to describe the quality of water. For example, at a campground you may see the word *potable* when the water is coming from a hose rather than from a water cooler. At the *conceptual* level of understanding, *potable* is one of many words used to describe drinkable beverages in addition to water. The word *potable* is an adjective that may apply to many different types of beverages such as chocolate, eggnog, ginger beer, punch, lemonade, as well as alcoholic drinks. At the conceptual level of understanding, students also understand why some beverages are potable and others are not potable. These students further understand the results of drinking water or some other beverage that was not potable.

As you begin to teach the word *potable*, you may want to simply define it with the synonym *drinkable*. After doing so, you can give the students many examples. You might say, "The water in the drinking fountains is potable, or drinkable." This means the water is good for drinking. You may give adverse examples by saying, "The water in some countries is not potable, and if you do drink it, chances are you will become sick." Now you are using the word in context.

If the students know the meaning of the word *edible*, you may want to compare the word

Expanding word meanings is one of your major daily responsibilities.

potable to the word *edible*. You can make the following analogy: *edible* is to food as *potable* is to water. Using this analogy may help students who understand the word *edible* to understand the word *potable*.

You might want to ask students to recall some direct experiences by having them tell where they saw the word *potable*. Some students have seen this word in the restrooms in airplanes, others have seen it at campgrounds, while others have seen it at mineral springs or near wells. You can provide some simulation experiences by having them make signs to put on the drinking fountains located in the school. The signs can simply say, "This water is potable." Students will enjoy watching others being puzzled by the signs!

Next you may want to have the students list some beverages that are potable and some that are not. In doing so, the students will indicate some of their favorite beverages and contrast these to poisonous liquids such as liquid chlorine.

You may want to have the students look at the meaning of the word in the dictionary to see if there is a description of the word origin. Some students who are studying foreign languages may be able to provide the foreign word that means the same as *potable* and point out similarities and/or differences.

If you want the students to remember the word and make it a part of their listening, speaking, reading, and writing vocabularies, you will have to provide many opportunities for them to use the word. It will be most helpful to use the word frequently during the next few days. You may come into the classroom tomorrow and say, "I had something that was potable." Have the students try to guess what you had that was drinkable. This will help them review the meaning of *potable*.

Evaluation:

You can evelute the students' knowledge of the meaning of the world *potable* by having them write a definition or by observing whether or not they use the word as a part of their speaking vocabularies. You might also notice whether or not the students use the word in writing and conversing with each other.

Did you notice that the above lesson plan used a variety of activities? The teacher defined the word for the students, provided opportunities for the students to give definitions, used the word in sentences, used a synonym and an analogy, provided a simulation activity, and had the students classify ideas associated with the word. Instead of just saying, "Look up the word *potable*," the teacher used many different instructional activities to fix the word in the students' minds.

Practicum Exercise

Now it is your turn to select activities from those listed in this Study Guide. Choose a word in your content area that you want all students to understand. Write a definition of this word at each of the three levels of understanding. Now go through the activities for each level of understanding and select those you could use to teach the meaning or meanings of the word. Try to incorporate a variety of activities. Make sure you list activities for each level of understanding because your students probably have different levels of definitions for the word you have chosen.

Answers to the Practicum Exercise

It is impossible for us to provide an exact answer to this Practicum Exercise, since the words you have chosen are different. We will provide a sample answer, and you can analyze the response to determine if your response meets the criteria of providing a variety of activities to help students understand words.

Let us suppose that you are an English teacher and you have had the students read a short story written by an author from London. In this short story the author used the word *perambulate*. The word was used in the following sentence: "After dinner they decided to *perambulate* around the garden."

In discussing the selection with the students, you asked them what the word *perambulate* means. As the students shared their definitions, you listened for understanding of the word at the specific, functional, or conceptual level. A student at the specific level of understanding defined *perambulate* as "to walk or to stroll." At the functional level of understanding, a student defined *perambulate* as "a movement that may or may not have a purpose." The student further explained that perambulate can be to stroll about without any particular purpose in mind, or perambulate might be to move about as you take a survey of some property. At the conceptual level of understanding, a student said that *perambulate* is a verb that designates moving about, through, over, or around, especially in examining or inspecting something. The student gave examples— you can perambulate in order to fix the boundaries of a forest as well as to scour the ground or to track a course. On the other hand, *perambulate* might mean simply to go for a walk or to push a baby carriage or pram, which is sometimes called a perambulator. A student who understands *perambulate* at the conceptual level will be able to compare it to other words that mean or indicate movement or travel, such as *jogging, roaming, driving, hiking,* and *meandering.*

You may want to write *perambulate* on the board and pronounce it for the students. You can then tell them that you are going to *perambulate*. At this time begin to stroll around the classroom. Ask the students to try to determine what you are doing. As the students describe what you are doing write the descriptions on the board. For example, some of the students may say you are walking, some may say you are strolling, others may say you are examining. Through these definitions you can have them define the word *perambulate*.

You may want to have the students look at the origin of the word. You can tell the students that the word *perambulate* comes from the root word *ambulare*, which means to walk or to move. The prefix *per* means *through*. So the word *perambulate* means walk through, especially as in examining or inspecting something.

At this time you may want to ask what the opposite of *perambulate* is. The students may indicate "to stay put or stationary." They are giving you the antonym for *perambulate*. At the same time you can ask the students for synonyms for *perambulate*. When the students provide words such as "go over the ground, go for a walk, pace, or cover territory," they will be indicating their understanding of the word *perambulate*.

If you have some pictures of people perambulating you may show these to the students. Throughout the day you may provide opportunities for students to perambulate, and then ask, "Who is that *perambulating* around our class?"

Finally, you may want to have the students look up the word in the dictionary to see the definitions that are provided. Continue to use the word frequently throughout the day in many types of context. You can give sentences with definition clues such as, "They perambulated around the block." This means that they were strolling or walking about the block. You can also provide synonym clues such as, "They were perambulating or walking about the school grounds." If you continue to use the word in many different contexts throughout the next few days, the students will be using it soon, too.

Posttest

Directions: Read each following statements and complete each Posttest item.

1. You must strive to develop the broadest meanings of words specific to your subject area. List and describe the three levels of word meaning, and write a definition of the word *barrier* at all three levels of word meaning.

2. To be more effective and efficient in the teaching of new words and their meanings, you need to follow certain instructional guidelines identified through research and practice. List the six major guidelines for teaching word meanings to ensure the effectiveness of vocabulary instruction.

3. You have become familiar with a number of commonly used activities for teaching word meanings. You will recall that the activities used to introduce the meaning of a word can determine the level at which that word is eventually understood. Read the following list of nine instructional activities for teaching word meaning. Specify the level of word meaning developed by each activity. Use the letter *S* to indicate specific level of word meaning, the letter *F* to indicate functional level of word meaning, and the letter *C* to indicate conceptual level of word meaning. Then decide which two activities are considered best for developing the fullest meanings of words.

_____a. Suggesting synonyms
_____b. Using context clues
_____c. Providing real experiences
_____d. Looking up words in a glossary and writing sentences
_____e. Studying relationships among prefixes, suffixes, and stems
_____f. Memorizing Latin roots
_____g. Playing word identification games
_____h. Using vocabulary exercise books
_____i. Using films

Posttest Answers

1. The three levels of word meaning and a description of each follow:
   a. *Specific instance or association level.* At this level the student has only one object, event, observation, or definition associated with a word. Some possible ways of defining the word *barrier* at the specific level are (1) "a fence"; (2) "mountains out there"; (3)"the reef in the ocean."

b. *Functional level.* At this level the student is able to describe a major use of the word and/or use the word in a sentence that demonstrates his or her understanding. The following are some ways of using *barrier*: (1) "It is like when you put a fence as a barrier in front of a house to keep dogs out." (2) "The mountains were a barrier that made it difficult for the early settlers to get to California from the east coast of the United States." (3) "A barrier reef separates deep from shallow water or warm from cold water."

c. *Conceptual level.* At this level the student has many facts and ideas associated with the word. He or she recognizes and uses the word in many different sentences or contexts. For example: "There are many types of barriers. Barriers to physical movement, barriers to developing personal relationships, and more. Almost anything can be used as a barrier if it is used to block or inhibit something else."

2. The six major guidelines for effective teaching of word meaning follow:

   a. New words are learned best when taught as labels for direct experiences.

   b. Vocabulary development must have the continued and systematic attention of all classroom teachers.

   c. Many encounters with a word in like and differing contexts are necessary before the fullest meaning of the word can be acquired.

   d. The teacher's attitude toward vocabulary improvement and superiority of the teacher's own vocabulary are contagious and vital factors in improving student vocabulary.

   e. Study of a limited number of words in depth is more productive than superficial acquaintance with lists of words.

   f. It is possible, but perhaps foolish practically, to teach words that are not part of the verbal community in which students live. The lack of opportunity for use must result in eventual atrophy.

3. The nine instructional activities for teaching word meaning have been categorized into the three levels of word meaning. The circled letters designate the two activities that will develop the fullest meaning of words. (*S* = specific level of word meaning; *F* = functional level of word meaning; *C* = conceptual level of word meaning.)

   F   a. Suggesting synonyms.

   F   b. Using context clues.

   C   (c.) Providing real experiences.

   S   d. Looking up words in a glossary and writing sentences.

   F   e. Studying relationships among prefixes, suffixes, and stems

   S   f. Memorizing Latin roots

   S   g. Playing word identification games

   S   h. Using vocabulary exercise books

   C   (i.) Using films

Selected Bibliography

Abbass, M. "The Vocabulary of Application Forms." *Reading Improvement* 16, no. 1 (Spring 1979): 28–31.

Bergman, J. R. "Reducing Frustration by An Innovative Technique for Vocabulary Growth." *Reading Improvement* 14, no. 3 (Fall 1977): 172–74.

Bloom, B. S.; Hastings, J. T.; and Madaus, G. F. *Handbook on Formative and Summative Evaluation of Student Learning.* New York: McGraw-Hill, 1971.

Bruland, R. A. "Learnin' Words: Evaluating Vocabulary Development Efforts." *Journal of Reading* 18, no. 3 (1974): 212–14.

Chance, L. "Using a Learning Stations Approach to Vocabulary Practice." *Journal of Reading* 18, no. 3 (1974): 244–46.

Dale, E.; O'Rorke, J; and Bamman, H. A. *Techniques of Teaching Vocabulary.* Palo Alto, California: Field Educational Publications, 1971.

Gipe, J. P. "Investigating Techniques for Teaching Word Meaning." *Reading Research Quarterly* 14, no. 4 (1978–79): 624–44.

Goldfield, B. "Semantics: An Aid to Comprehension." *Journal of Reading* 16, no. 4 (1973): 310–13.

Johnson, D. D. and Pearson, P. D. *Teaching Reading Vocabulary.* New York: Holt, Rinehart, and Winston, 1978.

McKenna, M. "Etymologies in the Reading Process." *Reading Improvement* 14, no. 1 (Spring 1977): 55–56.

Manzo, A. V., and Sherk, J. K. "Some Generalizations and Strategies for Guiding Vocabulary Learning." *The Journal of Reading Behavior* 4, no. 1 (1971–72): 78–89.

Pachtman, A. B., and Riley, J. D. "Teaching the Vocabulary of Mathematics Through Interaction, Exposure, and Structure." *Journal of Reading* 22, no. 3 (1978): 240–44.

Petty, W. T.; Herold, C. P.; and Stoll, E. *The State of Knowledge About the Teaching of Vocabulary.* Champaign, Illinois: National Council of Teachers of English, 1968.

Thomas, E. L., and Robinson, H. A. *Improving Reading in Every Class: A Sourcebook for Teachers.* Boston, Massachusetts: Allyn and Bacon, 1972.

Thorndike, E. L., and Lorge, I. *The Teacher's Word Book of 30,000 Words.* New York: Teachers College Press, Columbia University, 1944.

Usova, G. M. "Improving Vocabulary Through Wide Reading and Context," *Reading Improvement* 14, no. 1 (Spring 1977): 62–64.

MODULE **6**

Helping Students
Comprehend

Contents

Prospectus
   Rationale
   Objectives
   Resources and Time Required
Pretest
Branching Program Alternatives for Pretest Responses
Enabling Element 1: *Comprehending Comprehension*
Enabling Element 2: *Preparing Reading Questions*
Enabling Element 3: *Strategies for Obtaining Improved Answers To Questions*
Enabling Element 4: *Teaching Question-Answering Strategies*
Posttest
   Posttest Answers
Selected Bibliography

Prospectus

Rationale

As students progress through the educational system, the reading materials they use become increasingly more technical. Because of the increased technical nature of the writing, increased demands are placed upon the reader's comprehension skills. For many students the demands eventually overtake their comprehension competencies. Unless these students are provided with some assistance in obtaining meaning from the printed material in subject areas, their performance will dwindle and they may eventually fail.

Subject area teachers are generally the most qualified persons on the school faculty to help these students with their comprehension needs in the subject areas. No other teachers are better acquainted with the nature of the reading material, style of writing, and the strategies for content analysis than subject area specialists. Subject area teachers also know the qualifications of subject area writers and the subtleties with which they communicate. Subject area teachers are the most qualified teachers in our secondary schools to teach subject-area-related reading comprehension skills. *In short, subject area teachers are the best readers of the materials in their respective areas. And the best readers should teach students how to read in their subject areas.*

To help students improve their comprehension of subject area material, subject area teachers need only to make minor instructional changes. This module deals with four basic competencies subject area teachers need to have in order to improve the comprehension achievement of their students. First, teachers need to know the basic comprehension behaviors. Second, they need to know how to prepare questions to assess the comprehension behaviors. Third, they need to know how to analyze the questions they ask to determine the procedure or thinking processes needed to obtain answers. Throughout this module we refer to this procedure for obtaining answers as a ''question-answering strategy.'' Fourth, teachers need to plan ways to teach question-answering strategies that will improve their students' comprehension. The purpose of this module is to provide subject area teachers with these four competencies.

Objectives

Terminal Objective

You will prepare a lesson plan to improve the comprehension achievement of students in your subject area.

Specific Objectives

1. You will name and describe the six major categories of questions in the Classification Scheme for Reading Questions.
2. You will write one question for each of the six categories in the Classification Scheme for Reading Questions.
3. You will write the step-by-step procedure used for answering a question.
4. You will list the steps in a plan for teaching question-answering strategies, and you will prepare a lesson plan designed to teach a strategy for answering a specific type of question on a reading assignment.

Resources and Time Required

In addition to paper and a writing instrument, the participant will need a copy of his or her subject area textbook to complete this module. Other materials required for completing this module are provided. The estimated time to complete the starred core Enabling Activities is four to six hours.

Pretest

Directions: For each question, determine the word that indicates your belief regarding your competency. If you are in doubt, choose NO.

1. It is important for teachers to have students read material and answer   YES   NO
   specific questions about the material. Can you name and describe six
   major categories of questions in a classification scheme for reading
   questions?

2. Students must be asked questions by their teachers at various levels in a   YES   NO
hierarchy of questions. Can you write one question for each of six
categories in a classification scheme of reading questions?

3. Teachers have a responsibility to help students figure out the answers to   YES   NO
questions the teachers ask. Can you list the steps you mentally go
through to determine the answer to questions you ask?

4. By slightly altering present instructional approaches, subject area   YES   NO
teachers can improve their students' comprehension of textual materials. Can you list the steps in a plan for teaching question-answering
strategies and prepare a lesson plan designed to teach students how to
answer specific types of questions?

Branching Program Alternatives
for Pretest Responses

1. If you can name and describe the six major categories of questions in the Classification Scheme for Reading Questions, you are ready for Enabling Element 2. If not,
Enabling Element 1 will provide you with this useful information.

2. Knowing how to write questions at various levels of difficulty is an important
prerequisite for teaching comprehension. If you can write questions for each of six
categories in a classification scheme for reading questions, you are ready for
Enabling Element 3. If not, Enabling Element 2 will help you develop this important
competency.

3. If you can write in detail the procedure you follow for answering questions, you are
ready for Enabling Element 4. If not, Enabling Element 3 will help you understand
your question-answering strategies.

4. The reading comprehension of your students will improve when they know how to
answer the questions you ask them. If you can list the steps in a plan for teaching
question-answering strategies and prepare a lesson plan to teach a specific question-
answering strategy, you are ready for the Posttest. If you cannot, Enabling Element 4
will be of interest to you.

Enabling Element 1
Comprehending Comprehension

Specific Objective 1

You will name and describe the six major categories of questions in the Classification
Scheme for Reading Questions.

Enabling Activities

*1. After completing Study Guide 1, list the six major categories of questions in the Classification Scheme for Reading Questions.

*2. Share the Classification Scheme for Reading Questions with your colleagues. Together determine if there are types of questions pursued in your subject area that are not included in this scheme. If there are, add them to the appropriate list.

*3. Randomly select questions from lesson plans in your subject area textbook. Compare them with the questions in the classification scheme. Are there types of questions proposed by the textbook author(s) that are not listed in the Classification Scheme for Reading Questions? If so, add them to the appropriate list.

 4. As you examine the questions asked by your textbook author(s), tally the number that fall into each of the six categories of the classification scheme. You may be surprised at how few questions fall into certain categories. It is not uncommon to find that most questions fall into the Recognition and Recall or Translation categories.

*5. Use the Classification Scheme for Reading Questions to prepare questions for a future reading assignment. Duplicate the questions and distribute them to your students. Direct your students to use these questions as purposes for reading. Determine if having purposes that require different levels of comprehension make the reading assignment more interesting for your students.

Study Guide 1

Most often students in your subject area will demonstrate their comprehension of printed material by some type of oral or written response. Generally the response comes as a result of a question you have asked. Each day as you are working with students you will ask many questions and receive hundreds of answers.

If an inventory were prepared of all the questions subject area teachers ask, the inventory could be used to demonstrate the comprehension behaviors required for success in content areas. Once the questions were inventoried, they could be classified into a few basic types of questions. These basic types of questions could probably be arranged into a hierarchy from rather simple recognition and recall questions to rather difficult and complex evaluation questions. Once such a classification scheme had been developed, it could be used by subject area teachers for developing reading questions. It could also be used to illustrate for students the types of reading comprehension behaviors they must possess in the various subject areas.

A sample classification scheme is included in this Study Guide. The Classification Scheme for Reading Questions is a collection of questions classified into six categories. The categories are arranged in approximate order from the simplest to the more difficult and complex. The scheme was developed by Nativadad Santos. She developed it after a thorough examination of taxonomies prepared by Bloom and Sanders.

---

*Indicates core Enabling Activities.

The Santos Classification Scheme for Reading Questions is included in this Study Guide because it is a valuable tool for both assessment and instruction of comprehension behaviors. It has these specific advantages:

1. It includes nearly all questions that can be asked.
2. It is divided into six major categories of questions.
3. Each category requires a different comprehension behavior.
4. The categories are arranged in approximate order from simple recognition and recall to the more difficult and complex evaluation.

At this point it is necessary for you to become familiar with the Classification Scheme for Reading Questions, which follows. First, skim the classification scheme to identify the six major categories of reading questions. Next read the introductory statement following each category. As you do so, ask yourself, ''What type of thinking or comprehension behaviors are required to answer questions that fit this category?'' Last, look at the specific types of questions that fit under each category. Now go ahead and examine the classification scheme for the three purposes identified.

Classification Scheme for Reading Questions

A. Recognition or Recall Questions. A reading question falls under the recognition or recall category if it can be *answered verbatim* with specific information found in the selection read, and if it requires the reader to locate or repeat the information. A teacher who asks a student to answer a question by reading to locate what the author said is asking a recognition question. The teacher who asks a student to answer a question by remembering what the author said is asking a recall question. Recognition questions require a student to locate an answer; recall questions require the student to use only memory. Teachers use recognition or recall questions when asking students to do the following tasks.

1. Respond to direct factual questions in which the fact is given in the selection read;
2. Enumerate or make a list of information presented in the selection read;
3. Quote the author or character in the selection;
4. Recall who said a given quotation taken verbatim from the selection read;
5. Recite a stanza of a poem, an essay, a rule, from memory;
6. Read aloud the part that answers a factual question, or the part called for.

B. Translation Questions. A reading question falls under the translation category if it requires the reader to answer a question by *restating* in his or her own words what the author said. The reader must keep the author's idea and not change any facts. When asking a student to give the answer to a question in his or her own words, a teacher is asking a translation question. Teachers use translation questions when asking students to do the following tasks.

1. Explain in the reader's own words the meaning of technical terms, vocabulary words, and stated meanings;

2. Restate a problem, generalization, principle, rule, or procedure the author has described;

3. Paraphrase or summarize a selection;

4. Retell a selection; describe or retell parts or events of a selection to prove a point;

5. Explain printed directions;

6. Change poetry to prose or vice versa;

7. Change a statement to a question;

8. Illustrate or draw information presented verbally;

9. Describe a picture, poster, sketch, drawing, painting, or object;

10. Present information through a graph, diagram, chart, table, or map.

C. Application Questions. A reading question falls under the application category if it requires the reader to *use previously learned information* to explain a situation or solve a problem. Asking a student to use information the student has already acquired to give a new explanation or solve a new problem is asking an application question. Teachers use application questions when asking students to do the following tasks.

1. Make use of previous knowledge to make comparisons, observations, and explanations, or to answer a question;

2. Apply information or principles learned from the selection read to explain a phenomenon or a problematic situation;

3. Use a theory or principle to predict outcomes;

4. Apply rules for (a) classifying or grouping, (b) indexing, (c) outlining, (d) rearranging a set of ideas in alphabetical, chronological, or some other proper sequence;

5. Apply arithmetical procedures and skills to solve and/or explain arithmetical problems;

6. Give examples to fit a previously stated definition or abstraction;

7. Locate elements of style used in a selection read, such as rhyme, free verse, and satire;

D. Analysis Questions. A reading question falls under the analysis category if it requires the reader to *identify the parts* of a communication and/or to explain the relationship between the parts. An example of an analysis question is giving a student a statement and asking the student if the statement is a correct inference based upon the facts and opinions in the story. An analysis question requires the student to separate parts when looking for information to answer a question. Teachers use analysis questions when asking students to do the following tasks.

1. Analyze a given communication to find supporting opinions and/or facts.

2. Analyze main ideas, inferences, and conclusions to find their supporting statements.

3. Predict outcomes or implications from evidence presented.

4. Identify in a given communication what information is given, what is not given, and/or what is to be solved in a story problem;

5. Identify clues from which inferences may be drawn, as in (a) connotative expressions, (b) character's actions, traits, remarks, (c) the setting, (d) figurative language, (e) semantic variations;

6. Identify relationships, as in (a) cause-effect relationships, (b) sequential relationships, (c) logical relationships (analogies, antecedents), (d) past-present relationships, (e) main idea—details relationship, (f) central theme—main idea relationship;

7. Indicate whether ideas are similar, different, contradictory, supportive, relevant, related, irrelevant, essential, extraneous, in proper sequence;

8. Identify author's purpose and point of view;

9. Identify parts of a given communication that make the communication false.

E. Synthesis Questions. A reading question falls under the synthesis category if it requires the reader to *combine information* to create a new communication, devise a new procedure, or propose new relationships. Asking a student to generalize over a set of information to create a main idea statement, conclusion, or inference is an example of a synthesis question. Teachers use synthesis questions when asking students to do the following tasks.

1. Form main ideas, conclusions, and inferences from information provided by a writer;

2. Rearrange a given set of ideas into unique sentences or paragraphs; substitute words or phrases to make ideas more correct;

3. Write an original rhyme, poem, essay, story, play, paragraph, or sentence;

4. Read aloud the part called for and give the passage his or her expression; dramatic reading; choral reading;

5. Pantomime; retell or dramatize a selection or parts of it using one's own words and expressions; present a pageant;

6. Use a personal experience and something read to give a new insight;

7. Discuss or give a short talk or extemporaneous speech on a given topic; tell an original story;

8. Submit a plan for a project needing construction, an experiment, a program, a skit, or a dramatization;

9. Suggest solutions to a problem; list possible problems that might sum up a situation;

10. Suggest different titles to a given communication; suggest scenes or events pictured from a given communication;

11. Formulate rules to observe in performing or judging a performance or presentation;

12. Give different endings to a given communication;

13. Relate a general problem to a local situation;

14. Give an opinion or make decisions without justifying one's views.

F. Evaluation Questions. A reading question falls under this category if it requires the student to determine whether a given communication *meets standards* set up by that student or presented to the student. It also requires the student to make decisions and to support the views in his or her own words. Asking a student to establish evaluation criteria, gather facts to compare with the criteria, judge how well each fact matches a given criterion, and form an evaluation is an example of an evaluation question. Teachers use evaluation questions when asking students to do the following tasks:

1. Evaluate a given communication for:

accuracy	completeness
authenticity	practicability
relevancy	reasonableness
adequacy	authoritativeness
value	logical consistency
imagination	truth
falsity	merit
agreement	appropriateness
suitability	objectivity, etc.

2. Evaluate pictures for accuracy, appropriateness, suitability, richness of imagination, and justify one's views;

3. Evaluate suggested endings to a story, summaries, a performance, a declamation, an oration, a speech, etc., and justify one's views and/or suggest ways of improvement;

4. Evaluate statements for ambiguities, overspecificity, omissions, distortions, inconsistencies, inaccuracies, overstatements, and justify one's views;

5. Evaluate to determine if a conclusion, inference, main idea, or thesis logically follows the facts presented; select the best conclusion, inference, etc., from a set of suggested conclusions, inferences, etc., and justify one's view;

6. Evaluate to form an opinion or to take a stand on an issue;

7. Judge agreement between ideas or sources of information, and justify one's views;

8. Judge and prove the truth or falsity of statements by pointing out supportive statements or evidence, and justify one's views;

9. Judge ideas as similar, different, contradictory, supportive, related, relevant, essential, or in proper sequence, and justify one's views;

10. Judge the relative merits of information from different sources, or sources of information, and justify one's views;

11. Judge characters in a story, and justify one's views.

The Classification Scheme in Review

As you read the Classification Scheme for Reading Questions, you noticed there were six major categories of questions each requiring its own comprehension behaviors, "thinking strategies." You noticed that each level of the strategy tends to be built upon the preceding level, suggesting a true hierarchy. The remainder of this section contains a review of some of the main ideas you should have obtained from your examination and study of the Classification Scheme of Reading Questions.

Recognition or Recall questions was the first category presented in this classification scheme. Questions of this type require the reader to identify or recall from the reading passage exact statements in order to provide verbatim answers. Since the comprehension behaviors required at this level are rather simple, the question-answering strategy is not very elaborate.

Translation questions are closely related to Recognition and Recall questions. The chief difference is that the translation questions require the reader to answer the questions in his or her own words, and not verbatim. Translation questions require a higher level question-answering strategy than Recognition or Recall questions because they require the reader to tell the answer in his or her own words.

Application questions require that the learner use in some new situation the information obtained through reading. This information can be used in any way as long as a change takes place in something as a result of the use of the information. The information can be used to make comparisons, to outline, or to locate information, to mention just a few of the ways specified under this section of the classification scheme. Application questions require a still higher level question-answering strategy because they require that the reader use the information in some way to alter some situation or product.

Analysis questions require that the learner analyze what he or she has read to identify the organization of the material, the basic components of the communication, and the relationships between those components. Basic components are such things as assumptions, inferences, and connotative expressions, to mention a few. Analysis questions require a still more complex question-answering strategy because they require the reader to separate the communication into parts, which are then analyzed.

Synthesis questions form the fifth category. Synthesis questions require that the learner obtain information from reading and combine it with information from other sources (background of experience, discussions, books, magazines, lectures, and the like) to form a new or different idea or product. The idea or product must be new or different and be greater than its parts. The synthesis question-answering strategy builds upon but is different and more complex than the preceding strategies because it requires the reader to combine information from various sources to form something new.

Evaluation questions form the sixth and final category in the classification scheme. Evaluation questions require the learner to make a decision. The decision is made after reading for information relative to the question and reading to obtain criteria for evaluating the information. The decision, information gathered, and evaluation criteria must be justified by the reader. The evaluation question-answering strategy is the most complex and difficult one for students to master. It requires the reader to identify important information, to evaluate the information in terms of specified criteria, and to make a decision, which he or she must defend.

Figure 6 provides a graphic summary of factors in the Classification Scheme for Reading Questions. This Summary Form demonstrates the interrelatedness and increased complexity of comprehension behaviors as questions move from Recognition and Recall to Evaluation.

Figure 6

Summary form: Classification scheme for reading questions

Question Categories	Type of response required					
	Recognize or recall answer verbatim	Change verbatim answer to own words	Use information to alter some situation or product	Separate communication into parts for analysis	Combine information for various sources to form something new	Evaluate and justify the decision
Recognition or Recall	X					
Translation	X	X				
Application	X	X	X			
Analysis	X	X	X	X		
Synthesis	X	X	X	X	X	
Evaluation	X	X	X	X	X	X

This form demonstrates the interrelated nature and hierarchy in the Classification Scheme for Reading Questions

If you will reflect for a minute, you will probably realize that the Classification Scheme for Reading Questions is a rather complete model of the reading comprehension requirements of your subject area. The classification scheme probably contains most of the questions you ask, answer, or ask your students to answer in your subject area. Because of its comprehensiveness, the classification scheme should be invaluable to you for preparing questions that will stimulate thinking among your students.

If you can now name and describe the six major categories for classifying reading questions from the Classification Scheme for Reading Questions, you are ready for Enabling Element 2. If not, complete the task before moving on. If you are having difficulty, reexamine this Enabling Element or see your instructor.

Enabling Element 2
Preparing Reading Questions

Specific Objective 2

You will write one question for each of the six categories in the Classification Scheme for Reading Questions.

Enabling Activities

*1. Read Study Guide 2. Prepare one question for each of the six categories on the reading selection, "Comprehension is the Cornerstone of Education."

*2. Identify some reading selections from your subject area textbook. Prepare two or three questions for each of the six categories of reading questions. Use these questions for establishing purposes for reading the assignment.

  3. Make copies of the Classification Scheme for Reading Questions available for your students. Familiarize them with the various kinds of reading questions that can be constructed. Have your students construct questions for each of the six categories that can be used for establishing purposes for reading.

  4. Exchange copies of questions with other staff members who have prepared, from common reading assignments, questions on each of the six categories. You may find that some teachers are better than others at writing certain types of questions.

*5. Get together with a group of colleagues in your subject area and, using the classification scheme, identify the more important types of questions for your subject area. Arrange the questions in a hierarchy from the least difficult to the most difficult. This activity will leave you with a classification scheme for reading questions specific to your subject area. Use this scheme for developing questions when you are planning future reading assignments.

Study Guide 2

Your first step toward improving the comprehension achievement of your students is to write a variety of questions. Not only is a variety of questions necessary, but the questions should be on a hierarchy from Recognition and Recall to Evaluation. The Classification Scheme for Reading Questions contains the desired hierarchy. It was introduced in Enabling Element 1 and will be used for preparing questions in this Enabling Element.

It is now time to begin writing questions using the Classification Scheme for Reading Questions. At this point, it would be valuable for you to reacquaint yourself with the classification scheme, particularly the variety of questions that can be prepared under each classification. When you have completed this task, read the following selection, "Comprehension is the Cornerstone of Education." When you have finished reading this selection, we will discuss the preparation of questions and ask that you prepare one question for each of the six levels in the classification scheme.

Comprehension Is the Cornerstone of Education

Comprehension of subject matter materials is one of the major objectives of public and private education. As a major objective of education, it becomes one of the chief responsibilities of every teacher. Many teachers, however, teach as if they believe comprehension to be an innate ability, which students have or have not. Their teaching behavior leads an observer to conclude that developing comprehension abilities is the objective of the student and not of the teacher. Teachers such as these make no attempt to explain the processes involved in

---

*Indicates core Enabling Activities.

obtaining information from textual material. They merely make assignments and leave it to the student to discover the intricate processes that lead to understanding. Given that human beings are our most important natural resource, we can no longer allow miseducation such as this to take place. In the future, subject area teachers will have to assume their rightful responsibility for developing the comprehension skills indigenous to their specific subject areas.

You will recall that the classification scheme contains six basic categories for questions. Under each category are descriptions of questions that can be classified in the category. If you look at each category closely, you will notice that it is highly unlikely that all the questions provided in the category could be applied to one reading selection. The nature of the selection and the author's purpose will be different for each selection. Therefore, the type of question that can be used will vary among selections.

Following this paragraph is a series of questions about the selection, "Comprehension is the Cornerstone of Education." There are questions for each of the six categories, but the number that could be prepared for each category is not the same. The reason for this is that some questions are appropriate for this passage and some are not. Next to each question is a code number that corresponds to a category on the Classification Scheme for Reading Questions. For example, question A1 corresponds to 1 on the scheme, "respond to direct factual questions in which the fact is given in the selection read." Compare each of our questions with its appropriate classification. From this comparison, you should recognize the ease with which questions can be prepared using the scheme.

Also notice that we have provided some code numbers for additional questions that could be prepared under each category. We have not provided the additional questions, but you may want to look at the categories designated for additional questions. By doing so, you will learn which additional categories lend themselves to questions you could prepare.

Outline for Preparing Questions, Form A
"Comprehension Is the Cornerstone of Education"

A. *Recognition or Recall*

   1. According to this author, what is one of the major objectives of public and private education?

   3.

   6.

B. *Translation*
   1. In your own words, define *comprehension*.
   4.

C. *Application*
   2. Does this selection offer an explanation for the observation that comprehension scores on standardized tests do not continue to improve as students go through high school? Explain.
   6.

D. *Analysis*
   1. What major facts presented by the author underlie his conclusion regarding future responsibilities of subject area teachers?
   2.

   8.

E. *Synthesis*
   3. Prepare a one-act play containing two characters to perform the roles of the two types of teachers described in this selection. What are the chief differences between the two characters?
   10.

F. *Evaluation*

    1. Did the author objectively present his point of view?

    6.

Practicum Exercise

Now it is your turn to write some questions. On the Outline for Preparing Questions, Form A, we provide code numbers for questions under each classification. Following some of the code numbers are questions; following others there are no questions. Your assignment is to formulate questions for the categories where questions do not presently exist. Using the selection, "Comprehension is the Cornerstone of Education," and the Classification Scheme for Reading Questions, write at least one question for each of the six categories. We are sure you will find the task sufficiently easy to be encouraged to design additional questions under the Recognition and Recall classification and the Analysis classification. You may want to examine the classification scheme provided to determine if still more questions could be prepared. When you have completed your task, begin reading with the following paragraph.

Answers to the Practicum Exercise

Now that you have completed your task, we are sure you will agree that the classification scheme makes it easy to prepare the questions. It is now time for you to compare your questions with those we prepared. Look at the six categories of questions in the Outline for Preparing Questions, Form B, which follows. Compare your questions with the questions we prepared. A comparison should demonstrate to you the adequacy of your questions as well as reinforce our point that the classification scheme makes writing questions an effortless task.

Outline for Preparing Questions, Form B
"Comprehension is the Cornerstone of Education"

A. *Recognition or Recall*

    1. According to this author, what is one of the major objectives of public and private education?

    3. What did the author say the behavior of many teachers leads an observer to conclude?

    6. Read aloud the sentence in which the author states the future responsibilities of subject area teachers.

B. *Translation*

    1. In your own words, define *comprehension*.

    4. List in order the major points made by the author.

C. *Application*

    2. Does this selection offer an explanation for the observation that comprehension scores on standardized tests do not continue to improve as students matriculate through high school? Explain.

    6. If you were to observe teachers such as those the author spoke of, what would you expect to see?

D. *Analysis*

    1. What major facts presented by the author underlie his conclusion regarding future responsibilities of subject area teachers?

    2. What is the author's main idea?

    8. What was the author's purpose or motivation for preparing this selection?

E. *Synthesis*

    3. Prepare a one-act play containing two characters to perform the roles of the two types of teachers described in this selection. What are the chief differences between the two characters?

    10. What could be another title for this selection?

F. *Evaluation*

    1. Did the author objectively present his point of view?

    6. How would you defend the author's conclusion?

Now that you are familiar with the Classification Scheme for Reading Questions and can use this scheme to prepare questions in each of the six categories, it is time to look at strategies for answering questions.

Enabling Element 3
Strategies for Obtaining
Improved Answers to Questions

Specific Objective 3

You will write the step-by-step procedure used for answering a question.

Enabling Activities

    *1. Read Study Guide 3, and list the steps in your question-answering strategy for an inference question.

---

*Indicates core Enabling Activities.

*2. For a passage of your choosing, write six questions at the various levels identified in the Classification Scheme for Reading Questions. When you have finished, list the step-by-step procedure you went through to answer each question.

*3. Arrange a meeting with a group of colleagues to discuss and refine strategies for answering questions. Share the sample strategies from this Study Guide to initiate the discussion. Group discussion is probably the best way to refine thinking on question-answering strategies.

4. Reproduce the sample question-answering strategies provided, and distribute them to your students. Use the various strategies as a basis for discussing comprehension improvement in your subject area.

5. Discuss with other colleagues in your subject area the various types of strategies used by students for answering questions. How well students answer certain types of questions should provide some insight into which types of questions should be stressed in future reading assignments.

Study Guide 3

Each question you prepared for the reading selection in Enabling Element 2 has its own unique answer. Likewise, each question requires a different procedure or thinking process to obtain an answer. We call this procedure or thinking procedure for obtaining answers to questions a *strategy*. Specifically we refer to it as the *question-answering strategy*.

It is your responsibility as a teacher to improve the question-answering strategies of students in your subject area. Your strategies have become highly refined as a result of years of reading and studying in your specialty. Therefore, you are the most appropriate teacher to improve these strategies.

However, before you can help your students improve their question-answering strategies, it is necessary for you to become more familiar with your own strategies for answering questions. This will take some time because your strategies are likely to be executed automatically when you are confronted with a question. It is unlikely that you typically think in the detail that will be required of you to improve the comprehension of your students. The following Practicum Exercise will help you develop an awareness of your question-answering strategies.

Practicum Exercise 1

Directions: (1) Read the question that establishes a purpose for reading the selection. (2) Read the essay. (3) Determine your answer to the question. (4) List the step-by-step procedure you followed to arrive at your answer.

Purpose for reading: Why did the author write this essay?

A Civil Air Patrol Cadet

Hello! My name is Robbie DuBois and I am a cadet major in Civil Air Patrol. Civil Air Patrol is a volunteer civilian auxiliary of the United States Air Force. I am the cadet unit leader of the Riverside, Florida, Squadron of Civil Air Patrol. Civil Air Patrol is open to boys and girls, ages fifteen to twenty. In Civil Air Patrol we learn search and rescue procedures so we can assist in locating military and civilian aircraft. We go on flight practice missions. We also learn how to get along with others and to be good citizens. I think every high school boy or girl should learn these things. That is why I enjoy my volunteer job and serve as a member of Civil Air Patrol.

Write your answer to the purpose-setting question here.

Write the steps in your question-answering strategy here.

Answers to Practicum Exercise 1

Did you write your answer? Did you list the step-by-step procedure you used to arrive at your answer? If you did, compare your question-answering strategy and answer with ours.

1. We surveyed the question and the passage to be sure they contained no unfamiliar words, expressions, or ideas. Many questions are misunderstood or answered incorrectly because the reader does not take time to clarify an unfamiliar word, expression, idea, or the like.

2. Next, we read the question to be sure the intent was clear. Many questions are answered incorrectly because they are misunderstood. Sometimes restating the question in another form helps. In this case, ''Why did the author write this story?'' can be changed to ''What was the writer's purpose for writing this story?''

3. Then we examined the passage for all the facts relevant to the question and disregarded those facts not relevant to the question under investigation. The relevant and verifiable facts are:
   a. The writer is a member of Civil Air Patrol.
   b. The writer is a cadet major and unit leader.
   c. Civil Air Patrol is a volunteer organization for boys and girls.

4. Next we studied the facts to determine if all or some of the facts needed to answer the question had been identified. All the facts necessary to answer the question posed at the beginning of this story are not stated in this story. At this point we had a hunch about the answer to the question.

5. If our examination of the facts had suggested that all the facts necessary to answer the question were available, we would have reached a conclusion and answered the question accordingly. When all the facts are present, the reader reaches a conclusion. Conclusions are final statements or decisions reached when all the facts are present. In a conclusion all the facts are identifiable. Since all the facts were not identified, a conclusion could not be drawn.

6. After our examination of the facts, we determined that all the facts necessary to answer the question were not available. It was then necessary to determine which facts were missing. What is missing is a statement asking others to join or explaining that a membership drive is now open. After all, this could merely be an information blurb on Civil Air Patrol.

7. Background of experience, discussion with others, additional reading, hunches, and the like were used to supply the missing facts. These missing facts are really hypothesized facts that are not verifiable in the selection. Background of experience suggests that this style of writing is often used in recruitment campaigns. Reading other personal-appeal recruitment reports led us to believe that the real intent was recruitment. This intent was further substantiated by the fact that this is a volunteer organization, and volunteer organizations always seem to be looking for more members.

8. The verifiable facts and hypothesized facts were combined to answer the question.

Since all the facts are not present in the selection, a conclusion cannot be reached and an inference has to be drawn. The question, ''Why did the author write this story?'' requires that the reader analyze the component parts of the communication to make an inference. (See the Classification Scheme for Reading Questions, Synthesis 1.) Inferences are final statements made by combining verifiable facts from the reading with hypothesized facts from other sources. The answer we inferred was ''to entice boys and girls ages fifteen to twenty to join Civil Air Patrol.'' Since all the facts are not present in the selection, our answer is an inference and not a conclusion.

Does your strategy agree with the strategy listed here? If it did not, how did it differ? It is quite possible that your answer agrees with ours even though you used a different strategy. Strategies may differ even though the answers may not. We do not know enough about the way in which people think to conclude that only one strategy exists for answering a particular type of question. When the answers are in agreement, it makes little difference that the strategies differ. The fact that question-answering strategies differ is only important when the answers differ; for that is when the teacher provides the student with a new strategy to assist him or her in answering a question. You will learn more about using your own strategy to help students develop question-answering strategies in the next Enabling Element.

Occasionally, equal support can be found and arguments can be made for two or more answers to the same question. When this impasse is reached, both answers should be accepted as possibilities of equal merit. However, remember that your goal is to develop whenever possible sufficient evidence to identify the one *best* answer. Emphasizing the need to identify the best answer encourages precise thinking among students.

You have now had an opportunity to read our question-answering strategy and to compare your strategy with ours. If you think your strategy is incomplete, now is an excellent time to refine your strategy so that it will be useful to you when you teach.

Practicum Exercise 2

At this point you are familiar with the process for writing questions and the process for examining your step-by-step procedure for answering these questions. Using the following selection, formulate one question for each category in the Classification Scheme for Reading Questions. Then examine the following Sample Question-Answering Strategies. Using the sample strategies as guides, create a specific question-answering strategy for each of the questions you prepared. This activity will further develop your insight into your question-answering strategies and, as a result, will enhance your effectiveness in working with the comprehension problems of your students.

Fish Propulsion

Fish, like humans, do not all use the same method for propelling, or moving, through the water. Some fish move through the water with snakelike motions. These snakelike motions are caused by muscle contractions throughout the body. Other fish propel through the water using a combination of muscle contraction and the side motion of their caudal, or tail, fin. The third type of swimmer uses the caudal fin almost exclusively. This swimmer keeps its body almost rigid while moving through the water. One category of fish has a unique way of propelling through the water. The flying fish emerges from the water, spreads its large pectoral fin, and glides over the water for hundreds of feet. The method used for propulsion seems to be related to the size of the fish and the speed at which the fish swims.

Directions: Using the preceding selection, create one question for each category in the Classification Scheme for Reading Questions.

Recognition or Recall question:

Translation question:

Application question:

Analysis question:

Synthesis question:

Evaluation question:

When you have finished preparing questions, read the following Sample Question-Answering Strategies. Follow the directions that appear after the sample strategies.

Sample Question-Answering Strategies

Included in this section are sample question-answering strategies for the six categories of reading questions. These are *general* strategies for each category. Question-answering strategies for specific questions within each major category will differ slightly from the sample strategies, which follow. The strategies will be slightly amended to fit the intent of each question. These strategies are provided as samples for your examination and study, and as models for creating your own question-answering strategies.

Recognition or Recall Strategy

1. Check the question and passage to be sure they do not contain unfamiliar words, expressions, or ideas. If an unfamiliarity is detected, clarify it before proceeding.
2. Be sure the intent of the question is clear. Rephrasing the question sometimes serves as a check on understanding.
3. Read the selection and identify the precise statement(s) that answer the question.
4. Reread the selection to verify that you have identified all the information necessary to answer the question.
5. Answer the question in precisely the same words as in the passage.

Translation Strategy

1. Survey the question and passage to see if they contain any unfamiliar words, expressions, or ideas. If an unfamiliarity is detected, clarify it before proceeding.
2. Be sure the intent of the question is clear. Rephrasing the question sometimes helps to ensure clarity.
3. Read the selection and identify the precise statement(s) that answer(s) the question.
4. Check the passage to be sure that you have identified everything necessary for answering the question.
5. Answer the question in precisely the same words as in the passage.
*6. Restate the answer in your own words.
*7. Compare your restated answer with the quoted answer to be sure it contains all of the facts or ideas.

Application Strategy

1. Determine whether or not the question or passage contains unfamiliar words, expressions, or ideas. If it does, clarify before going further.
2. Obtain a clear understanding of the specific problem or situation contained in the question. Be sure to understand how the information to be obtained from the reading will be applied to the specific problem or situation. Identify and state the problem or situation. Restate the question so it specifies what information must be obtained to solve the problem or change the situation.

---

*Indicates new step(s) not contained in preceding strategy.

3. Read and locate the precise information required by your restated question.

4. Reread the selection to be sure all available information has been obtained.

5. Examine the obtained information to be sure it does not contain new or inaccurate information.

*6. Using the information obtained from reading the selection, solve the problem or change the situation as directed by the question.

*7. Check the answer to be sure the problem or situation has been solved or changed appropriately.

Analysis Strategy

1. Examine the question and passage to identify any unfamiliar words, expressions, or ideas. Clarify before proceeding.

2. Be sure the intent of the question is understood. Restate the question if necessary to clarify the intent.

*3. Read the selection to identify the parts of the communication and/or the relationship between the component parts.

*4. Read and locate information required by your question.

*5. If necessary, gather additional information from various sources.

*6. Look for the relationships between information from various sources.

7. When you have obtained all the necessary information, prepare an answer.

8. Test the answer for accuracy against the selection and other sources of information.

Synthesis Strategy

1. Check the question and passage for unfamiliar words, expressions, or ideas. Clarify them before going further.

2. Be sure the intent of the question is clear. Restate the question if necessary.

3. Identify all relevant information available from the passage.

4. Supply information from other sources as needed.

*5. Synthesize the information from various sources, and compose an answer to the question. The answer should be new, different, and broader than the sum of its parts.

*6. Test the answer to be sure it is sufficient to cover the information gathered.

Evaluation Strategy

1. Check the question and passage to be sure that it does not contain any unfamiliar words, expressions, or ideas. Clarify as necessary.

2. Be sure the intent of the question is understood. Rephrase the question if necessary to substantiate that you understand the intent of the question.

---

*Indicates new step(s) not contained in preceding strategy.

3. Identify important information from the passage.

*4. Establish the evaluation criteria.

*5. Evaluate each basic unit of information in terms of the appropriate criteria.

*6. Examine all evaluations and prepare a final decision.

*7. Justify the information gathered, evaluation criteria, and your final decision.

Directions: As previously directed, formulate the answer to each of your questions and list the steps in your question-answering strategy.

Recognition or Recall answer

and strategy

Translation answer

and strategy

---

*Indicates new step(s) not contained in preceding strategy.

Application answer

and strategy

Analysis answer

and strategy

Synthesis answer

and strategy

Evaluation answer

and strategy

Answers to Practicum Exercise 2

Because we could not anticipate the questions you wrote, it was impossible for us to
provide you with strategies for each of your questions. However, we think that by now

you should be able to evaluate your own strategies. To do this, compare your strategies with the sample strategies we provided. Since your strategies are specific to questions within each category, and ours are *general strategies* for each category, your strategies will probably contain steps in addition to those we have listed. If you are having difficulty listing the steps in your strategy or feel uncomfortable with the strategy you have developed, we suggest that you reread appropriate components of this Study Guide, complete additional Enabling Activities, examine reference sources by Bloom or Sanders in the selected bibliography, or see your instructor.

You should now be able to prepare questions and develop question-answering strategies. You are now ready to discuss improving the reading comprehension of your students in your subject area. Enabling Element 4 addresses itself to this topic.

Enabling Element 4
Teaching Question-Answering Strategies

Specific Objective 4

You will list the steps in a plan for teaching question-answering strategies, and you will prepare a lesson plan designed to teach a strategy for answering a specific type of question on a reading assignment.

Enabling Activities

*1. Read Study Guide 4. When you have finished reading it, list the steps to follow when teaching such a strategy.

*2. After completing Study Guide 4, prepare a lesson plan designed to teach a strategy for answering a specific question.

*3. Using reading material you will soon be assigning to your students, prepare a number of questions at each of the six levels in the classification scheme. Assign the questions to your students. From the answers they give, identify students who have difficulty answering specific types of questions and group the students according to the difficulty of the questions they could not answer. Teach the students a question-answering strategy following the procedure suggested.

*4. Organize open discussion groups wherein students can meet informally and discuss their reading habits and strategies.

 5. Teach your aides or more capable students how to teach the question-answering strategies. Have them work along with students who need the additional instruction.

 6. Share your lesson plans and materials with your colleagues. By so doing, each of you will gather an excellent collection of lesson plans.

---

*Indicates core Enabling Activities.

Study Guide 4

Now that you are familiar with the classification scheme, can prepare questions at different levels in a hierarchy, and have examined your own processes for answering questions, you are ready to teach. Teaching your students to comprehend your subject area material by studying strategies for answering different types of questions is not a long or involved process. Nor does it detract from the study of your subject area. In fact, teaching students to comprehend reading assignments for different purposes will enhance their understanding and appreciation of your subject area.

This Study Guide introduces a plan for teaching question-answering strategies. It is a simple plan that draws heavily upon the background and reading style of the subject area teacher. The plan is based upon the assumption that subject area specialists are the best readers of their own subject area materials.

The plan for teaching question-answering strategies consists of five steps. These five steps are

1. **Set the purpose for learning.** This step is designed to substantiate for your students their need for instruction.
2. **Assess the comprehension strategy.** This step is designed to determine the precise steps in the learner's strategy for answering a specific type of question.
3. **Teach the comprehension strategy.** This step is designed to teach a strategy to obtain the best answer to a question.
4. **Apply the comprehension strategy.** This step is designed to determine whether or not the strategy you taught is understood by the learner.
5. **Generalize the comprehension strategy.** This step is designed to enable the learner to use the strategy to answer a specific type of question in a variety of subject area materials.

The procedure for using the plan for teaching question-answering strategies follows, along with a more substantial discussion of its components and its application. The format is the same one you would follow when teaching students how to comprehend subject area material. The instructional plan is set into motion when a student *incorrectly* answers a number of questions of the same type: Recognition and Recall, Translation, Application, Analysis, Synthesis, or Evaluation. Your study of the instructional plan should begin by surveying the five-step outline to identify the five major steps in the instructional plan. Then read the material under each step to determine precisely what you must do to improve your students' comprehension.

Plan for Teaching Question-Answering Strategies

A. *Set the purpose for learning.* The purpose of this step is to substantiate the need for instruction. It is assumed that if a lesson is to be taught, it is because a group of students had difficulty answering two or more questions of the same type—probably in similar material. The material the students had difficulty comprehending would be the material used for teaching this lesson. Point out to the students that their difficulty in answering a particular type of question is the reason for this lesson. Further explain that after some instruction the students will be able to answer such questions and, as a result, will improve their comprehension achievement.

B. *Assess the comprehension strategy.* The purpose of this step is to determine the step by-step procedure the students followed when they answered the question incorrectly.

1. The teacher starts by restating one or two questions and supplying the answers provided earlier by students. As an alternative, the teacher may ask students to state their own answers. It is advisable to write the answers on a surface for continued reference by all students.

2. Ask one of your students for a step-by-step explanation of how the student arrived at his or her answer. You may wish to repeat this procedure with another student.

3. As the students reveal their question-answering strategies, list the steps in these strategies on a chalkboard, or some other surface.

4. Do not accept "I don't know" answers. Continue to question the students to obtain the specific steps they followed, which led them to their incorrect answers.

C. *Teach the comprehension strategy.* The purpose of this step is to teach the necessary components in a strategy designed to identify the best answer to a question.

1. Using the passage wherein the students demonstrated their original difficulty, direct the students to observe while you read the passage aloud.

2. As you read the passage aloud, describe and demonstrate how you are determining the preferred answer to the question that your students answered incorrectly.

3. As you describe and demonstrate your strategy, write the steps on a chalkboard. (Remember, you learned these strategies in Enabling Element 3.)

4. When you have finished reading, describing, and demonstrating your strategy, review the steps with your students. After your review, cover or remove the steps from your students' view.

5. To be sure they understand the question-answering strategy you just taught them, ask selected students to list and explain the steps in the procedure you described.

6. Next, have the students compare their original strategies with your strategy to identify like and different steps and explanations.

7. Discuss with your students how they must modify their strategies in order to obtain the most desired answer to questions of the type being studied.

8. Have your students explain how they would apply the new strategy to similar questions.

9. The students must *understand* and be able to explain the strategy before the teacher goes to the next step.
   Special Note: A student may arrive at the preferred answer using an equally acceptable but different strategy than did the teacher. If this is the case, the teacher should not attempt to change the student's strategy. Cognitive styles differ, and desired answers can be obtained in a number of different ways.

D. *Apply the comprehension strategy.* The purpose of this step is to determine if the students understand and have acquired the strategy presented by the teacher.

   1. Provide the students with a reading assignment similar in reading level and content to the initial assignment.

   2. Have a number of questions prepared of the same type as those with which the students experienced difficulty.

   3. Direct the students to read the passage silently to find the answer to one of the questions.

   4. When they have finished reading, have the students explain what they did as they looked for the answer to the question.

   5. The students should eventually arrive at or near the preferred answer. In some cases, students fail to provide an improved answer. If this is the case, the teacher should return to the teaching step and reteach the strategy through additional demonstrations. Reteaching is most effective when it is done with new material; but when new material is not available, it is permissible to use the same material.

   6. When the students can apply the strategy and obtain the preferred or best answer, go to step E—generalize the comprehension strategy.
   Special note: Students should be taught at the onset that often there exists a range of acceptable answers; but in any range, one preferred answer usually exists. Striving for the best possible answer is what refines the process of critical thinking.

E. *Generalize the comprehension strategy.* The purpose of this step is to provide students with opportunities to use the strategy with different subject area materials.

   1. Provide students with newspapers, magazines, and monographs used in your subject area. Assist your students in applying their strategies to the different types of subject area materials.

   2. The students should be led to realize that the question-answering strategy generally remains the same, even though the material may differ.

   3. Provide students with opportunities to answer similar questions in everyday classroom activities and assignments. Strategies are soon forgotten unless opportunities are provided for continuous application.

You should now understand the five steps in the plan for teaching question-answering strategies. To make the plan even clearer, in the next section we will provide an example of how a lesson may be taught using this plan.

The following Teaching Plan will explain how comprehension is improved through the study of a Synthesis (1—Inference) question. This instructional plan was developed using the following selection, "A Civil Air Patrol Cadet." You may want to refer to this selection as you read the Teaching Plan.

Question: Why did the author write this essay?

A Civil Air Patrol Cadet

Hello! My name is Robbie DuBois and I am a cadet major in Civil Air Patrol. Civil Air Patrol is a volunteer civilian auxiliary of the United States Air Force. I am the cadet unit leader of the Riverside, Florida, Squadron of Civil Air Patrol. Civil Air Patrol is open to boys and girls, ages fifteen to twenty. In Civil Air Patrol we learn search and rescue procedures so we can assist in locating lost military and civilian aircraft. We go on flight practice missions. We also learn how to get along with others and to be good citizens. I think every high school boy or girl should learn these things. That is why I enjoy my volunteer job and serve as a member of Civil Air Patrol.

Teaching Plan

A. *Set the purpose for learning.* Let us assume that a student answered the following question.

Question: "Why did the author write this story?"

Answer: "He wanted to tell us what Civil Air Patrol cadets do."

Because this answer is not the best answer to the question, the teacher points out the obvious need for instruction. The teacher also indicates that the instruction should improve the student's comprehension of the passage and help the student to answer other questions of this type.

B. *Assess the comprehension strategy.* If you do not have the student's answer to the question recorded, ask him or her to repeat the answer; record it on chalkboard, paper, etc. Ask the student to explain how he or she arrived at this answer. Record each step. Probe to obtain specific steps.

A recorded strategy elicited from a student may appear as follows:

1. "I read the passage."

2. "I found statements that say what cadets do."

3. "I concluded that he wanted to share these things."

C. *Teach the comprehension strategy.*

1. Give the student a copy of the essay, "A Civil Air Patrol Cadet." Direct the student to read silently as you read aloud.

2. As you read, describe and demonstrate each step in *your* strategy. (Remember, the strategies are in Enabling Element 3.)

   a. Be sure there are no unfamiliar words, expressions, or ideas and that the intent is clear.

   b. Gather the relevant and verifiable facts.

   c. Decide whether or not all the necessary facts are supplied. If not, a conclusion cannot be drawn. Instead, an inference will have to be drawn.

   d. Determine what facts are missing.

   e. Use your experience, conversations with others, outside reading, and best hunches to supply the missing facts.

   f. Combine verifiable and hypothesized facts that are relevant, and formulate your inference.

Tell your students how you arrive at answers.

3. Write each step on the chalkboard, etc., as you proceed.
4. When you have finished, review your strategy to provide a total overview. Remove the strategy from the chalkboard, or cover it.
5. Ask the student to list and explain each step to check on his or her understanding.
6. Compare strategies and point out likenesses and differences.
7. Have the student explain how his or her strategy needs to be modified.
8. Have the student explain how he or she would handle a similar question in another passage.

D. *Apply the comprehension strategy.*

1. Prepare two questions of similar type dealing with one passage from similar reading material. If necessary, the same material may be used.
2. Direct the student to read the material silently to answer one question.
3. When the student has finished reading, ask for his or her answer. Also ask the student to explain what he or she did to answer the question. The explanation should be the strategy you have taught.
4. Repeat step 3 with a second question to provide additional practice.

E. *Generalize the comprehension strategy.*
Assist students in applying the question-answering strategies to all the different types of reading materials used in your subject area (i.e., magazines, newspapers, another textbook, to mention just a few. Provide daily practice opportunities to answer similar questions in classroom activities and assignments. Such opportunities should be provided until the skill is at the automatic performance level.

Practicum Exercise

Now it is your turn. *First*, use the Classification Scheme for Reading Questions to prepare a number of questions over a reading assignment that you will soon assign to your students. Prepare some questions for each of the six major levels of the classification scheme.

Second, provide your students with these questions and the reading assignment. After they have completed the assignment, ask them to write their answers to the questions. If you wish, you may use a group question-answer discussion technique, but it is easier for students to mislead you with this technique. Analyze the students' answers to the questions. Students who have given fuzzy, incomplete, or incorrect answers can be placed in small groups for instruction.

Third, select one group of students having difficulty with a specific type of question, and prepare a lesson following the guidelines provided. An outline form for developing a teaching plan follows.

Fourth and finally, provide instruction following the steps provided in the following teaching plan.

Teaching Plan

A. Set the purpose for learning.

B. Assess the comprehension strategy.

C. Teach the comprehension strategy.

D. Apply the comprehension strategy.

E. Generalize the comprehension strategy.

Answers to the Practicum Exercise

We hope your lesson went well. If not, refer to the discussions to determine why you had difficulty or see your assigned instructor. Since every plan would be different, it is not possible to anticipate answers; therefore, no answers for this Practicum Exercise are provided.

If you are familiar with the plan for teaching question-answering strategies and can prepare a plan for teaching a question-answer strategy, you are ready for the Posttest. If not, refer to the appropriate Enabling Elements or see your instructor.

Posttest

Directions: Read each of the following statements and complete each Posttest item.

1. As part of this module, you were introduced to the Classification Scheme for Reading Questions. Name and describe each of the six major categories of questions in this classification scheme.

2. The Classification Scheme for Reading Questions is a useful tool for writing questions. Write one question for each of the six categories using the following selection.

Sleep
Sleep is an unconscious state from which a person can quickly be aroused. During sleep the function of most vital organs is reduced. This reduction causes a person to become cool and require covers for comfortable sleeping. A sleeping person goes through periods of light and heavy sleep. The person also goes through periods when he or she does and does not dream. Dreaming seems to have an effect upon the quality of sleep. Although the necessary number of hours of sleep varies from person to person, most adults sleep approximately six to eight hours a day. Sleep cannot be stored in a body like energy in a flashlight battery, and therefore most people need to sleep sometime during each twenty-four-hour period.

3. Before you can help students understand their question-answering strategies, you must understand your own. Write the step-by-step procedure for answering the evaluation question that you prepared for the preceding selection.

4. The plan for teaching question-answering strategies is an instructional plan for helping students to improve their question-answering abilities. First, list the steps in the Teaching Plan. Second, prepare a brief statement describing what takes place at each step during the instructional process.

Posttest Answers

1. The six categories and their descriptions follow:

    a. Recognition and Recall questions. Questions in this category require a verbatim answer.

    b. Translation questions. Questions in this category require the learner to locate the exact answer and then translate the answer into his or her own words.

    c. Application questions. Questions in this category require the learner to apply what he or she has read to solve a problem or change a situation.

    d. Analysis questions. Questions in this category require the learner to separate the selection into parts and analyze each part.

    e. Synthesis questions. Questions in this category require the learner to combine information to create a new idea or product.

    f. Evaluation questions. Questions in this category require the learner to evaluate what has been read and then make a decision using a specified set of criteria. The learner must also justify his or her information, decision, and the evaluation criteria.

2. Compare each question you wrote with the Classification Scheme for Reading Questions. If you have prepared at least one question for each of the six categories, you have demonstrated the required competency.

3. Compare your question-answering strategy with the following evaluation strategy taken from the Sample Question-Answering Strategies in Enabling Element 3. If your strategy contains the same steps, you have demonstrated the required competency.

    Answering Strategy for Evaluation Questions

    a. Check the question and passage to be sure that it does not contain any unfamiliar words, expressions, or ideas. Clarify as necessary.

    b. Be sure the intent of the question is understood. Rephrase the question if necessary.

    c. Identify important information from the passage.

    d. Establish the evaluation criteria.

    e. Evaluate each basic unit of information in terms of the appropriate criterion or criteria.

    f. Examine all evaluations and prepare a final decision.

    g. Justify the information gathered, evaluation criteria, and your final decision.

4. *Teaching Plan*

    a. Set the purpose for learning. At this step, the teacher establishes the need for instruction.

    b. Assess the comprehension strategy. Here the teacher asks the students to explain how they answered a question. The purpose of this step is to assess the adequacy of the learners' strategy for answering a specific type of question.

    c. Teach the comprehension strategy. This step contains the procedures for teaching the question-answering strategy.

    d. Apply the comprehension strategy. This step is designed to determine if the strategy taught is understood by the learners.

    e. Generalize the comprehension strategy. At this step, the teacher teaches the students how to use the strategy with various kinds of subject area materials. The teacher also provides daily practice sessions to raise students' performance in the application of this strategy to the automatic response level.

Final Comment

You have now acquired a competency that will help you improve substantially the comprehension achievement in your subject area. Using this competency requires only minor instructional effort by most subject area teachers. We hope you will make this minor adjustment.

    If you have satisfactorily completed all Posttest items, you are ready to move to another module. If not, refer to appropriate Enabling Elements, see your instructor, or refer to the Selected Bibliography.

Selected Bibliography

Altick, R. D. *Preface to Critical Reading*. 4th ed. New York: Holt, Rinehart, and Winston, 1967.

Axelrod, J. "Some Flaws in Commercial Reading Comprehension Materials." *Journal of Reading* 17, no. 6 (1974): 474–79.

Bloom, B. S. et al. *Taxonomy of Educational Objectives: Handbook I, Cognitive Domain*. New York: David McKay, 1956.

Burmeister, L. E. *Reading Strategies for Secondary School Teachers*. 2d ed. Reading, Massachusetts: Addison-Wesley, 1978.

Dale, E. "Develop Critical Reading." *Reading Improvement* 13, no. 1 (Spring 1976): 30–33.

Dixon, N. P. "A Test to Help Improve Instruction in Reading Comprehension." *Reading Improvement* 17, no. 1, (Spring 1980): 22–25.

Durkin, D. "What Classroom Observations Reveal about Reading Comprehension Instruction." *Reading Research Quarterly* 14, no. 4 (1978–79): 481–533.

Galloway, P. "How Secondary Students and Teachers Read Textbooks." *Journal of Reading* 17, no. 3 (1973): 216–19.

Manzo, A. V. "Guided Reading Procedure." *Journal of Reading* 18, no. 4 (1975): 287–91.

Mize, J. M. "A Directed Reading Strategy for Teaching Critical Reading and Decision Making." *Journal of Reading*, 22, no. 2 (1978): 144–48.

Moore, W. E. *Creative and Critical Thinking*. Boston: Houghton Mifflin, 1967.

Newton, B. T. "Higher Cognitive Questioning and Critical Reading." *Reading Improvement* 15, no. 1 (Spring 1978): 26–27.

Ortiz, R. K. "Using Questioning as a Tool in Reading." *Journal of Reading* 21, no. 2 (1977): 109–14.

Sinatra, R. C. "The Cloze Technique for Reading Comprehension and Vocabulary Development." *Reading Improvement* 14, no. 2 (Summer 1977): 86–92.

Smith, C. B.; Smith, S. L.; and Mikulecky, L. *Teaching Reading and Subject Matter in the Secondary School*. New York: Holt, Rinehart and Winston, 1978.

Helping Students Use Study Skills and Strategies

Contents

Prospectus
  Rationale
  Objectives
  Resources and Time Required
Pretest
Branching Program Alternatives for Pretest Responses
Enabling Element 1: *Teaching Basic Study Skills*
Enabling Element 2: *The SQ3R Study Strategy for Social Sciences*
Enabling Element 3: *The PQRST Study Strategy for Physical Sciences*
Enabling Element 4: *The SQRQCQ Study Strategy for Mathematics*
Posttest
  Posttest Answers
Selected Bibliography

Prospectus

Rationale

To read a textbook, your students must have both study skills and a study strategy. In fact, to read in a number of content area textual materials, your students must have a number of study skills and strategies. Study skills are necessary for locating information or materials, for understanding various types of graphic or visual aids, and for adjusting rate and style of reading. Study strategies are plans for reading textual materials that help the reader comprehend and retain more of the information. If you want your students to be effective and efficient readers of the textual materials you assign them, then you must teach the appropriate study skills and study strategies. In this module you will learn the major study skills and an appropriate study strategy for your content area. You will also learn how to teach them to your students.

Terminal Objective

You will specify the major study skills from your content area, prepare a plan for teaching a study skill, and apply three study strategies.

Specific Objectives

1. You will specify the major study skills in your content area and prepare a lesson designed to teach a study skill.

2. You will write the associated words for each step in the SQ3R Study Strategy, write a paragraph describing each step in the process of using SQ3R, and describe a plan for teaching the strategy.

3. You will write the associated words for each step in the PQRST Study Strategy, write a paragraph describing each step in the process of using PQRST, and describe a plan for teaching the strategy.

4. You will write the associated words for each step in the SQRQCQ Study Strategy, write a paragraph describing each step in the process of using SQRQCQ, and describe a plan for teaching the strategy.

Resources and Time Required

To complete the core Enabling Activities in this module, you will need blank paper, a writing instrument, and one of your subject area textbooks. The estimated time required to complete the core Enabling Activities is four to five hours.

Pretest

Directions: For each question, determine the word that indicates your belief regarding your competency. If you are in doubt, choose NO.

1. Every content area has its own reading and study demands. Can you   YES   NO
   specify the major study skills in your subject area and identify the steps
   in a plan for teaching a study skill?

2. Students who do poorly on follow-up tests based upon reading assign-   YES   NO
   ments in social science materials can improve their performance if they
   use the SQ3R Study Strategy. Can you name the key words for the
   SQ3R Study Strategy and write a paragraph describing each step in the
   process of using SQ3R?

3. Students who have difficulty with reading assignments in physical   YES   NO
   science materials can improve their performance if they use the PQRST
   Study Strategy. Can you name the key words for the PQRST Study
   Strategy and write a paragraph describing each?

4. Similarly, students who have difficulty with math problems requiring   YES   NO
   reading can improve their performance if they use the SQRQCQ Study
   Strategy. Can you name the key words for the SQRQCQ Study Strategy
   and write a paragraph describing each step?

Branching Program Alternatives for Pretest Responses

1. You will need to teach the specific study skills for effective and efficient study of your required textual materials. If you know the major study skills in your content area and how to teach them, you are ready for Enabling Element 2. If not, Enabling Element 1 will be of interest to you.

2. Every student takes social science courses. Social studies, government, economics, and psychology are but a few of those courses offered under the broad curriculum area of social sciences. Every student needs a study strategy for reading in the social sciences. If you can name a study strategy for the social sciences and write a paragraph describing each of the steps in the strategy, you are ready for Enabling Element 3. If not, you will find Enabling Element 2 helpful.

3. All students receive some instruction in the physical sciences with emphasis on physics, chemistry, physiology, and the like. When reading material from the physical sciences, all students need a reading study strategy. If you can name a study strategy for the physical sciences and write a paragraph description of each step in the strategy, you are ready for Enabling Element 4. If not, Enabling Element 3 will familiarize you with such a strategy.

4. Mathematics is emphasized at every school curriculum level. Many students who do not have difficulty with straight computation problems have difficulty with reasoning problems that require reading. Students can be more successful with such reasoning problems if they know and can apply a study strategy for mathematics reading. If you can name a study strategy useful for mathematics and write a paragraph description of each step in the strategy, you are ready for the Posttest. If you think you need additional information, Enabling Element 4 will be helpful to you.

Enabling Element 1
Teaching Study Skills

Specific Objective 1

You will specify the major study skills in your content area and prepare a lesson designed to teach a study skill.

Enabling Activities

*1. Read Study Guide 1 to identify the major study skills in your content area and the steps in a plan for teaching a study skill.

*2. Refer to Module 4, Diagnosing Reading Skill Needs, to identify additional impor-

---

*Indicates core Enabling Activities.

tant study skills for your content area. Add these study skills to the list in Study Guide 1. Complete Practicum Exercise 1.

*3. After reading Study Guide 1, prepare a plan for teaching one of the study skills from your content area. Complete Practicum Exercise 2.

4. Examine your textbook to determine all the study skills needed by students to understand the material in your content area. List the skills.

5. Together with your colleagues, identify the study skills required for understanding and using the various textual materials in your subject area. Divide the responsibility of developing plans for teaching the study skills. Share the plans with each other. After the plans have been used in class, meet with your colleagues to revise the plans as needed.

6. Ask your students how important it is for you to teach them the study skills necessary for locating and understanding textual materials in your subject area. Let the students' comments guide you as you prepare future plans for teaching study skills.

Study Guide 1

In addition to being able to understand word meanings, comprehend ideas, and pronounce multisyllable words, students need to understand the basic skills required to locate information or material, to read graphic material, and to adjust their reading rates. We refer to that large cluster of skills necessary for locating information and material, reading graphics, and adjusting rate as *study skills*. Basically, study skills are techniques students use when they study.

Students must skillfully use many techniques in order to study. If you fan through the pages of any textbook in your area, you will notice they are full of information, pictures, graphs, charts, diagrams, work sheets, and other useful aids. The textbook also has a table of contents, and probably an index, glossary, and other front and back matter sections that are important for students to use effectively and efficiently when they study. Now consider that the textbook is only one source of information the students use when they study. They use other sources such as dictionaries, encyclopedias, thesauruses, references and guides. You can see that students need to master many study skills in order to effectively and efficiently study. Your students must be taught the specific study skills required for reading textual materials in your content area. Teaching these skills is your job because you are the most qualified person to do it. You know how to use the study skills in your content area. Through demonstration, your students will learn to study your content area the way you do. Before we see how this is done, you will need to identify the important study skills for your content area.

Study Skills

We have listed some of the major study skills common to most textual materials. However, there are study skills that are unique to specific textual materials or subject areas. To make a complete list of these study skills, you need to examine your own textual materials. Some of the more important study skills for thirteen content areas are identified and listed in Module 4. To identify the study skills for your subject area you should (1) examine the study skills for your content area in Module 4; (2) examine the study skills that follow to determine if there are still other study skills that need to be taught in your content area; and (3) examine the textual materials in your subject area to find any additional, necessary skills. Make a list of all these study skills. Later you will systematically teach them to your students.

General Study Skills

1. Locating specific reference materials
2. Reading diagrams
3. Reading illustrations
4. Reading graphs
5. Reading charts
6. Reading specific types of worksheets and/or balance sheets
7. Arranging materials or information in sequence by alphabetical order, number, or other designated procedure
8. Using the card catalog
9. Using the *Reader's Guide to Periodical Literature*
10. Organizing ideas into an outline
11. Summarizing information
12. Using a dictionary to locate, pronounce, and define words
13. Using encyclopedias
14. Using a thesaurus
15. Using textbook aids such as title page, copyright page, table of contents, preface, index, glossaries, vocabulary lists, and others
16. Interpreting drawings, cutaway patterns, diagrams, and the like
17. Reading labels to note ingredients, cautions, and directions
18. Locating, reading, and compiling information from a number of sources on a specific topic
19. Reading tables using square roots, or common logarithms of numbers
20. Reading and interpreting pictographs and flowcharts
21. Interpreting pictures and similar graphics
22. Remembering the meanings of symbols and abbreviations
23. Interpreting maps and diagrams
24. Using library skills to locate and research information from journals, government publications, and other common references

Practicum Exercise 1

Directions: List here the five most important study skills for your content area. Be sure to examine all the sources of study skills identified above before making your list.

1.

2.

3.

4.

5.

Answers to Practicum Exercise 1

If you (1) referred to the list of study skills provided in Module 4, "Diagnosing Reading Skill Needs," (2) referred to the list provided in the Study Guide, (3) examined your textual materials for still other important study skills, and then (4) listed the five major study skills, you have a very good list of study skills. Read on!

Teaching Study Skills

When you introduce your content area textbook to your students, share with them the various study aids that are part of the textbook. Most textbooks minimally contain aids such as a title page, copyright page, table of contents, glossary, and an index. Many of them also contain pictures, graphs, charts, and similar graphic aids. When you introduce the textbook, the first set of study skills you should teach students are those that relate to understanding the purposes and uses of the title page, copyright page, table of contents, glossary and index. As you move through the textbook, you will want to teach students how to use specific graphic aids necessary for understanding information presented in the various chapters.

When you introduce your textbook, ask your students questions about the various textbook aids and identify those students who do not understand the use of the aids. Then prepare a skills test following the suggestions in the module on diagnosis to determine how well these students understand the use of the aids. When you have finished, you will have identified a group of students who need some instruction in how to use basic textbook aids. Then you can use the following lesson plan outline to prepare a lesson. Finally, with a lesson plan and a textbook in your hands and copies of the textbook in the students' hands, you can proceed to teach them how to use the textual aids.

The basic lesson plan for teaching study skills contains four steps. They are (1) purpose, (2) instruction, (3) evaluation, and (4) extension activities. A sample lesson plan is provided to show you how to teach a study skill. Read the plan to see how the instruction takes place. This plan could be used with a total class or simply with those students who are not able to demonstrate performance of the skill.

Demonstration Lesson Plan

Purpose

The first step in any plan or lesson is to state your purpose or objective. To do this, you need to determine what your students should be able to do after a lesson that they could not do before the lesson. Let us suppose that the students were not able to answer questions about the various sections of your textbook. Maybe it is because this is the first time they have seen a textbook of this type, or because they have never been taught to use the study aids provided in similar textbooks. The objective of the lesson becomes "Given a textbook, the students will identify the major study aids and state the purpose of each."

Instruction

Here are some steps you can follow for helping your students accomplish the stated objective:

1. Ask the students to survey the textbook to identify its various sections or parts. As they are identified, list them on the chalkboard. Such things as these should be identified: front cover, title page, copyright page, preface, table of contents, chapters, glossary, index, cover, and possibly others specific to your textbook.

2. Ask the students to share what they know about each of these sections of the textbook. As key points are brought out for each of the sections, write them after the section title on the chalkboard. For example:
   a. Front cover—tells the name of the book and the author.
   b. Title page—tells the name of the book, name of the authors, location of the authors, and the publishing company and their location.
   c. Copyright page—gives the added information of the date the book was copyrighted, which is assumed to be the date the book was first available. It also tells if the book was previously copyrighted, which shows that this is a newer version of an older book.
   d. Preface—where the author explains the purpose for writing the book. The author may also identify the audience for which the book was written and acknowledge those who helped him or her.
   e. Table of contents—an outline of the various chapters or topics, showing how the book is organized.

f. Glossary—the author defines the generic and/or technical words he or she believes are important for understanding the ideas in the book.

g. Index—an alphabetical listing of the various topics covered within the book. It is a much finer breakdown of the topics than is found in the table of contents. Often, the names of people, places, or things mentioned in the book are also included in the index.

3. Now lead the students through an examination of each of the book's sections. As you examine each section, discuss with the students the information found there as well as how that information could be used to help them more effectively and efficiently use the textbook. As time permits, continue in this manner until you have moved throughout the entire textbook.

4. As you work through the textbook sections, it will be obvious to you that some of your students do not know how to use some of the more technical sections such as a glossary and index. These students will need to be grouped together for an additional study skills lesson at a later time. We will talk about that in a moment.

Evaluation

To determine how effective the instruction was, you will need to evaluate. You can do so by calling upon students and asking them to explain the various sections of the textbook.

Extension Activities

1. To reinforce what the students have learned about the various sections of the textbook, you will want to give them assignments requiring them to use these textual aids. For example, you may want to give them a list of questions that refers them to the table of contents or index to find the sections of the book where they can read to answer the questions. Some of your questions may ask them to define words located in their glossaries. Also ask them questions to see how well they can read the copyright page or the title page.

2. Have your students look through other content area textbooks to determine if they contain the same textual aids. Ask the students how these textual aids will be useful to them, and then allow them to verify or refute their beliefs by examining the textual aids.

Practicum Exercise 2

One lesson usually leads to another, and it is very likely that you will have a number of students who now understand the various sections of a textbook but do not understand how to use the more technical textbook aids such as a glossary or an index. Suppose the students do not know how to use the index in your content area textbook. On the sample lesson plan that follows, write an objective for a lesson that would be designed to teach them how to use the index. Do it now.

LESSON PLAN

Objective:

Instruction:

Evaluation:

Extension Activities:

Next, decide what you are going to demonstrate to your students as well as what you are going to have them do to gather an understanding of an index. Write in outline form what you will do, say, and require your students to do to accomplish your objective. Do so under the section called *Instruction* in the lesson plan.

When you have finished teaching, you will need to evaluate the effectiveness of your instruction. Write what you will do to evaluate how well your students have learned both the purpose and the use of an index. Not only will this be an evaluation of how well your students have learned, but it will also be an evaluation of the effectiveness of your instruction. Write your evaluation ideas under *Evaluation*.

Finally, you will need to provide your students with some activities designed to reinforce and extend what they have learned about an index. Under *Extension Activities* in the lesson plan, specify your ideas for helping students to solidify their understanding of an index and to become more skillful in using an index.

Answers to Practicum Exercise 2

Of course, there are many different ways to teach students what an index is and how to use it. The following lesson plan is one example. Compare it with your responses to see if you have provided a clear objective, appropriate instructional activities, useful techniques for evaluation, and extension activities that truly reinforce and develop skill in index use.

Purpose

    Given a textbook index, the students will state its purpose and demonstrate how to use the index to locate specific material within a textbook.

Instruction

1. Have the students refer to the table of contents of the textbook to locate the page on which the index begins. Then have the students turn to the index. Point out to them that each page consists of two or more columns of information.

2. Have the students use their index fingers to guide them as they skim down each of the columns on each of the pages of the index. As they do, point out that the index is organized in alphabetical order.

3. Next have the students read the columns of information on the first page of the index. As they do, lead them to understand that both major topics and subtopics are included in an index. The major topics are capitalized and align on the far left of every column. The subtopics are usually not capitalized and are indented under major topics. Also bring out that there are page numbers for both major topics and subtopics.

4. Direct the students to any topic that has a number of subtopics. The students should first read the topic and subtopics and then refer to the various pages on which the subtopics appear. Lead the students to understand that a major topic may be dealt with in a number of places in a textbook and that various page numbers after the major topic show which pages contain information about the topic. The various subtopics are ideas that relate to the major topic; they too may be discussed on various pages in the text, and the numbers following the subtopics in the index indicate the text pages on which the subtopics are mentioned.

5. Have the students skim the major topics to see what kinds of information are included in the index. Point out that your index may contain such information as names, places, and topics dealt with in the textbook.

6. Point out any other features of the index in your book.

7. Ask the students to tell where they would locate information in their textbooks on various topics. Such an exercise gives students practice in rapidly locating topics and subtopics using the index of your textbook.

Evaluation

    Question your students to determine if they understand the purpose of an index. Then give each student a topic, and watch as the student uses the index to locate the pages on which that topic is discussed. As you watch the students use the index, evaluate them for effectiveness and efficiency.

Extension Activities

1. At another time, ask your students to locate information using the indexes of their textbooks.

2. Incorporate into your assignments activities that require your students to locate information in their textbooks using an index.

3. Hold time drills in which your students compete with each other to locate information in their textbooks.

Now you should understand the basic study skills that are important for independent study by students in your content area. You should also know how to prepare a lesson plan to teach the use of these various study skills. Remember, some of the study skills need to be taught when a textual source is introduced, and others should be taught when the need to use them arises. The best time to teach study skills is *when the students need them.*

Now that you are familiar with the basic study skills in your content area and know how to teach them, you are ready to learn about strategies. You will learn about three study strategies in the following three Enabling Elements.

Enabling Element 2
The SQ3R Study Strategy

Specific Objective 2

You will write the associated words for each step in the SQ3R Study Strategy, write a paragraph describing each step in the process if using SQ3R, and describe a plan for teaching the strategy.

Enabling Activities

*1. Read Study Guide 2, to identify the five key words associated with this strategy and to learn how to use each step in SQ3R with a reading assignment in social science and humanities materials.

*2. Select a reading passage from a student textbook in the social science or humanities subject area. The reading passage should be approximately six to ten pages in length *or* require approximately twenty to thirty minutes of sustained silent reading by your students. Follow the recommended procedures in ''Using the SQ3R Study Strategy,'' and study the selection.

*Indicates core Enabling Activities.

*3. Practice using the SQ3R Study Strategy with reading assignments containing few or no side headings. Prepare a plan for teaching students how to use this strategy with reading assignments containing few or no side headings.

*4. Use the recommended procedure in "Teaching SQ3R" to prepare a plan for teaching SQ3R. Following your plan, teach SQ3R to a group of students.

5. Reproduce the section entitled "The Components of SQ3R," and distribute it to your colleagues. Discuss the possibilities for teaching the use of this study strategy in all social science and humanities courses.

6. Compare the reading rate and comprehension scores after reading two similar assignments, one using SQ3R and the other using your present reading strategy. What do your findings suggest?

Study Guide 2

An educator by the name of Francis Robinson was concerned about the reading comprehension level of his students. He found that the typical reader remembers only about half of what he or she is asked for on a quiz immediately following the reading assignment. He found this to be true for both average and superior high-school students.

Recognizing this problem, Francis Robinson devised the SQ3R Study Strategy as a technique for increasing immediate understanding and prolonging retention. The SQ3R Study Strategy he devised is well supported by results obtained from studies investigating the learning process.

SQ3R represents the five steps in the study strategy. The five steps are *Survey, Question, Read, Recite,* and *Review.* The first three steps evolved from research that demonstrated (1) the value of skimming over and summarizing headings before reading and (2) the value of knowing the comprehension questions before reading an assignment. Skimming to obtain an overview of the textual material provides an orientation to the material and provides clues to what information will be presented. Questions provide specific purposes for reading and directions on how to read. Furthermore, the questions are generally connected by a thread of logic that make them easier to remember. Because questions reveal to us the specific information we are looking for, they are valuable in assisting us in remembering the information.

When Robinson's students applied the first three steps, Survey, Question, and Read, to reading assignments, the result was a higher level of immediate understanding. However, this result did not totally satisfy Robinson for he knew that approximately 80 percent of what was read would be forgotten within two weeks. He also knew that retention could be improved by test-type reviews after the reading assignment. When test-type review sessions were used following reading, forgetting was reduced from 80 to 20 percent after a two-week period. Because of this substantial change in retention, Robinson added the final two components to his study strategy: Recite and Review.

The SQ3R Study Strategy introduced thirty years ago by Francis Robinson has withstood the test of time. It has been widely accepted because the study strategy is designed to serve as an advance organizer, provide specific purposes for reading, provide self-comprehension checks, and fix information in memory. The SQ3R Study

Plan several lessons to help your students use SQ3R.

Strategy does not require additional reading time; in fact, it generally requires less reading time after the technique is mastered.

The Components of SQ3R

There are five basic components or steps in the SQ3R Study Strategy. The student follows the steps in the same order as they occur in the formula statement SQ3R: Survey, Question, Read, Recite, and Review. Here is an overview of the five components:

SURVEY. When the reading material includes side headings, the Survey consists of reading all side headings and the final or summary paragraph. If the reading material does not have side headings, the Survey consists of skimming paragraphs for topic sentences until a transition point is located. When a transition point is located, the reader is advised to stop and reflect on the ideas in the last set of paragraphs read. A question is then formulated about those ideas. This process is continued until the end of the assignment is reached.

QUESTION. Now the headings or major points are changed into questions. A question is used because of all sentence forms it probably provides the reader with the most specific direction. The questions serve as an advance organizer for the total assignment, and each specific question provides immediate and specific direction for reading.

READ. Taking each question in turn, read to locate the answer. The reader may skim, skip, or reread material as he or she chooses. The style of reading should vary with the purpose for reading.

RECITE. Recitation is used to check on clarity of ideas and to fix ideas in memory. After an answer to a question has been located or reasoned out, the reader should pause and recite the answer. Most students should recite their answers aloud. Students, like most of us, are more critical of their ideas when they are spoken aloud.

REVIEW. A review is used to fix in memory the overall organization as well as the specific ideas. Generally, one review should occur immediately following completion of the reading assignment. A second review should take place within the next twenty-four hours and a third, twenty-four hours later. Students with memory difficulties should periodically review throughout the reading assignment as well as continue the daily reviews.

Now that you are aware of how SQ3R was developed and are familiar with the five components of the study strategy, it is time for you to use the study strategy.

Using the SQ3R Strategy

Before you can teach SQ3R to others, you must understand how to use this study strategy. To ensure that you will have no difficulty teaching this strategy, follow our suggestions for using the strategy on a reading assignment in one of the student textbooks in your subject area. We can get started as soon as you get the textbook.

Practicum Exercise

Identify a six- to ten-page selection in the textbook. The reading assignment should take approximately twenty to thirty minutes for your average reader to complete. Choose a selection you would like your students to read because later we will ask you to use this passage with your students.

1. *Survey*. Begin by surveying the headings, charts, graphs, and pictures, and then reading the final paragraph or summary. Surveying consists of a rapid reading of side headings or topic sentences. This provides the reader with an overview of the content and the thread of organization. Stop reading and complete this step. When it is complete, begin reading step 2.
2. *Question*. When the survey has been completed, use the information you have obtained from headings and topic sentences to formulate questions. For most of us, questions provide a clearer focus than other types of sentence constructions. A well-formulated question cuts down considerably on the amount of time it takes to locate information. Stop reading and complete this step; then begin reading step 3.

3. *Read*. Now read to locate the answers to your questions. Reading is not defined here as looking at every word on every line of every page. It is perfectly legitimate to skim material, to skip material, and to reread material. You must remember that the objective is to obtain the information necessary to answer your questions. Your style of reading should vary dramatically as the nature of your questions change. Just as there is more than one type of question, there is also more than one style of reading. Stop reading and complete this step. When it is completed, begin reading step 4.

4. *Recite*. After you have located the answer to each question, look away from the textbook and recite the answer in your own words. It is important to recite the answer in your own words to be sure you understand what you have read and to avoid parroting. Depending on how important the information is, you may want to write a brief phrase to assist you with the future recall of the information. Stop reading and complete this step. When it is completed, begin reading step 5.

5. *Review*. When you finish the assignment, review the ideas obtained from your reading. Remember, immediate recitation followed by periodic reviews is what reduces memory loss from 80 to 20 percent at the end of a two-week period. Stop reading and complete this step. When it is completed, begin reading the next paragraph.

Answers to the Practicum Exercise

How was it? If you are like most teachers, you found it very easy to apply this study strategy. You also found that you remembered more of what you read. If you timed yourself, you probably found it took you less time than you expected to complete this assignment. You surely noticed that your reading style varied with the nature of the question you asked—and it should! Remember, effective and efficient readers vary their reading style with their purpose for reading.

You are now familiar with the SQ3R Study Strategy and have applied it to a textbook in your teaching area. Now it is time to move on to a discussion on teaching the SQ3R Study Strategy.

Teaching SQ3R

Now it is time to prepare yourself to teach the SQ3R Study Strategy. The instructional procedures are divided into five steps, each of which is explained in detail.

Select Materials.

1. Select a reading assignment six to ten pages in length or one requiring twenty to thirty minutes of sustained silent reading by your students. Select reading assignments from textbooks suitable for your students. For your first lesson, you may use the material you identified for the practice lesson from the Practicum Exercise in Study Guide 2 if the selection is suitable.

2. Prepare and duplicate copies of "The Components of SQ3R." You will need a copy for each student.

3. Collect copies of nontextbook materials without side headings. You will need one copy for each student in your group. All students should have a copy of the same material if the material is suitable.

Apply SQ3R.

1. Read the six- to ten-page textbook selection using the SQ3R Study Strategy.

   a. *Survey* the selection.

   b. *Question* the material.

   c. *Read* and answer the questions.

   d. *Recite* answers.

   e. *Review* questions and answers.

2. Be sure to apply SQ3R with the same care and completeness you expect from your students.

Schedule Instruction. Schedule three fifty-minute periods for teaching the study strategy to your students. If possible, teach the three lessons within the same week.

Provide Instruction.

1. During the first fifty-minute period

   a. Explain to your students that you are going to introduce them to the SQ3R study strategy that is to be used when reading assignments in your class. Tell them the SQ3R strategy will raise their level of understanding, extend retention, and save study time. You may want to share other facts on how Francis Robinson developed the strategy.

   b. Distribute copies of "The Components of SQ3R" to each student. Discuss each component so your students understand its function.

   c. Demonstrate the application of SQ3R using the selection you prepared. Answer any questions your students have.

   d. Assign the same selection to your students. Direct them to apply SQ3R as they read the assignment.

   e. When your students have finished reading the assignment, record their reading time and check their comprehension. Use this information in the following discussion.

   f. Begin a group discussion in which SQ3R is compared with prior reading strategies. Point out the advantages of study strategies such as SQ3R.

2. During the second fifty-minute period

   a. Review the SQ3R components.

   b. Demonstrate the application of SQ3R with another textbook selection.

    c. Assign a different selection to be read than you used for demonstration purposes. Direct the students to apply SQ3R as they read.

    d. When the assignment is completed, record their reading time and check their comprehension. Review the advantages of SQ3R.

    e. Assign another, shorter selection to provide additional practice using SQ3R.

3. During the third fifty-minute period
    a. Discuss the application of SQ3R to materials without side headings.

    b. Demonstrate the application of SQ3R to materials without side headings.

    c. Assist students in using SQ3R with a reading assignment in a material that does not contain side headings.

    d. When the assignment is completed, record reading time and check comprehension. Discuss advantages of SQ3R with this type of material.

Practice. Schedule ten- to fifteen-minute class periods for additional demonstrations and student practice sessions. At least twenty teacher-directed practice sessions will be needed to raise this study strategy to the automatic performance level. It is just as easy on this level to apply SQ3R as it is to do anything else.

In stress situations, students have a tendency to resort to their most secure and automatic behavior patterns. This means that your students may apply SQ3R in practice activities but not in "reading" assignments unless you provide sufficient practice to raise the skill to the automatic level of behavior. We suggest that you encourage the use of SQ3R Study Strategy in every assignment. Do so by providing time for surveying and suggesting questions that can be used to guide reading. Whenever a new type of instructional reading material is used, demonstrate how you apply the strategy to this new material. Always stress and reward improved comprehension and extended memory as a result of using SQ3R.

You are now familiar with the major steps in a lesson plan designed to teach the SQ3R Study Strategy. Before we go on, review the five steps by listing them.

Recommended Steps for Teaching SQ3R

1.

2.

3.

4.

5.

We hope you now know how to use and teach the SQ3R Study Strategy. Take the next step and teach the strategy to someone. All the directions are provided, and you have already prepared the material.

Enabling Element 3
The PQRST Study Strategy for the Physical Sciences

Specific Objective 3

You will write the associated words for each step in the PQRST Study Strategy, write a paragraph describing each step in the process of using PQRST, and describe a plan for teaching the strategy.

Enabling Activities

*1. Read Study Guide 3 to identify the five key words associated with the strategy and write a paragraph describing each step in the procedure for using PQRST with a reading assignment.

*2. In student textual materials from various physical science subject areas, locate a number of selections appropriate for study by your students. Identify selections that are approximately six to ten pages in length or require approximately twenty to thirty minutes of sustained silent reading by your students. Follow the recommended procedures in "Using the PQRST Study Strategy" to study the selection.

*3. Identify some reading selections in physical science materials that do not contain side headings. Practice using the PQRST Study Strategy with these reading selections.

4. The teaching plan used for teaching SQ3R can be adopted for teaching PQRST. Write a paragraph that explains each of the basic steps you are to follow for teaching PQRST. Following your plan, teach PQRST to a group of students.

5. Share with your colleagues the section entitled "The Components of PQRST." Show them how you have used the strategy to improve comprehension and retention of information.

6. Contrast SQ3R and PQRST as study strategies to clarify how the strategies are applied differently to social science and physical science textual materials.

---

*Indicates core Enabling Activities.

Study Guide 3

Physical science materials are written in a style that may require the use of a unique study strategy. Although SQ3R may be useful for studying physical science materials, George Spache and Leo Fay recommend that the PQRST Study Strategy be used. We believe the difference between the SQ3R and PQRST Study Strategies is more than one of semantics; and therefore, we concur with Spache and Fay and recommend that PQRST be taught to students for studying physical science materials.

Before we explain the steps in the PQRST strategy and discuss its application to passages characteristic of science writing, a few points need to be made. First, scientific textual materials are written in a different style than most of the textual materials students are accustomed to reading. Science textbooks, for the most part, are not designed with the express purpose of imparting information. Their emphasis is upon developing a way of thinking often referred to as the *inquiry*, or *scientific*, *method*. Second, in science textbooks, the reader is generally required to follow a presentation of details that are formulated by the author into a generalization, theory, or concept. Once the generalization, theory, or concept has been formed, the student is shown how to test it through a series of experiments. Keep these points in mind as you read to understand the components of the PQRST Study Strategy, and as you see how the PQRST Study Strategy is applied to science textual reading materials. The science selections in this module are typical of, but shorter than, most selections found in science textbooks.

The Components of PQRST

Five steps form the PQRST Study Strategy. The reader applies the steps in the same order as they occur in the formula statement PQRST: Preview, Question, Read, Summarize, and Test. Here is an explanation of the five steps.

PREVIEW. The student begins by skimming the title, side headings, and all pictures and other graphics to identify the generalization or theory the writer is presenting and supporting. The student cannot move to the next step and form questions until the writer's generalization or theory has been identified.

QUESTION. Next, the student seeks out the questions the writer is going to answer to supply information in support of the generalization or theory being proposed. The student uses these questions as purposes for reading.

READ. Then the student reads the selection to obtain answers to the purpose-setting questions. When there are more questions and facts than the student can trust to memory, the questions and facts should be written down. Sometimes it is necessary for the student to complete experiments before answers to questions are obtained and understood.

SUMMARIZE. Now the student summarizes the information, preferably in written form. The facts related to each question are grouped together, and a summary statement is prepared for each question.

TEST. Finally, the student tests the generalization against the supporting information. This means the student must determine if the author answered the appropriate questions with sufficient information to support the generalization or theory being proposed. As students grow in age and scientific understanding, the criteria they use for testing generalizations will and should change.

You should now be familiar with the basis and components of the PQRST Study Strategy. Read on to see how the strategy is applied when reading scientific textual materials. First read the selection, ''Your Nervous System,'' and then the explanation of how you should apply the strategy.

Your Nervous System

In your body the nervous system regulates all other systems. The nervous system can be divided into three separate but related systems. First is the *central nervous system*, which includes the brain and the spinal cord. Second is the *peripheral nervous system*, which includes the outward extention of nerves from the spinal cord to the base of the brain. Third is the *autonomic nervous system*, which controls both the central and peripheral systems through conscious activity and sensations. When we think of these three systems, it is best not to think of them as separate systems; but rather as interrelated systems, the interrelationship of which is necessary to sustain good health and life.

Here is how you should use PQRST to study-read this passage:

PREVIEW. Skim the title and the selection to gain an overall impression. You notice that the selection deals with the *nervous system*. The generalization being made by the author is that the nervous system regulates all other systems in the body. The author has highlighted some important points for your attention. Anything that appears in capital letters or italics should be given special attention during the previewing.

QUESTION. There are at least one major and three minor questions that should be asked from this selection that are relevant to the author's basic generalization. What is a nervous system? How does the central nervous system relate to the nervous system? How does the peripheral nervous system relate to the nervous system? How does the autonomic nervous system relate to the nervous system?

READ. Using the questions as guides, slowly read the selection. Carefully attend to the facts that relate to your questions. Remember that facts are very important in scientific writing. Although many facts are needed to substantiate a theory, only a single fact is needed to refute it.

SUMMARIZE. Take the facts you have gathered and organize them into clusters around the four questions. First, summarize the facts around the three questions concerning the central nervous system, peripheral nervous system, and autonomic nervous system. Second, summarize all the facts related to the major question on the nervous system.

TEST. Examine the questions and answers to determine if the appropriate questions were asked and sufficient information was supplied to support the author's basic generalization. If the generalization passes the test, it can cautiously be accepted. If it fails, then additional information may be needed, or possibly the generalization should be rejected. Remember, as students grow in age and scientific sophistication, their criteria for testing generalizations or theories will and should change.

Practicum Exercise

Now it is your turn to apply the PQRST study strategy. Read the following selection using PQRST. The key words in the PQRST study strategy follow the selection; for each of the key words describe the procedure you used as you read "Weather Symbols."

Weather Symbols

The weather map used by meteorologists contains a variety of information. The quantity of information and ease of reading require that the information be codified. Three major classes of weather symbols are codified under (1) precipitation, (2) cloud cover, and (3) barometric change.

The precipitation code includes an asterisk for snow, a dot for rain, and an inverted triangle for showers. The symbols may be combined. For example, a dot over an inverted triangle means rain showers. An asterisk over an inverted triangle means snow showers.

The cloud cover code is a simple one. It uses only a circle. A clear circle indicates clearness or no clouds. A half-shaded circle indicates partly cloudy weather. A fully shaded circle means cloudy.

The barometric code is also simple. A horizontal line means steady. A line rising to the right indicates rising barometric pressure. A line falling to the right indicates falling barometric pressure.

Your knowledge of these signs will enhance your understanding of weather reporting. It will also improve your map-reading ability.

Preview:

Question:

Read:

Summarize:

Test:

Answers to the Practicum Exercise

The PQRST letter formula is a helpful mnemonic device for remembering key words that will assist you in understanding scientific writing. You should have found these key words helpful as you read "Weather Symbols." You should have applied the PQRST study strategy to this passage in the following manner.

1. *Preview.* You skimmed the title and the selection to gain an overall impression. As you were skimming, you noticed a sequence of three numbers used in the selection. The numbers should have alerted you to something important. If you stopped to read the sentence containing those numbers, you learned a great deal about the selection. You learned that the selection was a discussion of three different types of codes. A quick glance at each of the succeeding paragraphs should have verified that observation. The generalization you searched for is in the last paragraph, where the author proposed that your understanding of weather reporting will be enhanced by an understanding of weather symbols or signs.

2. *Question.* At least two major and three minor questions should have come to mind. Although your questions may not have been exactly like ours, they were probably somewhat similar. What are weather symbols? What are weather symbols used for? What are the weather symbols for precipitation? for cloud cover? for barometric change?

3. *Read.* Using the questions as guides, you read the selection slowly and carefully clustered your facts around your questions.

4. *Summarize.* You took the facts that you had gathered and organized them into clusters around the questions you raised. You summarized the minor questions and then summarized the major questions.

5. *Test.* You examined the questions and facts supporting each question to determine if they supported the generalization proposed by the writer. If the questions and their answers passed your test of reasonable support for the generalization, you cautiously accepted that generalization. If they did not pass the test, you reread the selection for additional questions and answers or sought additional information from other sources, or rejected the writer's generalization.

If your answers and explanations basically agreed with those presented here, you are ready to try PQRST on scientific material of your own choosing. We hope that after you try the strategy, you will share it with your students.

Teaching PQRST

The instructional procedures outlined at the end of Enabling Element 2 for teaching SQ3R are also appropriate for teaching the PQRST Study Strategy. To teach the study strategy, you first need to *select an appropriate reading assignment*. The assignment probably should be no more than six to ten pages in length or require no more than twenty to thirty minutes of reading time. Prepare and duplicate copies of ''The Components of PQRST'' found in this study guide; prepare sufficient quantities so that each student has a copy.

Second, be sure to apply the PQRST Study Strategy to the reading assignment you plan to use for teaching the students how to use the strategy. Apply all of the steps as you did in the preceding practicum activities.

Third, schedule the instruction. Instruction probably should occur over three fifty-minute periods. It is a good idea to provide all three lessons within the same week.

Fourth, provide the instruction by following the guidelines suggested for teaching SQ3R. Be sure your explanations and demonstrations are clearly understood by your students.

Finally, provide opportunities for the students to practice the PQRST Strategy both in their at-school and at-home reading assignments. Remember, at least twenty teacher-directed practice sessions will be necessary before the students become comfortable using the strategy. When this comfortable and automatic level is achieved, the students will likely use the strategy without your reminding or prodding them. To encourage the students to continue using PQRST, always stress and reward improved comprehension and memory that results from applying PQRST.

You now know how to use and teach the PQRST study strategy in physical science textual reading materials. Now teach it to someone to help him or her become a more effective and efficient reader. Read on to learn about a third study strategy useful for studying mathematics.

Enabling Element 4
The SQRQCQ Study Strategy for Mathematics

Specific Objective 4

You will write the associated words for each step in the SQRQCQ Study Strategy, write a paragraph describing each step in the process of using SQRQCQ, and describe a plan for teaching the strategy.

Enabling Activities

*1. Read Study Guide 4 to identify the six key words associated with this strategy and to write a brief description of each step in the strategy.

*2. Locate a number of math reasoning problems that require reading and following the recommended procedures in "Using the SQRQCQ Study Strategy." Read and solve the problems. Did you find the study strategy helpful for solving the problems?

*3. Demonstrate the use of the SQRQCQ Study Strategy to a small group of students. This will provide you with an opportunity to practice teaching the SQRQCQ Study Strategy in a controlled environment.

 4. Have students who successfully use the SQRQCQ Study Strategy explain and demonstrate it to students who are still mastering the study technique.

 5. Select two mathematical reasoning problems that require reading and are of equivalent difficulty. Assign students to read the first problem using their traditional reading approach and to read the second problem using the SQRQCQ Study Strategy. After the students have completed both, discuss the merits of using a study strategy and when it might or might not be appropriate to use one.

 6. Place your explanation of the SQRQCQ Study Strategy, as well as an example of how it is applied to solve a math reasoning problem, on an audio tape. Let students who are having difficulty answering reasoning problems and not consistently using the study strategy listen to the audio tape. Also, use the audio tape to introduce the strategy to new students who arrived after your initial explanation.

Study Guide 4

Students who have no difficulty with straight mathematics computations often have considerable difficulty solving mathematics problems requiring reasoning and reading. This difficulty begins to appear in the intermediate and middle-school grades and continues throughout the schooling years. For the most part, students have difficulty with math reasoning problems because they do not know how to systematically approach and solve these problems. Leo Fay proposed a strategy for helping students solve mathematics problems requiring reasoning and reading. His strategy follows the letter formula SQRQCQ.

The Components of SQRQCQ

There are six basic components or steps in the SQRQCQ Study Strategy. The student follows the steps in the same order as they occur in the formula statement SQRQCQ: *Survey, Question, Read, Question, Compute,* and *Question*. Here is a description of each of the six components:

---

*Indicates core Enabling Elements.

SURVEY. Begin by rapidly reading through the entire mathematics reasoning problem to determine what is to be accomplished. Ask yourself a question or two about the problem; this allows you to determine its intent.

QUESTION. Once you identify the intent of the problem, put the intent into question form. In addition, restate the problem, and attempt to further your understanding by visualizing, drawing, or speaking aloud.

READ. Next, read to find the facts and relationships necessary for solving the problem.

QUESTION. With the facts and relationships clearly in mind, decide upon the processes for reasoning through or solving the problem. To begin a search for these processes, ask yourself the question, "What mathematical processes must be followed to obtain the correct answer to this problem?"

COMPUTE. At this point, you are ready to do the actual computation. But before you can carry out the computation, you must set up the problem or problems on paper.

QUESTION. Finally, look at the answer to the problem and ask, "Does the answer appear correct?" "Was the original question answered?" To answer the first question, check the computation. To answer the second question, examine the answer to verify its relationship to the intent of the problem.

You can see how effective the SQRQCQ Study Strategy is by following its application to the following word problem.

Problem 1

John has been earning $55 a week working for Mr. Tomilson. With the money he earns, John wants to purchase a new motorcycle, which costs $330. How many weeks will John have to work to earn enough money to purchase the motorcycle on a cash sale?

Now follow the application of the SQRQCQ Study Strategy to the solution of this problem.

1. *Survey*. Read the complete problem rapidly but carefully to determine the intent or outcome. From a survey of this problem, we learn that (a) John wishes to purchase a motorcycle with his weekly earnings and (b) he would like to know how long it is going to be before he can obtain the motorcycle.

2. *Question*. Now that the intent or outcome is clear, put it into question form. Remember, a question is used because of all sentence forms, it probably provides the most specific direction to the reader. Questions also serve as an advance organizer for sifting and locating key information. The question raised by this problem is, "At John's present weekly earnings, how long will it take him to purchase the motorcycle he wishes to own?"

3. *Read.* Now it is time to look through the problem to identify the pertinent facts. The pertinent facts are (a) John earns $55 a week, and (b) the motorcycle John wishes to purchase costs $330. Although there are no other substantiated facts that are needed, there are some implied facts. First there is an assumption that there will be no weekly deductions from John's $55 salary. Second, it is assumed that his weekly earnings will continue at $55 a week as long as it takes him to accumulate sufficient money to purchase the motorcycle. Third, it is assumed that the motorcycle cannot be purchased for a discount, nor will it increase in cost during the time John is acquiring his money.

4. *Question.* Now it is time to ask oneself, "What mathematical process must be followed to obtain the correct answer to the question?" If the total cost of the motorcycle ($330) is divided by the weekly earnings ($55), we will obtain the number of weeks John has to work to accomplish his goal.

5. *Compute.* The computation is now carried out, and its result is an answer of six weeks.

$$
\begin{array}{r}
6 \text{ weeks} \\
55\overline{)330} \\
\underline{330}
\end{array}
$$

6. *Question.* At this point one should ask, "Does the answer appear to be correct?" A simple check can be made to determine the correctness of the answer. Realizing that division is verified through multiplication, the participant multiplies six weeks times a weekly earning of $55 and obtains a total earnings for the six weeks of $330.

Practicum Exercise

Now it is your turn to apply the SQRQCQ Study Strategy to a mathematics problem. By applying the strategy to the following problem, you will experience the power of this strategy.

Problem 2

Peter borrowed $95 from his father at an 8-percent-yearly interest rate. He agreed to repay the loan along with the interest at the end of three months. How much must he repay?

Describe the procedure you followed to solve this problem.

Survey.

Question.

Read.

Question.

Compute.

Question.

We are sure you found the letter formula very helpful for organizing your attack on this problem. You probably proceeded in the following manner:

Answers to the Practicum Exercise

Survey. Your quick but careful survey of the problem revealed to you that Peter borrowed money, which he would have to pay back at a specific time along with a certain amount of interest for its use.

Question. The question raised in this problem is, "What is the total principal and interest to be paid at the end of three months on a $95 loan at an 8-percent-yearly interest?"

Read. The facts are: (1) the total amount borrowed was $95, (2) the loan is to be repaid in three months, (3) the 8 percent interest is a yearly interest rate and Peter only has to pay interest on his loan for the three-month period of time he used his father's money. An assumed fact is that all the conditions of the loan will remain constant.

Question. Next you ask yourself, "What mathematical processes must be carried out to solve this problem?" First, what is the yearly interest at 8 percent? This is a multiplication task. Second, what fraction of one year is three months? This is a process of reducing fractions. Third, how much is the interest for three months? This is a division process. Fourth, how much is the total principal and interest for three months? This is an addition process.

Compute. The yearly interest at 8 percent is $7.60. Three months is equal to one quarter of a year. ($\frac{1}{4}$ of $7.60 = $1.90) ($95 + $1.90 = $96.90)

Question. At this step, ask yourself "Is the answer reasonable?" Next, check each step of your answer to see if it is correct. Your verification revealed that the total principal plus interest payment of $96.90 is correct.

We hope your answers and explanations agreed with those presented here. Now read on to learn how to use a modification of the teaching steps used for teaching SQ3R and PQRST to teach SQRQCQ.

Teaching SQRQCQ

Now it is time to learn how to teach SQRQCQ to those students who are having difficulty solving mathematics reasoning problems that require reading. An adaptation of the outline following for teaching SQ3R and PQRST can be used for teaching the SQRQCQ Study Strategy. The instructional procedures are divided into five steps, each of which is explained in detail here.

Select Problems.
1. Select a mathematics reasoning problem that requires reading and is typical of those with which your students are having difficulty. The best way to demonstrate to your students the value of the SQRQCQ Study Strategy is to show them how it makes the task of solving problems easier.
2. Prepare and duplicate copies of "The Components of SQRQCQ." You will need a copy for each of your students.

Apply SQRQCQ. Apply the study strategy to the reading problems with the same care you expect from your students. Be sure to do the following:
1. *Survey* the problem to determine what is to be accomplished.
2. Ask yourself a *question* that captures the intent of the problem.
3. *Read* to find the facts and relationships necessary for solving the problem.
4. Ask yourself a *question* regarding the mathematical processes necessary for solving the problem.
5. *Compute* as necessary.
6. *Question* the accuracy of your answer and its appropriateness for your original question.

Schedule Instruction. Schedule three fifty-minute periods for teaching the study strategy to your students. Your students will not master the application of the strategy after a single lesson, thus you will need to prepare additional lessons with other problems to help them develop this mastery.

Provide Instruction.

1. During the first fifty-minute period
   a. Begin by explaining to your students that you are going to teach them how to use the SQRQCQ Study Strategy, which is designed for studying mathematics reasoning problems. Tell them the SQRQCQ Study Strategy will provide them with a structure for effectively and efficiently answering mathematics reasoning problems.
   b. Distribute a copy of ''The Components of SQRQCQ'' to each student. Discuss each component so that your students understand its function.
   c. Demonstrate how SQRQCQ is used to solve a mathematics reasoning problem. Answer any questions your students may have.
   d. Now have your students work independently through the same problem, applying the SQRQCQ Study Strategy as they read to solve the reasoning problem.
   e. Have the students write a statement describing how they use each of the steps in the SQRQCQ Strategy to solve the reasoning problem.
   f. Hold a group discussion in which SQRQCQ is compared with prior reading strategies. Bring out the advantages of this study strategy.

2. During the second fifty-minute period
   a. Review the SQRQCQ components.
   b. Demonstrate the application of SQRQCQ with another mathematics reasoning problem.
   c. Assign a different mathematics reasoning problem to be read by your students using the SQRQCQ Study Strategy.
   d. When the assignment is completed, call upon the students to explain how they applied the various steps in the strategy. Discuss with the total group their feelings about how they have grown in effectiveness and efficiency by using SQRQCQ.

3. During the third fifty-minute period
   a. Again, discuss the components of SQRQCQ.
   b. Assign a number of reasoning problems to different individuals in the group. Tell the students to solve the problems using the SQRQCQ Study Strategy.
   c. As the students work, circulate among them to answer any questions they may have and to ensure that they are applying the steps in the strategy as you have taught them.
   d. When the assignment is completed, allow the students to share with each other how they applied the study strategy to solve the various problems you assigned.

Practice. Continue to provide students with opportunities to practice using SQRQCQ under your supervision. As with the previous study strategies we introduced, it will take at least twenty teacher-directed practice sessions before the students reach the automatic performance level with the SQRQCQ Strategy. You will know that they have reached the automatic performance level when they begin to apply the strategy without your reminder. Always stress and reward the improved mathematics reasoning that results from using SQRQCQ.

Now it is your turn to identify a mathematics reasoning problem that requires reading and to prepare a lesson for teaching SQRQCQ to a group of students. Having done this, you will have a good feeling about the new study strategy you have learned to teach. If you now understand and can apply SQ3R, PQRST, and SQRQCQ, you are ready for the Posttest. If you cannot, you should reexamine the appropriate Enabling Elements or talk with your instructor.

Some Cautions

A few words of caution are necessary before we leave this discussion of study strategies. SQ3R, PQRST, and SQRQCQ Study Strategies are all effective study tools for students to use. However, to be successful students must (1) be familiar with the vocabulary, (2) be able to comprehend ideas, and (3) be able to pronounce the words. For these strategies to be successful, the material must be generally suitable for the students. These strategies are not to be used to force students through material that is basically unsuitable for them. If textual materials are unsuitable, the only thing the teacher can do is to select new materials or to rewrite the old. The first is the better solution.

Of course, to apply PQRST, a student must also be familiar with the scientific method as applied to the various areas of the physical sciences. Similarly, to be successful in using SQRQCQ, the student must have mastered the basic mathematical operations.

Posttest

Directions: Read each of the following statements and complete each Posttest item as directed.

1. Study skills are techniques students use when they study. List the five major study skills in your content area. Then identify the components of a lesson plan designed to guide you as you teach study skills.

2. The SQ3R Study Strategy was introduced by Francis Robinson more than thirty years ago. We propose that this strategy be taught to students for studying reading in social science and humanities materials. Write the key words associated with each letter in the SQ3R formula statement. Also write a brief description of each step in the process of using SQ3R.

3. PQRST was introduced by George Spache almost twenty years ago. We propose this strategy be taught to students for studying reading in the physical sciences. Write the key words associated with each letter in the PQRST formula statement. Then write a brief description of how each step is to be followed.

4. SQRQCQ was proposed by Leo Fay more than fifteen years ago. This strategy is helpful for solving mathematical reasoning problems that require reading. Write the key words associated with each letter in the SQRQCQ formula statement. Then write a brief description of each step in the process of using SQRQCQ.

5. Identify and briefly describe the steps in the instructional procedure for teaching any one of the three study strategies.

Posttest Answers

1. Check your list of study skills against what you wrote for the Practicum Exercise in Study Guide 2. The four lesson plan components are: *objective, instruction, evaluation,* and *extension activities.*

2. The key words associated with the SQ3R formula statement are:
   Survey
   Question
   Read
   Recite
   Review

   The following are the recommended procedures for applying SQ3R to reading assignments:

   Survey.   Begin by making a quick survey of the reading assignment to obtain a general idea of the selection. Refer to side headings and/or topic sentences as appropriate.

   Question. Turn each heading into a question. If headings are not available, key topics should be turned into questions.

   Read.   Read to answer each question. Questions are answered in the order in which they occur.

   Recite.   Recite the answer to the question with the eyes averted from the passage. It is often beneficial to write key phrases in outline form.

   Review.   Review your questions and answers immediately following the reading assignment. Periodic reviews are advised to enhance retention.

3. The key words associated with the PQRST formula statement are:
   Preview
   Question
   Read
   Summarize
   Test

   The following are the recommended procedures for applying PQRST to reading assignments:

Preview.   Skim the selection to obtain an overall impression and to identify the generalization or theory presented by the writer.

Question.   Form questions to be used as purposes for reading.

Read.   Using the questions as guides, read the selection.

Summarize.   Organize information and summarize, preferably in written form.

Test.   Test the generalization or theory against the supporting information.

4. The key words associated with the SQRQCQ formula statement are:

   Survey
   Question
   Read
   Question
   Compute
   Question

The following are the recommended procedures for applying SQRQCQ to math problems requiring reading:

Survey.   Read rapidly to determine intent of the problem.

Question.   Determine what question the problem is asking or what problem needs to be solved.

Read.   Read for facts necessary to answer the question to solve the problem.

Question.   Decide upon the process to be used.

Compute.   Do computation.

Question.   Ask yourself, "Does the answer appear correct?" Check the answer against the problem and facts.

The five steps in the instructional procedure for teaching any one of the three strategies are:

a. *Select* materials or math problems.

b. *Apply* the strategy to the materials or problem.

c. *Schedule* instruction for appropriate number of periods or length of time so that the information can be thoroughly and comfortably taught.

d. *Provide instruction* following the suggestions provided.

e. *Hold practice sessions* following instruction to help students become automatic in the application of the newly acquired study strategy.

Selected Bibliography

Burmeister, L. E. *Reading Strategies for Secondary School Teachers*. Reading, Massachusetts: Addison-Wesley, 1978.

Fay, L. "Reading Study Skills: Math and Science." In *Reading and Inquiry*, edited by J. A. Figurel. Newark, Delaware: International Reading Association, 1965.

Harris, A. J. "Research on Some Aspects of Comprehension: Rate, Flexibility, and Study Skills." *Journal of Reading* 12, no. 3 (1968): 205–10, 258–60.

Herber, H. L., ed. "Developing Study Skills in Secondary School." *Perspectives in Reading*, vol. 2. Newark, Delaware: International Reading Association, 1965.

Lamberg, W. J. and Lamb, C. E. *Reading Instruction in the Content Areas*. Chicago, Illinois: Rand McNally, 1980.

Pyrczak, F. "Knowledge of Abbreviations Used in Classified Advertisements on Employment Opportunities." *Journal of Reading* 21, no. 6 (1978): 493–97.

Riley, J. D. and Pachtman, A. B. "Reading Mathematical Word Problems: Telling Them What to Do Is Not Telling Them How to Do It." *Journal of Reading* 21, no. 6 (1978): 531–33.

Robinson, F. P. "Study Skills for Superior Students in Secondary School." In *Improving Reading in Middle and Secondary Schools*, 2d ed., edited by L. E. Hafner. New York: Macmillan, 1974.

Robinson, H. A. *Teaching Reading and Study Strategies: The Content Areas*. Boston: Allyn and Bacon, 1975.

————, and Thomas, E. L., eds. *Fusing Reading Skills and Content*. Newark, Delaware: International Reading Association, 1969.

Roe, B. D., Stoodt, B. D., and Burns, P. C. *Reading Instruction in the Secondary School*. rev. ed. Chicago: Rand McNally, 1978.

Singer, H. and Donlan, D. *Reading and Learning from Text*. Boston: Little, Brown and Company, 1980.

Smith, C. B., Smith, S. L. and Mikulecky, L. *Teaching Reading and Subject Matter in the Secondary School*. New York: Holt, Rinehart and Winston, 1978.

Smith, C. F. "Read a Book in an Hour: Variations to Develop Composition and Comprehension Skills." *Journal of Reading* 23, no. 1 (1979) 25–29.

Spache, G. D. *Toward Better Reading*. Champaign, Illinois: Garrard, 1963.

Tadlock, D. F. "SQ3R—Why it Works, Based on an Information Processing Theory of Reading." *Journal of Reading* 22, no. 2 (1978) 110–12.

Viox, R. G. "Evaluating Reading and Study Skills in Secondary Classroom." *Reading Aids Series*. Newark, Delaware: International Reading Association, 1968.

MODULE **8**

Helping Students
Pronounce
Multisyllable Words

Contents

Prospectus
  Rationale
  Objectives
  Resources and Time Required
Pretest
Branching Program Alternatives for Pretest Responses
Enabling Element 1: *A Word-Pronunciation Strategy*
Enabling Element 2: *Assessing Word Pronunciation*
Enabling Element 3: *Teaching Word-Pronunciation Skills*
Posttest
  Posttest Answers
Selected Bibliography

Prospectus

Rationale

One characteristic of subject area textual material is its unique vocabulary. Generally speaking, this vocabulary consists of hundreds if not thousands of multisyllable words, such as *dispensation, tambourine,* and *horticulture.* Your students must learn to pronounce these words as well as acquire their meanings. Module 5 explained how to develop word meanings for the technical words in your subject area. This module addresses itself only to the pronunciation of those technical words.

Most middle-school and secondary-school students will have acquired the necessary word-pronunciation skills to pronounce the many new multisyllable words. However, there is very likely to be a group of students who have not acquired these abilities. These students will rely upon you to provide them with the necessary word-pronunciation strategy to read the textual material in your subject area.

It is not the purpose of this module to acquaint you with the word-pronunciation skills taught in the primary grades. If you have students who need the primary-grade reading skills, Module 10 provides suggestions for helping these problem readers. For the most part, this latter group of students needs the help of trained reading specialists.

The purpose of this module is to provide subject area teachers with a brief but useful strategy for helping students pronounce multisyllable words. You will teach this strategy to students who for various reasons did not acquire this strategy in the upper-elementary grades. Soon you will be able to assign them reading materials that would have been difficult before they possessed this strategy.

Objectives

Terminal Objective

You will determine the word-pronunciation strategies used by students and help them use a strategy for pronouncing multisyllable words.

Specific Objectives

1. You will prepare a written list of steps that make up the word-pronunciation strategy presented in this module.
2. You will prepare and use the Quick Test of Word Pronunciation, Word-Pronunciation Strategy Test, and Class Record Form.
3. You will list each of the major organizational steps and their purpose in lesson plans designed to teach word pronunciation skills and strategy.

Resources and Time Required

Most of the materials required for completing the starred core Enabling Activities are provided. You will need to supply eleven three-by-five inch, white index cards, a single sheet of two-by-three foot newsprint, and a few sheets of white paper. The estimated time to complete the starred core Enabling Activities is three to five hours.

Pretest

Directions: For each question, determine the word that indicates your belief regarding your competency. If you are in doubt, choose NO.

1. During reading assignments, many students are confronted with mul-   YES   NO
   tisyllable words they cannot pronounce even though these words are
   often in their listening vocabulary. Can you list the steps in a word-
   pronunciation strategy that can be taught to students to assist them in
   pronouncing subject area words they have heard but not seen?
2. It is not always easy to identify students who are having difficulty   YES   NO
   pronouncing multisyllable words. Do you know how to construct,
   administer, record, and use the results of tests for assessing word-
   pronunciation skills and strategies?

3. To enable students with word-pronunciation difficulties to achieve   YES   NO
optimally in your subject area, you may need to teach them certain
word-pronunciation skills and a word-pronunciation strategy. Can you
list each major organizational step and its purpose in lesson plans
designed to teach the word-pronunciation skills and strategies?

Branching Program Alternatives for Pretest Responses

1. Some of your students will be confronted in your subject area textual material with
multisyllable words they cannot pronounce. If you can list the steps in a word-
pronunciation strategy that can be taught to these students, you are ready for Enabling
Element 2. If you cannot, Enabling Element 1 presents a word-pronunciation strategy
you will find valuable.

2. Since all of your students will not need to be taught word-pronunciation skills or
word-pronunciation strategy, you will need to identify those who need this instruction. If you know how to construct, administer, record, and use the results of tests for
assessing these skills and strategy, you are ready for Enabling Element 3. If you do
not, Enabling Element 2 will help you achieve the objective.

3. Once you have identified students who need to acquire word-pronunciation skills and
strategy, you will need to plan for their instruction. Can you list each major
organizational step and its purpose in lesson plans designed to teach a skill and
strategy? If you can, you are ready for the Posttest. If not, Enabling Element 3 will
provide you with this information.

Enabling Element 1
A Word-Pronunciation Strategy

Specific Objective 1

You will prepare a written list of steps that make up the word-pronunciation strategy
presented in this module.

Enabling Activities

*1. Read Study Guide 1, and prepare a list of the seven steps in the strategy.

*2. Obtain a sheet of two-by-three foot newsprint or similar material, and record on it the word-pronunciation strategy. Display the strategy in a permanent location in your classroom. As students have difficulty pronouncing words, refer them to the strategy. Your students will find your chart a valuable aid to word pronunciation. Look at the ''Strategy Chart'' provided at the end of this Study Guide for suggestions.

3. Students who struggle in their attempts to pronounce longer words may benefit from a discussion and examination of the more common prefixes and suffixes. Lists of common prefixes and suffixes are provided and may be used for this purpose.

4. You may wish to do a content analysis of your subject area material to identify the many prefixes and suffixes used in your subject area. A form, entitled Subject Area Inventory, is provided at the end of this Study Guide to assist you with this task. Also, Appendix C of Burmeister's book (1978, pp. 364–88) includes an extensive list of prefixes and suffixes used in specific content fields. Exposure to the isolated prefixes and suffixes will help your students identify them in unrecognized words.

5. Provide small-group practice sessions for pronouncing multisyllable words from textual material. Spending one or two minutes daily in such groups will increase students' pronunciation effectiveness and efficiency.

6. Duplicate the word-pronunciation strategy on book markers and distribute them to every student in your class. Give the extras to the librarian or other teachers.

7. Use the word-pronunciation strategy to practice pronouncing these words: *temperature, legislature, dramatic, stationary exercise, inclination, bilingual, urbanize.*

Study Guide 1

By the end of the sixth grade, some students will not have acquired all the necessary skills to identify some of the longer, technical words found in the various content areas. If you wish to assign your content area reading material to this latter group of students, it will be necessary for you to provide them with some word-pronunciation instruction. If you provide this instruction, you will find that your students will complete more reading assignments.

Characteristics of Problem Words

There are undoubtedly some students in your classes who struggle with their reading assignments because they cannot pronounce all the words. If you analyze the words the students have difficulty pronouncing, you will discover the following:

---

*Indicates core Enabling Activities.

1. Many of the words begin with a prefix and/or end with a suffix.

2. Many of the words contain stems that are composed of two or more syllables. A stem is a base word or unit to which a prefix and/or suffix is affixed such as *pay* in re*pay*ment.

3. If you observe students who have difficulty pronouncing words, you will notice that they approach unrecognized words in a haphazard way rather than with a definite strategy.

4. Furthermore, your observation of these struggling word pronouncers will reveal that many of the students have the elementary phonics skills to pronounce the common one- and two-syllable words.

The Word-Pronunciation Strategy

Using what we know about the kinds of difficulties struggling word pronouncers have, we can develop a strategy that will help many of them pronounce the longer and more complex words. The components of such a strategy follow and are in the appropriate order. Students should use them when attempting to pronounce words which may at first appear unfamiliar.

Word-Pronunciation Strategy

1. Look for a prefix.
2. Look for a suffix.
3. Locate the stem.
4. Divide the stem into syllables.
5. Try the word in context.
6. Look in the glossary or dictionary.
7. Ask someone how to pronounce the word.

Since this word-pronunciation strategy may be new to you, a comment or two about each component seems warranted.

Prefixes are language units that occur before a stem and change its meaning. Examples are *un* in *uncertain*, and *pre* in *preview*. Many of the longer words that perplex struggling readers contain prefixes. Since prefixes are easy to spot, occur frequently in words that present pronunciation problems, and have a highly reliable pronunciation, it seems that teaching prefixes is the likely place to begin a strategy.

Suffixes are also language units, but they occur after the stem to change the function of a word. Examples are *able* in *portable*, *ly* in *miserly*, and *tion* in *education*. Many of the longer and more perplexing words also contain suffixes. Since suffixes are also easy to spot, occur frequently, and have highly reliable pronunciations, they are placed second in the strategy.

What remains when the prefix and suffix have been removed from a word is the *stem*. The stem is the next component of the word that must be identified. It is a base word to which a prefix and/or suffix may be added; it is the underlying language unit.

Some examples are *dance* in *dancer*, *fair* in *unfairly*, and *skill* in *unskillful*. However, a stem may not always be recognized as a word. Some examples of this are *trac* in *subtraction* and *cep* in *perception*.

Once the stem has been isolated, the reader must determine whether the stem has more than one syllable. If the stem is only a single syllable, chances are the student can pronounce the syllable so this step can be skipped. Stems containing more than one syllable have more than one vowel, which are usually separated by one or more consonants. Some examples are mis-*cal-cu-late*, re-*fur-bish*, and uni-*lat-er-al*. When the stem is two or more syllables, it is necessary to divide it into separate syllables before pronouncing it . Guiding rules that are helpful for dividing stems follow:

1. Stems following the consonant-vowel-consonant / consonant-vowel-consonant (CVC/CVC) pattern are usually divided between the double consonants. Some examples are *but/ton*, *can/cel*, and *nor/mal*. This rule works very well as long as the middle two consonants are not consonant clusters (*ch, ph, th, bl, st, cr.*) Such natural clusters are usually not divided.

2. Stems following the consonant-vowel/consonant-vowel (CV/CV) pattern are usually divided after the first vowel. Some examples are *la/bor*, *fla/grant*, and *fi/nite*. Once the stem has been divided into syllables, the student can pronounce each syllable using those reading skills acquired in the earlier grades.

3. Sometimes stems that follow the consonant-vowel/consonant-vowel (CV/CV) pattern are not divided after the first vowel but rather after the consonant that follows the vowel. Some examples are *cab/in*, *pun/ish*, *trag/ic*, *plan/et*, and *man/age*. When CV/CV does not work, the students should be encouraged to try CVC/V.

When the prefix, suffix, and stem have been identified and pronounced, the word should be returned to the sentence and read. *Sentence sense*, or *context clues*, can be the most useful and reliable word-pronunciation clues as long as the word is in the student's listening vocabulary.

If the steps discussed thus far in the word-pronunciation strategy do not help a student pronounce a word, the student should be directed to use a subject area textbook glossary or a dictionary to obtain the pronunciation. If this fails, he or she should be directed to ask someone for the correct pronunciation of the word.

Now you have the components of the word-pronunciation strategy. If you have students in your classes who are struggling with this problem, now you know what to teach them. A number of instructional aids are provided here to assist you as you teach this strategy. They are:

1. *The Strategy Chart*. This is a useful, abbreviated list of key components of the word-pronunciation strategy. If you wish, you may duplicate the strategy and distribute it to students or use it to construct a larger chart for display on a bulletin board.

Key Terms to Remember
1. Prefix
2. Suffix

    3. Stem
    4. Syllables
       a. CVC/CVC
       b. CV/CV or CVC/V
    5. Context
    6. Glossary or Dictionary
    7. Ask

2. *List of Most Common Prefixes*. This is a helpful list you can bring to the attention of your students to ensure that none of these prefixes is causing word-pronunciation difficulties (Stauffer, 1942).

ab	dis
ad	en
be	ex
com	in
de	pre
pro	sub
re	un

3. *List of Most Common Suffixes*. This list can also be introduced to students to ensure that none are causing word-pronunciation difficulties. Pronunciation difficulties occur more often with suffixes than with prefixes (Thorndike, 1941).

ness	ant	ing	ed (d)
er	ment	ful	ly
tion	est	able	ed (ed)
ily	al	ed (t)	ent
y	ive	ance	ous

4. *Subject Area Inventory*. This is a useful form for examining subject area materials to inventory prefixes and suffixes. Once identified, these prefixes and suffixes can be used to familiarize students with additional causes of word-pronunciation difficulties.

Subject Area Inventory

Source:			*Source:*	
Prefixes	Suffixes		Prefixes	Suffixes

Keep in mind that the technical words you want your students to pronounce in their textual materials must be in their listening vocabulary before they can be successfully pronounced using the word attack strategy. This means you must first introduce the words orally in sentences. Second, you should write these words on the chalkboard for your students to see and study. Third, have your students say the words aloud to hear how the words sound when they say them. Finally, for those words that are likely to be most troublesome, have the students write the words for further reinforcement of your instruction.

Practicum Exercise

Now look through some textual materials in your content area to identify 20 words that are potentially difficult words for your students to pronounce. Write those words here. Then use the seven-step word-pronunciation strategy to see how it would help your students pronounce words such as these. To use the context-clues step in the strategy, you will need to read the sentences in which the words were used.

Answers to the Practicum Exercise

The answers will vary with the words you chose, so check them over with a colleague and as necessary with your instructor.

If you know the steps in the word-pronunciation strategy, you are ready for Enabling Element 2. Enabling Element 2 will help you identify those students who need to further develop their strategy. If not, return through the elements as necessary or talk with your instructor.

Enabling Element 2
Assessing Word Pronunciation

Specific Objective 2

You will prepare and use the Quick Test of Word Pronunciation, Word-Pronunciation Strategy Test, and Class Record Form.

Enabling Activities

*1. Read Study Guide 2. Then prepare the Quick Test of Word Pronunciation, Form A; Word-Pronunciation Strategy Test; and Class Record Form.

*2. Prepare the Quick Test of Word Pronunciation, Form B. Follow the same guidelines as for preparing Form A.

*3. Administer the Quick Test of Word Pronunciation and the Word-Pronunciation Strategy Test to two students from your subject area. Appropriately fill out the Class Record Form for these two students.

4. After providing your students with some instruction following the suggestions in Enabling Element 3, administer Form B of the Quick Test of Word Pronunciation to see how they have grown in word pronunciation achievement. Similarly, readminister the Word-Pronunciation Strategy Test to see how they have grown in their awareness of the strategy.

5. Construct and use tests of word pronunciation with different prefixes, suffixes, and syllabication generalizations.

6. You may discover that a number of your students lack the basic word-pronunciation skills taught in the primary grades. You may want to refer to *Phonics in Proper Perspective* by Arthur Heilman to obtain suggestions for teaching these skills. (This reference is listed in the Selected Bibliography.)

Study Guide 2

One of the characteristics of subject area material is the introduction of specialized vocabulary—words used to label the concepts in each subject area. Specialized vocabulary is one of the components that differentiate one subject area from another.

Generally, specialized vocabularies consist of multisyllable words formed through the use of prefixes, suffixes, and compound stems. Prefixes are useful for altering the meaning of words, suffixes for changing the function of words, and compound stems for forming new words.

Often, students learn to pronounce new subject area words by looking at the words while listening to their teachers pronounce them. If there are only a few new words to learn, it is not difficult for a student to memorize these words. However, when there are numerous new words to learn, memorization is an inappropriate technique for most students. Students then must have another method or strategy to help them pronounce words.

Many students during their elementary-school years acquire adequate methods or strategies for pronouncing unfamiliar words. These students quite likely will not need additional instruction. Those students who have not acquired a strategy will need your assistance to acquire a workable word-pronunciation strategy. If you will take the time to identify these students and teach them the strategy presented in this module, your students will be better able to accomplish your course objectives.

*Indicates core Enabling Activities.

This Study Guide will familiarize you with simple tests you can use to identify students who need to be taught word-pronunciation skills and strategy. Enabling Element 3 contains detailed lesson plans for teaching word-pronunciation skills and strategy.

Preparing Tests and Record-Keeping Materials

1. *Quick Test of Word Pronunciation, Form A*

   Print or type each of the following nonsense words on the unlined side of a three-by-five inch, white index card. Print or type the "dictionary" respelling on the back of each card.

Front of Card	*Back of Card*
pronabment	pro/năb/ment
abstraimance	ab/strāĭm/ance
comteationly	com/tēă/tion/ly
subsumptarant	sub/sŭmp/tär/ant
demomenence	de/mō/měn/ence or de/mŏm/ĕn/ence

   Form B of the *Quick Test of Word Pronunciation* is provided at the end of this Study Guide. You may want to use this form for students who were absent or to evaluate achievement after you provide instruction.

2. *Word-Pronunciation Strategy Test*

   Take one three-by-five, white index card and print or type the following question on one side.

   > When you come to a word in a sentence that you do not immediately recognize, how do you go about pronouncing that word? (What do you do first, second, third, etc., may be asked if further elaboration is necessary.)

3. *Class Record Form*

   Prepare a Class Record Form such as figure 7 for recording the word-pronunciation difficulties of your students. You will need one record form for each class.

Figure 7
Quick Test of Word Pronunciation
Class Record Form

Names of Students	Skills Unknown						Strategy Not Known
	Prefix	Suffix	Single Syllable Stems	Multiple CVC/CVC Stems	Multiple CV/CV CVC/V Stems	Context Clues	

**Test Administration, Interpretation,
and Record Keeping**

1. On one of the Class Record forms you prepared, record the name of every student in the class you have decided to test.

2. Arrange your class schedule to provide approximately three minutes for testing each student.

3. Each student must be tested separately. You will need to test the students where other students cannot hear what is said. It is not necessary to be out of the sight of other students.

4. When the student arrives at the testing center, explain that you would like to determine whether he or she has the necessary word-pronunciation skills and a strategy for pronouncing the longer words in your textual material.

5. Begin by exposing, one at a time, the cards containing the multisyllable nonsense words. Explain that these are nonsense words and you would like the student to pronounce them as if they were real words.

6. As the student pronounces each nonsense word, look for the following difficulties. As a difficulty is identified, place a check after the student's name under the appropriate category on the Class Record Form. Do this for all five nonsense words.

Nonsense Word	Sources of Difficulty
pronabment	pro—prefix
	nab—stem
	ment—stem
abstraimance	ab—prefix
	straim—stem
	ance—suffix
comteationly	com—prefix
	tea—stem
	tion—suffix
	ly—suffix
subsumptarant	sub—prefix
	sumptar—stem (CVC/CVC)
	ant—suffix
demomenence	de—prefix
	momen—stem (CV/CV or CVC/V)
	ence—suffix

What follows are the nonsense words as pronounced by a student. Look at the errors, and then see how they are classified in the following Class Record Form.

Nonsense Word	Pronounced by Student	Errors
pronabment	pro/nab/ent	1 suffix
abstraimance	ab/strum/ent	1 stem; 1 suffix
comteationly	com/tea/tal/ty	2 suffixes
subsumptarant	sub/sumpt/ent	1 CVC/CVC; 1 suffix
demomenence	de/mome/nence	1 CV/CV; 1 suffix

The errors are recorded on the Class Record Form in figure 8.

Figure 8

Quick Test of Word Pronunciation
Class Record Form

Names of Students	Skills Unknown						Strategy Not Known
	Prefix	Suffix	Single Syllable Stems	Multiple CVC/CVC Stems	Multiple CV/CV CVC/V Stems	Context Clues	
Jack		✓✓✓ ✓✓✓	✓	✓	✓		✓

7. To determine whether students are using context clues to pronounce words, you might have to observe them as they read as well as ask them if they use the clues. Students who use context clues should also be able to demonstrate how they use them.

8. Next, take the single three-by-five card containing the Word-Pronunciation Strategy Test and place it in front of the student. Ask the student to read aloud and answer the question on this card. It is acceptable to read the question to the student. (It may be necessary to query the student to obtain his or her most complete answer.) Compare the student's answer with the strategy presented in this module:

   a. Look for a prefix.
   b. Look for a suffix.
   c. Locate the stem.
   d. Divide the stem into syllables.
   e. Try the word in context.
   f. Look in the glossary or dictionary.
   g. Ask someone who knows.

   It is not necessary for the student's answer to contain precisely the same words or the same number of steps or have the steps in the same order. There are many acceptable ways of stating this strategy, and you will have to use your own best professional judgment to determine whether the expressed strategy is adequate. You will become better at this as you practice. If the student should omit any one of the steps, place a check (√) after the student's name under the column Strategy Not Known. For example, we asked Jack, "When you come to a word in a sentence that you do not immediately recognize, how do you go about pronouncing that word?" He responded, "Look for a beginning and ending that I know and divide the word into syllables." When Jack was asked to tell more about how he pronounced words, he said "That's all I know." Jack appeared to be aware of prefixes, suffixes, and syllabication. Since he did not demonstrate an awareness of context clues, glossary or dictionary, and his responsibility to ask for the pronunciation of an unknown word, a (√) should be placed under Strategy Not Known.

Now it is time for you to identify word-pronunciation skill and strategy errors and to classify them appropriately in the Class Record Form (see figure 9).

Figure 9
Quick Test of Word Pronunciation
Class Record Form

Names of Students	Skills Unknown						Strategy Not Known
	Prefix	Suffix	Single Syllable Stems	Multiple CVC/CVC Stems	Multiple CV/CV CVC/V Stems	Context Clues	
Jack		√√√ √√√	√	√	√		√
Mary							

Practicum Exercise

Mary pronounced the following words as indicated. Her strategy is also presented. Classify her errors in the Class Record Form provided in figure 9.

Nonsense Word	Pronounced by Student	Summary of Errors
pronabment	pro/na/bent	_____
abstraimance	ab/strum/any	_____
comteationly	com/toe/ton/ty	_____
subsumptarant	sub/sumt/ance	_____
demomenence	de/mon/en/ed	_____

Mary said her strategy is "I look for a beginning that I know and guess."

Mary did not appear to use context clues to pronounce unrecognized words. When asked, she agreed with the observation.

Answers to the Practicum Exercise

An examination of Mary's errors revealed the following. Checks (√) should appear in the appropriate columns on the Class Record.

Nonsense Word	Pronounced by Student	Summary of Errors
pronabment	pro/na/bant	1 stem; 1 suffix
abstaimance	ab/staim/any	1 stem; 1 suffix
comteationly	com/tea/ton/ty	2 suffixes
subsumptarant	sub/sumt/ance	1 CVC/CVC; 1 suffix
demomenence	de/mon/en/ed	1 CV/CV; 1 suffix; 1 context clues

Mary's strategy is inadequate. Her strategy is limited to looking for prefixes and guessing. A check (√) should be placed in the Class Record Form (see figure 10) under Strategy Not Known.

Figure 10
Quick Test of Word Pronunciation
Class Record Form

Names of Students	Skills Unknown						Strategy Not Known
	Prefix	Suffix	Single Syllable Stems	Multiple CVC/CVC Stems	Multiple CV/CV CVC/V Stems	Context Clues	
Jack		√√√ √√√	√	√	√		√
Mary		√√√√ √√	√√	√	√	√	√

Retesting

From time to time you will want to retest your students to determine if they have improved in word-pronunciation skills and strategy. Since the students may be familiar with the nonsense words used for Quick Test of Word Pronunciation, Form A, we have provided you with an equivalent test to use for retesting. Quick Test of Word Pronunciation, Form B, should be prepared in the same manner and using the same format as Form A. It is not necessary to prepare another Word-Pronunciation Test or Class Record Form.

1. *Quick Test of Word Pronunciation, Form B*
   Print or type each of the following nonsense words on the unlined side of a

three-by-five, white index card. Print or type the ''dictionary'' respelling on the back of each card.

Front of Card	Back of Card
premeply	pre/mĕp/ly
exscreemest	ex/scrē¢m/est
subpeedtionous	sub/pē¢d/tion/ous
unpetsuming	un/pĕt/sum/ing
besimenable	be/sī/mĕn/able or be/sĭm/ĕn/able

Nonsense Word	Sources of Difficulty
premeply	pre—prefix
	mep—stem
	ly—suffix
exscreemest	ex—prefix
	screem—stem
	est—suffix
subpeedtionous	sub—prefix
	peed—stem
	tion—suffix
	ous—suffix
unpetsuming	un—prefix
	petsum—stem (CVC/CVC)
	ing—suffix
besimenable	be—prefix
	simen—stem (CV/CV or CVC/V)
	able—suffix

2. *Word-Pronunciation Strategy Test*

   Use the three-by-five, white index cards that you prepared for this test to go along with Form A. Since this test is basically a question that the student answers, it can be used with both Form A and Form B.

3. *Class Record Form*

   Use the same Class Record Form you used for testing with Form A to record the results obtained on Form B. In this way, you can rapidly identify the growth areas for each student tested.

   If you have prepared the Quick Test of Word Pronunciation, Forms A and B, Word Pronunciation Strategy Test, and Class Record Form and have classified the errors correctly in the Practicum Exercises, you are ready for Enabling Element 3. Enabling Element 3 will provide you with directions and lesson plans for teaching word-pronunciation skills and strategy. If you have had difficulty with any of the Enabling Elements, reexamine them or see your instructor.

Enabling Element 3
Teaching Word-Pronunciation Skills

Specific Objective 3

You will list each of the major organizational steps and its purpose in lesson plans designed to teach word-pronunciation skills and strategy.

Enabling Activities

*1. Read Study Guide 3 to learn the major organizational steps in seven lesson plans designed to develop a strategy for pronouncing multisyllable words.

*2. Teach the seven plans to one or two students needing this instruction.

*3. Look through your textual material and locate prefixes and suffixes not included in the lesson plans contained in this Study Guide. Modify the plans to include these prefixes and suffixes.

4. If you have an aide or school volunteer, familiarize him or her with the instructional procedure in this Enabling Element. Have the aide teach students who need to acquire the word-pronunciation strategy.

5. You may want to use some of your better students as tutors. Peer teaching has been found to be very effective in many situations.

Study Guide 3

The Word-Pronunciation Strategy

The lessons in this Study Guide are designed to develop a precise word pronunciation strategy. The strategy is designed to be applied to longer, multisyllable words that often perplex subject area students. These are words in students' listening vocabularies but *not* in their reading vocabularies. If a word is missing from students' listening vocabularies, the problem is word meaning, not word pronunciation. If this is the case, refer to Module 5, "Teaching Word Meanings," for ideas on developing word meaning. If the problem is word pronunciation, the lesson plans in this Study Guide will help you assist selected students in improving word pronunciation.

The lesson plans are designed to develop an understanding of specific word-pronunciation skills and the steps in a word-pronunciation strategy. When all the lessons

---

*Indicates core Enabling Activities.

have been presented to students, the following skills and strategy will have been developed:

Word-Pronunciation Strategy

1. Look for prefix.
2. Look for suffix.
3. Locate the stem.
4. Divide the stem into syllables.
5. Try it in context.
6. Refer to glossary or dictionary.
7. Ask someone.

There are seven lessons in the instructional set. Each lesson requires between twenty and thirty minutes to teach. The time varies according to the amount of teacher direction and discussion provided. The lessons should be taught in the same sequence in which they are presented in this instructional set. Each lesson contains complete directions for instruction.

There are three major organizational steps in each lesson plan. *First* is the *Purpose* step. You can use the information provided in the purpose section to substantiate the need or purpose for this skill. *Second* is the *Instruction* step. This contains directions and information for developing word-pronunciation skills and strategy. *Third* is the *Generalization* step. At this step the student is led to conclude that the word-pronunciation skill he or she has just acquired is one of a number of skills that form the strategy. The student will soon learn that with each succeeding lesson the generalization gets longer until it consists of all seven steps in the strategy.

Choosing Your Lessons

Not every student will need to be taught every lesson in this set. For example, the Class Record in Study Guide 2 reveals that Mary needs instruction in identifying suffixes, identifying single syllables, and with all syllabication generalizations. She also needs to be familiarized with the steps in the word-pronunciation strategy. Mary does appear to recognize prefixes and use context clues, so she does not need instruction in these word-pronunciation skills. Since Mary does not know the word-pronunciation strategy, her first instructional lesson should be an overview of the total strategy. This means she should be shown how to use all seven steps in the strategy to recognize a word that is in the listening vocabulary but not recognized. Then Mary should receive instruction in suffix recognition (lesson 2), single syllable stems (lesson 3), and syllabication generalizations (lessons 4 and 5). Begin with the suffix lesson plan and proceed in the order the lesson plans are presented.

When students are fully familiar with the word-pronunciation strategy and have only specific skill difficulties, only the specific skill lessons that correspond to their difficulty need to be taught. They should be taught in the precise order in which they occur in the lesson plans that follow. When students know all the specific word pronunciation skills but are unfamiliar with the strategy, then only the strategy needs to be shown to them. Now complete Practicum Exercise 1 to demonstrate that you understand these last guidelines for planning instruction.

Practicum Exercise 1

If Marty demonstrates the following needs (see figure 11), where and how should you begin instruction?

Figure 11
Quick Test of Word Pronunciation
Class Record Form

Names of Students	Prefix	Suffix	Single Syllable Stems	Multiple CVC/CVC Stems	Multiple CV/CV CVC/V Stems	Context Clues	Strategy Not Known
				Skills Unknown			
Jack		✓✓✓ ✓✓✓	✓	✓	✓		✓
Mary		✓✓✓✓ ✓✓	✓✓	✓	✓	✓	✓
Marty				✓	✓		✓
Bob					✓		

Answers to Practicum Exercise 1

Since Marty does not know the word-recognition strategy, you must review this strategy with him. Then begin teaching, using lesson 2 for suffixes, lesson 3 for single syllable stems, and lessons 4 and 5 to teach the basic syllabication generalizations.

Practicum Exercise 2

Now look at the information recorded in the Class Record Form (see figure 11) for Bob. In Bob's case, how would you provide instruction?

Answer to Practicum Exercise 2

Bob is aware of all the steps in the word-pronunciation strategy. He is having difficulty with one word-pronunciation skill. He needs instruction in the generalization of CV/CV and CVC/V for syllabication.

Asking someone to pronounce a word should be the last step in a word-pronunciation strategy.

Now you are familiar with how the Class Record Form is used to differentiate instruction for your students. You are also aware that some students will need to be taught only the word-recognition strategy, and others will need to be taught both the strategy and specific word-pronunciation skills. Still others will need to be taught only specific skills. You are now ready to read the seven lesson plans in the instructional set. Read each lesson, giving your full attention to the three organizational steps and to the directions and information found under each step.

Word-Pronunciation Lessons

Presentation: Prefix   **LESSON 1**

A. *Purpose:*
   Being able to detect a common prefix often enables a student to unlock a previously unknown word. This lesson is designed to: (1) acquaint students with a number of commonly recurring prefixes and (2) build recognition of prefixes as word-pronunciation units.

B. *Instruction:*
   The following instructional procedure is recommended:
   1. Write the following stems on the chalkboard. Have your students read them. Afterwards discuss the meaning of *stem* as a base word to which a prefix and/or

suffix is added. You may wish to have your students locate additional examples in the dictionary.

sent	come	verb	press	grace
fine	done	side	forest	fix
noun	ability	act	camp	

2. Here are some prefixes commonly found in reading material. Write each prefix on the chalkboard. Direct your students' attention to each prefix as you pronounce it for them. You may wish to discuss the meaning of the prefix, but this is not necessary since the primary purpose of this lesson is prefix identification and pronunciation.

ab	ad	be	com	de	pro	re
dis	en	ex	in	pre	sub	un

3. Attach the common prefixes to the known root words presented in step 1. Now have your students pronounce the new words.

absent	become	adverb	compress	disgrace
define	undone	subside	reforest	prefix
pronoun	inability	exact	encamp	

4. Now that your students are familiar with the common prefixes and have had an opportunity to see them in words, a practice activity should be useful. Place the following words on the chalkboard. As you do so, direct your students for each word to (a) identify and pronounce the prefix, (b) identify and pronounce the stem, and (c) blend the two to pronounce the affixed word.

abnormal	defame	prorate	adjoin	degrade
adjust	prewar	export	beside	bespeak
commit	unwed	disarm	input	submit

5. Tell your students many words begin with patterns that look exactly like the prefixes studied. In some cases the beginning patterns are not prefixes, but nevertheless some of these words can be pronounced in the same way as the prefixed words. (Example: *pr*each, *per*k, *de*al, *de*an.)

6. Locate words in your subject area materials that contain other prefixes. Teach these prefixes in the same manner as was done in this lesson.

C. *Generalization:*

Through discussion, lead your students to conclude that looking for prefixes is the first step in a word-pronunciation strategy. You may wish to record this step on a chart or chalkboard for reference before introducing the second lesson. You may wish to have your students record this step on a sheet of notebook paper they are reserving for the word-pronunciation strategy. It should be recorded as follows:

1. Look for a prefix.

Presentation: Suffix   **LESSON 2**

A. *Purpose:*

Being able to detect one of the common suffixes often enables a student to unlock a previously unknown word. This lesson is designed to: (1) acquaint students with a number of commonly recurring suffixes and (2) build recognition of suffixes as word-pronunciation units.

B. *Instruction:*

The following instructional procedure is recommended:

1. Write the following stems on the chalkboard. Have your students read them. If there are students who are still unclear about the meaning of *stem*, clarify the meaning at this point. It may be necessary to have your students locate examples in a dictionary.

hope	happy	move	educate	walk
mail	high	skill	arm	act
love	talk	nerve	want	

2. Here are some suffixes commonly found in reading material. Write each suffix on the chalkboard. Direct your students' attention to each suffix as you pronounce it for them. You may wish to discuss the meaning of the suffix, but this is not necessary since the primary purpose of this lesson is suffix identification and pronunciation.

ness	ily	est	y	tion
ly	ous	er	ant	ent
able	ance	ed (ed)	ed (d)	ive
al	ing	ed (t)	ful	ment

3. Attach the common suffixes to the known stems presented in step 1. As you do so, ask selected students to pronounce the new words.

hopeful	higher	active	happily
mailable	talked (t)	nervous	happiness
lovely	movement	education	wanted (ed)
walking	army	happiest	skilled (d)

4. Now that your students are familiar with the common prefixes and suffixes and have used them to build words, a practice activity designed to build their recognition of prefixes and suffixes to the automatic recognition level is necessary. Write the following words on the chalkboard. As you do so, ask your students to (a) identify and pronounce the prefix, (b) identify and pronounce the suffix, (c) identify and pronounce the stem, and (d) blend and pronounce the affixed word.

reloading	prepayment	inactive	department
refreshment	enjoyment	preheated	unfairly
preschooler	abnormally	unskillful	prolonged

5. In your subject area materials, locate words that contain other suffixes. Teach these suffixes in the same manner as in this lesson.

C. *Generalization:*

Through discussion, lead your students to conclude that looking for suffixes is the second step in a word-pronunciation strategy. You may wish to record this step on a chart or chalkboard before introducing the third lesson so that your students may refer to it during the lesson. You may wish to have your students record this step on a sheet of notebook paper that they are reserving for the strategy. Show your students that at this point they have developed a two-step strategy, and have them record it as follows:

1. Look for a prefix.
2. Look for a suffix.

Presentation: Stems   **LESSON 3**

A. *Purpose:*

Identification of stems precedes their pronunciation. This lesson is designed to: (1) acquaint students with one- and two-syllable stems and (2) build recognition of stems as pronunciation units.

B. *Instruction:*

The following instructional procedure is recommended:

1. Place the following words on the chalkboard. Point out to your students that these words contain prefixes and/or suffixes. Identify the stems through analysis of each word, first for the prefix and second for the suffix. Point out to your students that once these elements have been identified, the word or syllable remaining is the stem.

camping	mainly	installment	entrenchment
discovering	enrichment	predisposition	undesirable
reboarding	unsinkable	removed	unknowingly

2. Point out to your students the procedure for pronouncing the above words. First, pronounce the prefix; second, pronounce the suffix; third, pronounce the stem; and fourth, blend and pronounce the word. Now direct your students to pronounce the above words using this strategy.

3. Either the teacher or the students may locate in subject area materials words that contain other prefixes and/or suffixes. These words can be analyzed using the strategy detailed in this lesson.

C. *Generalization:*

Through discussion, lead your students to conclude that the following strategy should be used when they encounter an unknown word in their reading. You may wish to record this third step on the strategy chart or chalkboard before introducing the fourth lesson so that your students may refer to it during the lesson. Or you may wish to have your students record this step on a sheet of notebook paper that they are reserving for the strategy. Their strategy should now contain these three steps:

1. Look for a prefix.
2. Look for a suffix.
3. Look for a stem.

Presentation: Syllabication CVC/CVC   **LESSON 4**

A. *Purpose:*

Often after a prefix and/or suffix has been identified, students find that they are faced with a multisyllable stem to pronounce. Having a few general guidelines for dividing such stems into syllables will be helpful in these situations. This lesson is designed to: (1) acquaint students with one of two commonly used techniques for dividing stems into syllables and (2) provide some practice in using this technique as an aid to word pronunciation.

B. *Instructions:*

The following instructional procedure is recommended:

1. Ask your students to listen closely as you pronounce some words. Tell them that you will be pronouncing two-syllable words and you want them to identify the separate syllables after you have pronounced each word. Elongate each syllable as you pronounce the following words:

   cargo   cattle   pencil
   person   summer   circus

2. After you have pronounced the words and the students have identified the separate syllables in each word, write the words on the chalkboard. Then review pronunciation and re-identify the separate syllables. Draw a slash mark (/) between the two syllables in each word.

   car/go   cat/tle   pen/cil
   per/son   sum/mer   cir/cus

3. Bring to your students' attention the fact that each word is divided between two consonants. Furthermore, each word follows the consonant-vowel-consonant / consonant-vowel-consonant pattern (CVC/CVC). Have your students draw from this observation a generalization that they can apply to similar words.

4. A generalization such as the following should be drawn: In multisyllable stems following the CVC/CVC pattern, the separate syllables are usually divided between the two consonants. (These exact words need not be used.)

5. Now that your students are familiar with the first syllabication technique, a practice activity is necessary to improve their skill in applying the technique. The following words are useful practice words for applying this technique.

   carrot   center   donkey   picnic   valley
   corner   settle   barrel   follow   grammar
   napkin   silver   garden   suggest   bottle

6. Have your students skim over the pages in their most recent reading assignment to locate multisyllable words following the CVC/CVC pattern. You may wish to locate words in your subject area materials that contain this pattern for additional practice for your students.

C. *Generalization:*

Through discussion, lead your students to conclude that the CVC/CVC pattern is useful for dividing multisyllable stems into their separate syllables. Record this step on a chart or a chalkboard, or have the students record this step in their notebooks. Point out to your students that the strategy is now one step longer.

   1. Locate the prefix.
   2. Locate the suffix.

3. Identify the stem.
4. Divide into syllables using CVC/CVC pattern.

Presentation: Syllabication CV/CV or CVC/V   **LESSON 5**

A. *Purpose:*

Even though a prefix and/or a suffix has been identified, the stem still can be difficult for a student to pronounce. This is generally true when it is two or more syllables in length. Three-syllable stems are unusual, but two-syllable stems are quite common. A syllabication technique has already been introduced. The purpose of this lesson is to (1) familiarize students with a second syllabication technique and (2) provide students with some practice in applying the technique.

B. *Instructions:*

The following instructional procedure is recommended:

1. Ask your students for their complete attention. Pronounce each of the following words, elongating and stressing each syllable as you do so. After you pronounce each word, have a student pronounce each syllable separately and indicate where the syllable division takes place.

CV/CV		CVC/V	
famous	station	river	habit
hotel	direct	damage	rigid

2. Now write the same list of words on the chalkboard. Then pronounce each word as you would in normal speech. Next, have a student pronounce the word and divide it into separate syllables on the basis of his or her auditory experience. Draw a slash mark between the separate syllables as in the following:

CV/CV		CVC/C	
fa/mous	sta/tion	riv/er	hab/it
ho/tel	di/rect	dam/age	rig/id

3. Show your students how multisyllable words following the CVCV pattern can be divided into syllables using either the CV/CV or CVC/V generalizations. Explain that often both generalizations must be applied to achieve the correct word pronunciation. Have the students draw a generalization from this observation that they can apply to similar words.

4. A generalization containing the following information is appropriate: Multisyllable words following the CVCV pattern are usually divided CV/CV or CVC/V. Try CV/CV first and then CVC/V.

5. Now that your students are familiar with the CV/CV and CVC/V patterns for syllable division, some practice to improve their skill is necessary. The following words lend themselves to division using these techniques.

pupil	locate	image	devil	blatant
spider	cement	pirate	dozen	timid
petal	seven	comic	final	novel

6. You may wish to locate other words that follow these patterns in your subject area material.

C. *Generalization:*

Through discussion, lead your students to conclude that the CV/CV and CVC/C patterns are useful for dividing multisyllable stems into their separate syllables. Record this step on a chart or a chalkboard, or direct your students to record it in their notebooks.

    1. Locate the prefix.
    2. Locate the suffix.
    3. Identify the stem.
    4. Divide into syllables using the CVC/CVC, CV/CV, or CVC/V pattern.

Presentation: Context Clues   **LESSON 6**

A. *Purpose:*

Sometimes a reader obtains a clue to the pronunciation of a word from the context surrounding that word. Context clues are phrases, sentences, or paragraphs that provide clues to an unknown word. This lesson is designed to acquaint students with such clues as a valuable aid to word pronunciation.

B. *Instruction:*

1. Place on the chalkboard the following two sentences, each of which contains a missing word. Point out to your students a word is missing, for a reason that will be revealed to them in a moment.

    (a) In order to pronounce an unknown word, all learners at all levels must learn how to _____ approach the unknown word. (systematically)

    (b) The _____ *strategy* being taught through these lessons is a systematic approach for identifying unknown words. (*pronunciation*)

2. Have each student silently read the sentences. Direct each student afterwards to write what he or she thinks is the missing word.

3. Discuss the various word choices for each sentence. Use discussion to build a logical and meaningful basis for selecting words to fill the blanks.

4. After the class has chosen fill-in words and agreed that the words are reasonable insertions, point out to your students that they have proven the value of using context clues. Remind them that context clues consist of all graphics, sentences, and/or paragraphs useful for word pronunciation.

5. Obtain a 500-word selection, and delete every seventh word. Duplicate the selection and give one copy to each student. Lead your students through the process of using graphic, sentence, and/or paragraph context clues to hypothesize and justify choices for the missing words.

C. *Generalization:*

Through discussion, lead your students to conclude that context clues are a valuable aid to word pronunciation. You may record context clues on the evolving word-pronunciation strategy chart, or on the chalkboard for future reference. You may wish to direct your students to record this step in their notebooks under the section they are reserving for this strategy. Point out to your students that their strategy now has five steps.

    1. Look for a prefix.
    2. Look for a suffix.
    3. Locate the stem.
    4. Divide into syllables using the CVC/CVC, CV/CV, or CVC/V pattern.
    5. Try it in context.

Presentation: Glossary, Dictionary, and   **LESSON 7**
           Knowledgeable Reader

A. *Purpose:*

This lesson is merely a set of necessary comments to be made to your students. Surely your students will want to know what they should do if the strategy does not work. This lesson is designed to answer that question.

B. *Instructions:*

The following instructional procedure is recommended:

1. Point out to your students that the five-step word-pronunciation strategy will not help them identify every word they do not recognize in their day-to-day reading. Sometimes the strategy will not lead them to the correct pronunciation of an unknown word because the word is not in their listening vocabulary or because they do not have sufficient word-pronunciation knowledge to pronounce the word.

2. Tell your students that, in order to have a near infallible strategy, they need two additional steps. Number 6 is the use of a glossary or dictionary. Number 7 is merely to ask someone who is familiar with the word how the word should be pronounced.

3. Be sure your students know how to use the glossary and dictionary to pronounce words. Module 7, "Study Skills and Strategies," explains how to teach the study skills for using the glossary and dictionary. Resist the temptation to tell your students to "look it up" before you have determined whether they have the necessary study skills to locate and pronounce the words in the reference to which you are sending them.

4. Caution your students against skipping the last two steps; these are as important as the first five. Words that are left unpronounced return to produce the same frustration on following pages. Generally the frustration is heightened as a result of still more new, unrecognized words.

C. *Generalization:*

At this point record the following generalizations on a chart or chalkboard, or have your students record them in their notebooks.

    1. Look for a prefix.
    2. Look for a suffix.
    3. Locate the stem.

4. Divide into syllables using CVC/CVC, CV/CV, or CVC/V pattern.
5. Try it in context.
6. Look it up in the glossary or dictionary.
7. Ask someone.

Practicum Exercise 3

You have now completed reading the seven lesson plans. You were asked to identify the three-step organization for every lesson plan. List each step, and describe what takes place at that step.

1.

2.

3.

Answers to Practicum Exercise 3

1. The first step is *Purpose*. Contained in this step is the information teachers need to establish a purpose for the instruction. At this step you tell the student what he or she will be able to do as a result of acquiring this new learning.

2. The second step is *Instruction*. This step contains the necessary directions and information to teach the specific skills.

3. The third step is *Generalization*. This step contains the information and procedure you need to follow to incorporate the new skill into the larger word-pronunciation strategy. This step shows the relationship of the individual skill to the overall strategy.

Final Comment

If your students will use the strategy, they will find it a valuable tool for pronouncing words. Ensuring that they apply the strategy is your responsibility. If you do not insist upon use of the strategy, your students will soon forget the strategy and all your instructional efforts will have been wasted. In order to reach the automatic application level, students need instruction, practice, and application opportunities under your direction.

If you have accomplished each of the three specific objectives in this module, you are ready for the Posttest. If not, complete them as directed. If you are having difficulty, return to appropriate Enabling Elements or see your instructor.

Posttest

Directions: Read each of the following statements and complete each Posttest item as directed.

1. You should now be completely familiar with a word-pronunciation strategy that can be taught to needful students. List in order of use the steps in such a strategy designed to help students pronounce multisyllable words.

2. Did you prepare and use the Quick Test of Word Pronunciation (Forms A and B), Word-Pronunciation Strategy Test, and Class Record Form to determine the word-pronunciation skill and strategy needs of students?

3. List and explain the three organizational steps in the word-pronunciation lesson plans.

Posttest Answers

1. The word-recognition strategy presented in this module follows. Each skill is listed in the order it should be used or taught.

   Word-Pronunciation Strategy

   a. Look for a prefix.
   b. Look for a suffix.
   c. Locate the stem.
   d. Divide the stem into syllables (CVC/CVC, CV/CV, CVC/V).
   e. Try the word in context.
   f. Look in the glossary or dictionary.
   g. Ask someone who knows how to pronounce the word.

   Your answer need not be stated exactly in these words, nor do you need to have the same number of steps. However, your answer should contain all the information presented in this strategy.

2. If you have *prepared* and *used* the Quick Test of Word Pronunciation (Forms A and B), Word-Pronunciation Strategy Test, and Class Record Form, you have satisfied this objective. If you have not completed all three, then you must do so before you can consider yourself as having satisfied the second objective of this module.

3. The major organizational steps for lesson plans designed to teach skills and strategy are as follows:

   a. Establish a purpose for learning. Tell the student why it is that he or she needs this instruction and what he or she will be able to do as a result of learning the skill you are about to teach.

   b. Provide instruction. This step contains the directions and information necessary to develop competency with a specific skill.

   c. Build a generalization. At this step, the student incorporates the new skill into a word-pronunciation strategy, which he or she will use when attempting to pronounce multisyllable words.

Selected Bibliography

Burmeister, L. E. "Selected Word Analysis Generalizations for a Group Approach to Corrective Reading in the Secondary School." *Reading Research Quarterly* 4, no. 1 (1968) 71–95.

————. *Word—From Print to Meaning*. Reading, Massachusetts: Addison-Wesley, 1975.

Cleary, D. M. "Reading Without Vowels: Some Implications." *Journal of Reading* 20, no. 1 (1976): 52–56.

Dawson, M. A., ed. *Teaching Word-Recognition Skills*. Newark, Delaware: International Reading Association, 1971.

Durkin, D. *Phonics, Linguistics, and Reading*. New York: Teachers College, 1972.

Elisiak, J. "There is a Need for Word Attack Generalizations." *Reading Improvement* 14, no. 2 (Summer 1977): 100–3.

Hafner, L. E., ed. *Improving Reading in Middle and Secondary Schools*. New York: Macmillan, 1974.

Heilman, A. W. *Phonics in Proper Perspective*. 4th ed. Columbus, Ohio: Charles E. Merrill Publishing Co., 1981.

Johnson, J. H., and Parades, E. "The Longest Tome Begins With a Single Phoneme." *Journal of Reading* 16, no. 5 (1975): 376–79.

Jones, D. R. "The Dictionary: A Look at 'Look It Up'." *Journal of Reading*, 23, no. 4 (1980): 309–12.

Kottmeyer, W. *Decoding and Meaning*. New York: McGraw-Hill, 1974.

Roe, B. D.; Stoodt, B. D.; and Burns, P. C. *Reading Instruction in the Secondary School*. Rev. ed. Chicago: Rand McNally, 1978.

Stauffer, R. G. "A Study of Prefixes in the Thorndike List to Establish a List of Prefixes That Should Be Taught in the Elementary School." *Journal of Educational Research* 32 (February 1942): 453–58.

Thomas, E. L., and Robinson, H. A. *Improving Reading in Every Class: A Sourcebook for Teachers*. Boston: Allyn and Bacon, 1977.

Thorndike, E. L. *The Teaching of English Suffixes*. New York: Bureau of Publications, Teachers College, Columbia University, 1941.

Motivating Reluctant
Readers

Contents

Prospectus
 Rationale
 Objectives
 Resources and Time Required
Pretest
Branching Program Alternatives for Pretest Responses
Enabling Element 1: *Motivation*
Enabling Element 2: *Factors Influencing Motivation*
Enabling Element 3: *A Motivation Strategy*
Enabling Element 4: *Preparing Reading Assignments*
Posttest
 Posttest Answers
Selected Bibliography

Prospectus

Rationale

How often have you heard your fellow teachers say, ''How do I get Alfonso and Marian to read their assignments?'' This is a question all teachers have about students at one time or another. Students like Alfonso and Marian, who have some reading ability but lack the motivation to complete their reading assignments, are reluctant readers.

As teachers, we have a responsibility to motivate reluctant readers. Motivation, from a teaching point of view, means manipulating variables in such a way as to entice students to read their assignments.

The ideas presented in this module are designed to help you accomplish this task. The suggestions provided for motivation can be implemented as part of a daily routine in any content area course. They require minimal changes in teacher attitude or instructional technique, and they initiate considerable student motivation. Ultimately, they lead to completed reading assignments.

Objectives

Terminal Objective

You will acquire and use the provided strategy for motivating reluctant readers.

Specific Objectives

1. You will write a one-word synonym for *motivation* and list two sources of motivation.
2. You will list the eight major affective and cognitive factors that influence motivation.
3. You will list the core factors in a motivation strategy and prepare a mnemonic device to be used for retaining the core factors in memory.
4. You will incorporate a motivation strategy into a subject area reading assignment.

Resources and Time Required

In addition to the module, the only other materials required are your subject area textbook, paper, and a writing instrument. The estimated time to complete the starred core Enabling Activities is three to four hours.

Pretest

Directions: For each question, determine the word that indicates your belief regarding your competency. If you are in doubt or know only part of the information for which you are asked, choose NO.

1. Many reluctant readers are merely unmotivated readers waiting for a spark. Can you state a one-word synonym for motivation and list the two principal sources of motivation?   YES   NO

2. How a student feels and what he or she thinks are important teacher concerns. Can you list the eight major affective and cognitive factors that influence motivation?   YES   NO

3. Every teacher needs a strategy for motivating students. Can you list the core factors in a motivation strategy and prepare a mnemonic device to aid you in their retention?   YES   NO

4. Knowing something about motivation does not guarantee application. Can you modify a subject area reading assignment to incorporate the motivation strategy presented in this module?   YES   NO

Branching Program Alternatives
for Pretest Responses

1. If you can supply a suitable one-word synonym for *motivation* and identify the two major sources of motivation, you are ready for Enabling Element 2. If you are not sure about the correctness of your synonym or of the two sources of motivation, Enabling Element 1 was prepared for you.

2. You are in good standing if you can list eight factors that bring about a motivated state in a learner; you may go to Enabling Element 2. If your list is incomplete, Enabling Element 2 will help you complete the list.

3. If you can list the core factors in a motivation strategy and have a mnemonic device to aid you in their retention, you are ready for Enabling Element 4. If not, you will find Enabling Element 3 valuable for formulating and helping you remember a motivation strategy.

4. Once you have a motivation strategy, incorporating the strategy into a reading assignment is the next thing you must do. If you have a strategy and can incorporate it into a reading assignment, you are ready for the Posttest. If you are unsure of just how this should be done, Enabling Element 4 will explain and demonstrate the procedure.

Enabling Element 1
Motivation

Specific Objective 1

You will write a one-word synonym for *motivation* and list two sources of motivation.

Enabling Activities

*1. Read Study Guide 1 to identify a one-word synonym for *motivation* and to discover two sources of motivation.

*2. Using the Sources of Motivation form (provided at the end of Study Guide 1), see if you can separate the intrinsic from the extrinsic students in one of your classes. Ask yourself what factors influence the motivation of students in the extrinsic group. You may find that you have discovered the very factors discussed in Enabling Element 2.

3. Discuss the extrinsically motivated students in your classes with other subject area teachers, and determine if the other teachers classify these students in the same way. Could some subject areas *spark* students more than others?

*Indicates core Enabling Activities.

4. Interview five of the highest achieving students on your intrinsic list. Ask them to tell you what motivates them to achieve. You may compare their answers to see if high achievers achieve for similar reasons. Compare their answers with the factors listed in Enabling Element 2.

*5. Distribute to your students the Incomplete Sentences form (provided at the end of Study Guide 1). Ask your students to complete each item to make a sentence that states how they feel about reading assignments. Compile their answers. Do your students' perceptions of your reading assignments agree with yours?

Study Guide 1

Motivation is often the explanation for why Angela completes her reading assignments but Ralph does not. Intelligence, language facility, cultural background, and many such factors may be insignificantly different for the two students. Motivational differences may be the significant factor.

Motivation, at one level of understanding, may be considered to be *need*. It is an individual need that causes a student to do something that will result in a satisfaction. Need comes from within the learner's environment; thus, teachers manipulate factors in an attempt to create needs.

All of us have had students like Angela who complete their assignments seemingly regardless of what we do. No matter how casual we are in making an assignment or how unclear we are about the purpose of the assignment, Angela always gets the job done. Students like Angela are motivated from within. Psychologists call them *intrinsically motivated*. Students like Angela have such a high need to succeed academically that they always complete their assignments. Teachers need to change the environment very little for students like Angela.

Teachers also have students like Ralph who occasionally complete their reading assignments. Ralph sometimes gets started, but too often he fails to reach completion. Many times Ralph does not even seem to be concerned by the fact that he has not completed his reading assignment. Students like Ralph are demonstrating low-level or nonexistent academic needs. They are not intrinsically motivated like Angela. Occasionally, however, Ralph does complete an assignment. He completes one when he has a need to do so, but the need is created by someone other than himself. Students like Ralph are either *extrinsically motivated*, or motivated by something in their environment. For these students, teachers need to be aware of the factors that influence or bring about motivation. Awareness of these factors followed by planned manipulation is likely to yield more completed reading assignments from reluctant students.

If you would like to identify the *intrinsically* and *extrinsically* motivated students in your class, the following form, "Sources of Motivation," should be helpful. The form contains a definition of *intrinsic motivation*, a definition of *extrinsic motivation*, and two columns for the names of your students. When you have your students divided by source of motivation, you may want to examine each group of students to see if you can identify specific motivation factors associated with either intrinsically or extrinsically motivated students.

If you wish to obtain some insight into the ways your students perceive your reading assignments, use the form entitled ''Incomplete Sentences.'' A compilation of your students' perceptions may provide you with additional clues to their sources of motivation.

You now have a definition of motivation and are aware of two sources of motivation. If you can list the motivational factors classroom teachers must manipulate to interest the extrinsically motivated students, go to Enabling Element 3. If you are unsure of the factors, Enabling Element 2 will identify and discuss them.

Sources of Motivation

Intrinsic motivation: self-starter; started from within; moved to complete a task by innate need.

Extrinsic motivation: externally started; start comes from outside the learner; moved to complete a task by outside influences that develop need.

Names	Names
1.	1.
2.	2.
3.	3.
4.	4.
5.	5.
6.	6.
7.	7.
8.	8.
9.	9.
10.	10.
11.	11.
12.	12.
13.	13.
14.	14.
15.	15.

Incomplete Sentences

Name _____

Class _____ Date_____

Directions: Complete each item to express how you feel about the many reading assignments you get in school each week. Try to make complete sentences from each of the following.

1. I complete my reading assignment _____
   _____ .

2. Long reading assignments _____
   _____ .

3. Teachers who assign only page numbers for reading assignments _____

_____ .

4. What annoys me most about my reading assignments _____

_____ .

5. Reading _____

_____ .

6. Reading to find the answer to a question _____

_____ .

7. People walking around the classroom when I am reading _____

_____ .

8. Reading at home _____

_____ .

9. Hard books _____

_____ .

10. Answering the teacher's questions correctly after completing my reading assignment _____

_____ .

11. Reading about something that interests me _____

_____ .

12. Reading textbooks _____

_____ .

13. When I use the information from my reading, _____

_____ .

14. Teachers make reading assignments _____

_____ .

15. Easy books _____

_____ .

16. When the teacher tells me I am wrong, _____

_____ .

17. Being right _____

_____ .

18. I would like to help my teacher _____

_____ .

19. Reading newspapers and magazines _____

_____ .

20. Reading is fun when _____

_____ .

Enabling Element 2
Factors Influencing Motivation

Specific Objective 2

You will list the eight major affective and cognitive factors that influence motivation.

Enabling Activities

*1. Read Study Guide 2, and compile a list of factors that influence motivation.

*2. In *one* of your classes, distribute the What Motivates Me form (included at the end of Study Guide 2). Ask the students to complete the form and turn it in for your future planning needs; or distribute the form and have the students use it as a basis for a discussion on motivational factors and learning.

 3. In another of your classes, discuss motivation individually with a few high- and a few low-achieving students. Ask them to list factors that motivate them to achieve in your classes. Did you acquire any new insight into the motives of your students?

 4. Think of one of your most reluctant readers. Write a one-paragraph description of this student using the motivational factors presented in Study Guide 2. This activity should provide you with factors you can change or manipulate to increase the work product of this student.

*5. Talk with other teachers who have the same student in class, and compare your description. Are there differences in perceptions among teachers? Could it be that some teachers have the *motivational keys* to some students, while others do not? Were any of the keys identified? Much can be learned about reluctant readers from talking with other teachers.

*6. Want to learn something about yourself as a teacher? Distribute the My Teacher form found at the end of Study Guide 2. Ask your students to complete the form and return it to you. No names are necessary. Tally and analyze the answers to the questions to see how you are perceived by your students.

Study Guide 2

The basic factors underlying motivation are no secret. Although these factors are well known and understood, they are all too often not applied. They can be divided into two categories, those that relate primarily to how students feel (affective factors) and those that relate to how students think (cognitive factors). A list of these basic factors follows:

Affective Factors	*Cognitive Factors*
Interest	Purpose for reading
Attitudes	Short-term goals
	Reading level
	Knowledge of results
	Success
	Usefulness of knowledge

Although these factors will be discussed separately, they operate together to bring about a motivated student.

---

*Indicates core Enabling Activities.

Affective Factors

The affective factors that influence motivation are *interest* and *attitudes*. These two factors interact to create a good or bad feeling in the learner about something and/or someone.

Interest refers to a curiosity or a concern about something—in this case a subject area. For most students, interest in a subject area does not bloom overnight like a spring flower; but rather it is developed in a subject area after many exposures to those intricacies that strike their curiosity. A social studies teacher who compares and contrasts the marriage customs and ceremonies in different countries with junior- and senior-high-school girls is appealing to their curiosity. Likewise, a mathematics teachers who deals with the consumption and cost of gasoline to determine cost-per-mile of automobile operation is appealing to the curiosity of high-school boys. Interest in a subject area is developed by teachers through continually relating the content of their courses to the curiosities of their students. This requires not only knowledge of the content area, but knowledge of the broader realm of the daily interests of students. The teacher who builds interest knows both the content area and the students; that teacher can relate one to the other.

Parents and teachers—in that order—have the most pronounced effect upon students' attitudes toward academic education. Parents create the initial attitude. Teachers refine the attitude toward school in general and their subject areas in particular. An attitude is a disposition or mental set toward something, which might be a subject area and/or a teacher. Attitudes may be either positive or negative. Students with positive attitudes toward their subject areas can be seen in the hallways carrying the subject textbook. They can also be seen in the libraries studying. Usually their assignments are complete and on time. Students with a negative attitude are also seen in the hallways. They are the students who carry few books, no notebook paper, and whose pencils always remain sharp. They too go to the library—to look at a newspaper, magazine, or to sleep. In class their assignments are rarely completed, and these students can usually be seen sitting in a reclined position with a dazed look on their faces. In order to create a positive attitude toward a subject area, a teacher has to be a special person. Through actions the teacher must relay to the students a feeling of concern for them as individuals. The teacher must be willing to accept their academic, emotional, and social level of development. He or she must be supportive of their smallest achievement and try very hard to withhold criticism. Attitude, like interest, is a pervasive quality that is developed only after a long period of pleasurable experiences. Finally, teachers who think positively about their students generally create students who think positively about their teachers and the content they teach.

Cognitive Factors

The cognitive factors that influence motivation are purpose, short-term goal, adjustment for reading level, knowledge of results, success, and usefulness of knowledge. These six factors interact to stimulate the cognitive, or thinking, processes of the learner.

Purpose. In order to be motivating, assignments must be given with a purpose. The purpose is a teacher's specific direction in an assignment. The teacher who at the end of a class tells the students to read text pages 27 through 54 for tomorrow is providing a very unrealistic purpose for learning. The student perceives the purpose as getting to page 54. Once the student reaches page 54, he or she thinks the purpose has been achieved. However, the teacher does not think that the student has achieved the purpose of the assignment until the student can satisfactorily answer the questions that will be raised over the material on the following day. Unfortunately for the student in this example, he or she will not find out what his or her purposes are for reading until the teacher begins to ask questions on the following day. Now suppose that a student who completes her assignment and reads pages 27 through 54 comes to class and is asked a few questions by the teacher. Suppose further that she is unable to answer the questions because she did not read the material for those purposes. In this case, the teacher would probably assume that the student did not read the material, since she could not answer the questions. After a few such assignments, the student discontinues reading any assignments. A better way for you to handle such an assignment would be to write on the chalkboard two, three, or more questions directed at the important points to be obtained from the reading. Then you tell the student to read whatever is necessary to answer the questions. This would provide specific purposes for reading and alert the student to precisely what is to be obtained from the reading assignment.

Short-Term Goals. The short-term goal is another important cognitive factor. When the goals are short-range, students perceive them as taking very little time and are therefore less reluctant to do the assignment. When you provide your students with a number of questions for which to read, you are providing them with short-term goals. Each question becomes a goal in itself, and before long the students complete their assignment not realizing the lapse of time or the amount of effort expended. The students probably read as much when assigned to read a specific number of pages, such as pages 27 through 54 in the previous example. The difference is that, given questions to answer, they know specifically what to read for. Each question becomes a goal by itself, which makes the assignment appear shorter.

Adjustment for Reading Level. The reading levels of all students need to be considered when making reading assignments. Assigning the same text material to students who read above, at, and below grade level is one way of making the reading assignment nonmotivating for perhaps the above- and surely the below-average reader. One way to avoid this pitfall is to select a number of textual materials with a range of readabilities. Module 3 provides suggestions for determining the suitability of material for various students. Module 1 suggests ways of determining readability, and Module 2 provides ways of altering the reading level. Given enough time, a school or county librarian can locate many materials on various reading levels. You may want to provide the librarian with the Graph for Estimating Readability to assist him or her in locating materials suitable for your students.

Knowledge of Results. None of us achieves unless we know what we have done right and *specifically* what we have done wrong. A student who is told that he used the right process to determine the latitude and longitude of Chicago on a globe assumes that the same process will apply for finding the latitude and longitude of Orlando, Florida. Pointing out the specific error made in the process and providing specific instructions help the student obtain the correct answer next time. Some teachers fail to tell students when they are correct, but consistently tell them when they are wrong. Knowing what is wrong tells us how *not* to respond the next time, but gives no clue on *how* to respond next time. Relative to the present discussion, the best advice for motivating students is to emphasize the positive and de-emphasize the negative. When you do emphasize the negative—BE SPECIFIC.

Success. In life, most people gravitate toward those vocations and avocations wherein they meet success. When we meet with repeated failure, we physically and mentally withdraw from the situation. Teachers who make reading assignments without providing a purpose are probably ensuring that their students will meet with failure when the assignment is due. A student could easily have read the material for one purpose, although the teacher had assigned it for another. A few such recurrences of this experience will create another subject-area mental dropout. Repeat the experience across subject areas and you may produce a physical dropout from school. The importance of success in motivation can be summed up by the statement, "No greater is a feeling than a feeling of success!"

Usefulness of Knowledge. "Knowledge for knowledge's sake is garbage!" If you do not like the brashness of this statement, we will supply you with the name of the student who made this contribution, and you can take it up with him. But he did make a point when he said this to his teacher. Knowledge acquired with no suggested application to daily problems or interests is fleeting knowledge indeed! For example, every teacher knows it is important to teach students the new vocabulary in the subject area. Now if vocabulary is taught by the teacher but no stress is placed upon application and use in the classroom, how long will the vocabulary last in the minds of students? And will the students be interested in additional vocabulary study? Finding ways of relating content to life is not easy. But it is essential, not only for motivation, but also for retention.

There are other factors, too, including the physical and cultural. The condition of the school plant and home also influence motivation. However, these factors often fall outside the realm of a classroom teacher. For the most part, the classroom teacher can only manipulate the affective and cognitive factors discussed in this Study Guide. As a result, manipulating these factors will not bring about success with every student, but should increase the motivation of many. In education, as in life, every little bit helps!

At the end of this Study Guide there are two forms you should find valuable. The first, entitled "What Motivates Me?" consists of a number of questions about motivating factors to which students answer YES or NO. It will take your students about ten minutes to complete. An analysis of your students' answers will help you identify the important motivational factors from the perception of your students. As an alternative, the statements on this form may be used as key statements for a class discussion of motivation.

The second form at the end of this Study Guide is entitled "My Teacher." This form contains a number of questions about you as a motivator of students and as a teacher. If you wish to learn something about yourself, reproduce copies of this form and distribute them to your students. The form will take approximately ten minutes for your students to complete. An analysis of the YES and NO responses will reveal the degree to which you are considering motivation factors when you prepare your reading assignments and lesson plans.

You are now familiar with a number of factors that affect motivation. If you can create a motivation strategy using the core factors from those identified in this Study Guide, you are ready for Enabling Element 4. If not, Enabling Element 3 should prove interesting as well as valuable.

What Motivates Me

Name _____

Class _____   Date _____

Directions: Read each of the following statements carefully and circle YES or NO for each one. Your answers will tell your teacher something about what motivates you to learn.

1. I read my assignments only when class time is provided to do so.   YES   NO
2. I like to know what I am to learn from an assignment.   YES   NO
3. I prefer one long assignment to two short assignments.   YES   NO
4. The more I like a subject, the more likely I will complete my reading assignment.   YES   NO
5. I like to be told if my answers to questions are correct or incorrect.   YES   NO
6. When it is noisy in the classroom, it is difficult to complete my reading assignments.   YES   NO
7. I complete my reading assignments even if the material is difficult for me to understand.   YES   NO
8. I like to read about things I can make or use in my daily life.   YES   NO
9. Other people moving around or talking in the classroom make it hard for me to concentrate.   YES   NO
10. I like to be able to answer correctly questions asked by my teacher.   YES   NO
11. When I do something right, someone should tell me so.   YES   NO
12. I like long reading assignments.   YES   NO
13. I like to receive a reward when I complete my reading assignment.   YES   NO
14. When I am right the teacher can tell everyone; when I am wrong the teacher should tell just me.   YES   NO
15. I like to help my teachers select my reading assignments.   YES   NO

My Teacher

Name _____

Class _____ Date _____

Directions: Your teacher would like to know more about himself as a teacher. Please read each of the following questions and then circle YES or NO after each question.

1. Does your teacher make fun of you when you are having difficulty reading? ... YES   NO

2. Does your teacher often get you so interested in your reading assignment that you talk about the assignment outside of class? ... YES   NO

3. When your teacher finishes telling you about your reading assignment, do you sometimes feel you want to go to the library to find out more about the assignment? ... YES   NO

4. Does your teacher make material that looks hard to read seem easier to read? ... YES   NO

5. Does your teacher tell you what you are to learn from your reading assignment before the assignment is due? ... YES   NO

6. Does your teacher ask interesting questions over the reading assignments? ... YES   NO

7. Does your teacher help you find material you can read for your assignments? ... YES   NO

8. Does your teacher give reading assignments from materials that are too difficult to understand? ... YES   NO

9. Does your teacher explain or define the new words in reading assignments? ... YES   NO

10. Does your teacher tell you when you did a good job on your reading assignment? ... YES   NO

11. When you are reading, does your teacher try to keep down the noise level in the classroom? ... YES   NO

12. Does your teacher give reading assignments that are too long? ... YES   NO

13. Does your teacher help you see the value of reading assignments to your daily life or to daily events? ... YES   NO

14. Does your teacher ever ask you what you would like to read to complete your assignment? ... YES   NO

15. Does your teacher ever let you decide how much reading you need to do to complete your assignment? ... YES   NO

16. Does your teacher know what you are interested in reading? ... YES   NO

Enabling Element 3
A Motivation Strategy

Specific Objective 3

You will list the core factors in a motivation strategy and prepare a mnemonic device to be used for retaining the core factors in memory.

Enabling Activities

*1. Read Study Guide 3 to identify the core components of a strategy to motivate reluctant readers.
*2. Read Study Guide 3 to acquire a mnemonic device useful for remembering the strategy presented in this Study Guide.
 3. Examine some of your subject area textbooks to determine if any motivation suggestions are provided. If your subject area books are like many others, you will find few suggestions on motivation. However, your textbook may be one of those in which the authors provide not only suggestions, but also a motivational strategy such as the one provided in this module. If your textbook includes a motivational strategy, you may want to try both strategies to see which is more effective.
 4. Discuss with colleagues the strategy provided in this module. Chances are they are also using the same strategy. A great deal can be learned from discussions of motivation.
 5. There are many textbooks and popular paperbacks available on the topic of motivation. You may find it beneficial to read one of these to further your understanding and ultimately enhance your techniques for handling students. Look at the bibliography for suggestions.

Study Guide 3

A number of factors associated with motivation were identified in Study Guide 2. All of these contribute to a student's state of motivation and therefore are important. However, it is probably unreasonable to expect that most teachers will keep in mind the eight or more factors mentioned in Study Guide 2. Therefore, in this module a brief but powerful four-step motivational strategy is presented.

The four-step motivational strategy is designed for general use when making reading assignments and employs the use of a mnemonic device that makes the strategy easier to remember. The strategy was developed by first identifying the many major

*Indicates core Enabling Activities.

factors that contribute to a student's state of motivation. Second, the factors were reduced to four core factors. When these core factors are considered in lesson planning, they will increase the probability of motivating students. To assist you in remembering the motivation strategy, the first letter from the key word in each of the core factors has been used to make up another word called an acronym.

The key letters, four core components of the motivation strategy, and implications for motivation follow:

P *Purpose*. Students acquire more meaning from what they read when they are provided with a purpose for reading. Providing students with purposes for reading defines what specific information and understandings are to be obtained as they read. Setting a purpose for reading also makes material more meaningful to the reader. Purposeful and meaningful assignments are motivating.

A *Attitude*. Students must acquire a positive attitude toward reading. This quality is developed through associations with teachers who have positive attitudes toward their students. Negative attitudes and reinforcement cause students to withdraw from teachers, their subject areas, and their assignments. Being an eternal optimist is difficult but nevertheless essential to teachers who wish to motivate students and teach important skills.

R *Results*. Students must be made aware of results through a teacher's stipulation of right and wrong responses. Providing students with knowledge of right and wrong is one way to teach students what they should and should not do the next time they find themselves in a similar situation.

S *Success*. Students, like teachers, do not repeat experiences unless they meet with some success. Every student needs to find some success in every lesson you teach and in every assignment you make. Accumulations of successes increase the likelihood of motivation for future assignments.

Additional suggestions for implementing each core component can be found at the end of this Study Guide.

Now if you will look at the acronym formed by the first letter of each key word in the core factors, you will see that it is a familiar word. *Par* is what most golfers hope to obtain on every hole on the golf course. *Pars* are what the golfer accumulates to signify satisfactory performance. Since satisfactory performance is every teacher's goal for every learner, PARS might be a useful acronym and mnemonic device for remembering the four core factors in the motivational strategy provided in this module.

You now have a strategy that can be applied when you make reading assignments. This strategy should be helpful for motivating many of the reluctant readers in your classroom. To further help you implement the strategy, a number of suggested activities are provided. The activities are listed under the core component descriptors—*Purpose, Attitude, Results,* and *Success.*

Allow time to effectively introduce reading assignments.

Activities for Implementing the Motivation Strategy

Purpose. Purpose provides direction for and meaning from what is read. Purposes for reading can be established through a number of activities.

1. Prepare a number of questions to be used for setting up a purpose and guiding students' reading. Write the questions on the chalkboard, and leave them there for the duration of the assignment.

2. Prepare a number of true and false questions over the assignment. Duplicate the questions and distribute them to your students. Ask the students to read their assignment and to answer the true–false questions.

3. Preview the reading assignment with the class. Ask the students to create questions based upon their previewing that can be used to guide their reading of the assignment. List the questions on the blackboard, or duplicate the questions and distribute them prior to the reading of the assignment. Module 7, Study Skills and Strategies, provides guidelines for creating questions through previewing.

4. Divide your class into small groups. Have each small group preview the reading assignment and prepare a number of questions over the assignment. Collect the questions and duplicate those you think are most important. Distribute these prior to the reading of the assignment.

5. Check the teacher's manual of your textbook to see which questions the authors think students should be able to answer at the end of a specific unit or assignment. Share these questions with your students after they have previewed the assignment and

created their own questions. Through discussion, agree upon a set of questions that will be used to guide the students' reading of the assignment. Assign factual-type questions to the less able readers and inferential questions to the more able readers.

6. Have the students individually preview the reading assignment and draw up their own purposes or questions for reading. Then have them read the assignment to achieve their own purposes. Afterwards, conduct a class discussion of the reading assignment and determine the agreement on reading purposes. Have the students explain their previewing techniques and their interest in the topic. Their interests will probably explain the different purposes.

Attitudes. Teachers have a responsibility to create positive dispositions toward school in general and their subject matter areas specifically. Positive attitudes are developed through teacher-pupil interactions.

1. Demonstrate to your students that you are aware of what they know as well as what they do not know. This is a demonstration of your concern for them as individuals.
2. Recognize the many excellent responses your students make to build positive attitudes and motivation.
3. Avoid berating and degrading students. Berating students builds negative attitudes toward the individual teacher and ultimately toward education in general.
4. Avoid berating the school or your colleagues. Teachers who berate their school and their colleagues in front of students build negative associations in the minds of their students. These negative associations ultimately turn into negative attitudes toward teachers and schools.
5. Speak positively about your subject area. It is difficult for students to become interested in a subject for which the teacher demonstrates no enthusiasm.

Results. Immediate and frequent knowledge of results is instrumental to motivation.

1. Prepare sheets students can use to check their own answers. These sheets will provide immediate and frequent feedback to the students. Such feedback initiates motivation.
2. Be sure that the learning from one assignment is added to previous learning so students can see their total growth in the subject area.
3. Do not overemphasize right or wrong responses. Such overemphasis does not contribute to motivation. A student who is right too often is not likely to be challenged. A student who is wrong too often is likely to become frustrated and give up the task. A teacher should emphasize rights more than wrongs, while always keeping in mind that one way in which students learn is from their errors.
4. When emphasizing what a student has done wrong, be sure to follow the emphasis with instruction that specifically tells the student what he or she needs to do to be right.
5. Students with poor attitudes toward subject areas need to have their correct responses recognized by their teachers in the presence of their classmates. Although teacher recognition is always important, peer approval means the most.

Success. Success breeds success. Without it there is no motivation.

1. Every day find a task in your subject area that every student can accomplish successfully.
2. Display the successes of poorly motivated students in your classroom for others to see.
3. Use individual assignments on a contractual basis. This is a good way to make sure that students meet with success in every assignment.
4. Reach an agreement with students regarding the purposes of assignments. If you and the student agree upon purposes for reading assignments, successes for the student are ensured.
5. Provide students with reading materials at their reading level.
6. Allow students to read more or less depending upon their interest in a topic.
7. Contract with students for a certain grade and a certain quality of performance in a reading assignment.
8. Pair a good reader with a reluctant reader to work cooperatively on an assignment.

You have now completed Study Guide 3 and are ready to apply the motivation strategy to a reading assignment. If you already know how to do this, go directly to the Posttest. If you are not sure of how to incorporate the motivation strategy into daily reading assignments, go to Enabling Element 4 to see how this is done.

Enabling Element 4
Preparing Reading Assignments

Specific Objective 4

You will incorporate a motivation strategy into a subject area reading assignment.

Enabling Activities

*1. Read Study Guide 4 to familiarize yourself with the procedure for incorporating a motivation strategy into your daily lesson plan.
*2. Examine the subject area reading assignment provided. Incorporate the motivation strategy into this assignment to enhance its appeal.
 3. Examine the reading assignments suggested by the author(s) of your textbook. Do

---

*Indicates core Enabling Activity.

these provide any material that can be used as one of the components of the motivation strategy?

*4. Sometimes authors provide discussion questions at the end of a unit. If your textbook has such questions, examine them. Determine whether or not they can be assigned before students begin reading in order to establish reading purposes.

*5. Incorporate the strategy presented in this module into one of your reading assignments. Be sure to evaluate the effectiveness of the lesson as a result.

Study Guide 4

The purpose of this Study Guide is to explain and demonstrate how the motivation strategy introduced in Study Guide 3 can be used to enhance the appeal of reading assignments. An assignment is an important part of a lesson plan. If it is not completed by the student, he or she will not have the necessary information for the following discussion. Due to a lack of information, the student will be unable to answer the teacher's questions, which means an ''F'' for the day. Such marks eventually lead to a failing grade for the grading period. Assignments are often not completed because they are not planned and presented in such a way as to create a need or to motivate the potential reader.

An examination of subject area teachers' plan books often reveals that reading assignments are given as follows:

Pages 127–152 for Tuesday. Continue discussion on WWII.

When the teachers' manuals for textbooks are examined, reading assignments such as the following often appear:

Pp. 127–152. This chapter describes the events leading up to the involvement of the United States in World War II. Important events, dates, places, and people are brought into perspective.

Both examples of reading assignments are not likely to appeal to your students. A few changes by the subject area teacher will make the assignment more motivating. Let us incorporate the motivation strategy (PARS) into this reading assignment to see how the likelihood is increased for achieving a motivated state in your students.

Stating the Purposes

First, we will need to obtain a *general purpose* for reading the assignment. General purposes are most meaningful and directive to students when they are stated as questions. So turn the statements into questions. Remember that the general topic under discussion

---

*Indicates core Enabling Activities.

is the events leading to the involvement of the United States in World War II. So our general purpose may be stated as the following question:

General Purpose for Reading
The United States generally does not want to fight others, and yet we were involved in a war. What major events led to the involvement of the United States in World War II?

This is a broad purpose that provides the student with direction for the reading assignment. Without such a broad purpose, students could become mired in details and lose sight of the broad organization of the reading assignment.

Second, *specific purposes* are needed to assist students in obtaining definite facts that eventually can be used to compile a list of major events leading to the involvement of the United States in World War II. Specific purposes are also most meaningful and directive when stated as questions. So write the specific purposes as questions. These questions serve as precise teacher directions for reading the textbook. Each question also serves as a short-range goal.

To get the reading assignment under way, all the teacher needs to do is to assign the general and specific purposes along with a *beginning* page number. The students are directed to read to obtain the necessary information. They are given no terminal page number. The following sample questions are arranged in the order of their discussion in the reading material and are designed to bring the reader into contact with *major events* asked for in the general-purpose question.

Specific Purposes for Reading
1. After World War I, the victorious Allies met in Paris, France, to arrange the terms of the peace treaty to be signed by the defeated Germans. Why were the German people unhappy with the terms of this peace treaty?
2. What was the economic and political situation in Germany following the signing of the peace treaty?
3. What conditions were present that allowed Hitler to come to power in Germany?
4. Why did Germany, Italy, and Japan join forces in World War II?
5. What was the reaction in the United States when Germany invaded Austria? Czechoslovakia? Poland?
6. What was the reaction in the United States when Germany invaded and conquered France and beat the British at Dunkirk?
7. Who were the candidates in the 1940 presidential election?
8. The winner of the 1940 presidential election interpreted his victory as a mandate from the American people to send aid to friendly, war-torn European countries. Why was this a significant event?
9. What did the Lend-Lease Act signal to the Germans, Italians, and Japanese?
10. What single event was responsible for the direct involvement of the United States in World War II?

Teacher Attitudes

The second component in the motivation strategy is *teacher attitudes*. Such beliefs regarding students and subject area are expressed by actions or dispositions. Although these attitudes and ensuing actions cannot be written like purposes into lesson plans, they are equally important. The teacher who differentiates reading assignments according to her knowledge of students' reading levels and interests, emphasizes *right* responses, avoids ridicule and degradation, and demonstrates enthusiasm for her subject area is building motivation and positive attitudes toward school and subject matter.

Knowledge of Results

The third component is *knowledge of results*. As was mentioned earlier in this Study Guide, immediate and frequent knowledge of results is instrumental to motivation. This component is easily incorporated into the reading assignment or lesson plan. After agreeing on questions to define purpose for reading, tell your students how they will be able to check upon the answers they obtain. You may want to consider providing prepared answers to the questions used for setting purposes. The students can then read the answers immediately after they complete their reading assignment. If their answers differ, provide them with an opportunity to reread parts of their assignment to see where they were misled. An alternative procedure for providing immediate feedback is to pair students or have them form small groups for comparing and discussing answers. Another technique you may wish to try is individual conferences with students to discuss and clarify their answers. Still another way is the customary class discussion of answers. For reluctant readers, reading assignments should be read partly in class and partly outside of class. Students who have a tendency not to complete assignments are often encouraged to do so when provided with an opportunity to start the assignment in class. This is especially true if provisions are made to show the reluctant readers how much progress they have made with their assignments in class and to assure them that they are obtaining the desired information.

Success

The fourth component is *success*. If you have established purposes for reading, demon-strated your belief in the dignity of your students and the value of your subject area, and made arrangements for immediate feedback, you have done most of what is necessary to ensure that every reader will meet with some success. To further ensure success, you may want to include in your reading assignment or lesson plan a few of the suggestions from the Success subsection of Activities for Implementing the Motivation Strategy (p. 268). A reading contract for a specified grade is a good way to assure success and motivate reluctant readers. Or you could ask reluctant readers to read their assignments for fewer purposes. Still another method is to assign only one purpose per period of reading time and to keep the reading unit short. Pairing a good student with a reluctant reader is an additional way to ensure the success of the reluctant reader. Remember, success breeds success and enhances motivation, but success must be planned for by the teacher. Planning success is essential for reluctant readers and cannot be left to chance.

You now see how the motivation strategy can be used to enhance the appeal of a reading assignment. Often, some changes in the nature of reading assignments and in our attitudes are necessary to achieve motivated students.

Practicum Exercise

Now it is your turn to modify a reading assignment. To complete this section all you need is a sheet of paper and a writing instrument. Answer each question in order, and then compare your answers with those provided in Answers to the Practicum Exercise.

Reading Assignment

Mr. Hernandez, an 11th grade biology teacher, is about to make a reading assignment to his students. The topic presently under discussion is the circulatory system of the human body. Pages 117–131 in the textbook discuss this topic. Mr. Hernandez has many reluctant readers in his class who consistently do not complete their reading assignments.

How would you advise Mr. Hernandez to prepare this reading assignment to enhance motivation?

Write down your answers to the following questions; when you have finished, compare them with the answers provided.

1. What are the key letters in the mnemonic device and key words in the motivation strategy that can be incorporated into this reading assignment?
2. The topic under study is the circulatory system, which includes the heart, blood, and blood vessels. What suggestions regarding *purpose* do you have for Mr. Hernandez?
3. What about the manner in which Mr. Hernandez makes the assignment? What are the important teacher attitude considerations?
4. Once Mr. Hernandez's students have completed their assignment, how can he provide for immediate feedback on results?
5. Mr. Hernandez has a reluctant reader for whom he wants to guarantee considerable success. What do you suggest?

When you have all your answers written down, compare them with the following answers.

Answers to the Practicum Exercise

1. The basic mnemonic device is PARS. The key words are *Purpose, Attitude, Results,* and *Success.*

2. Mr. Hernandez needs to set one general reading purpose related to the broad topic—the circulatory system. Then he needs to have approximately three specific reading purposes, one for each of the major components of the circulatory system—heart, blood, blood vessels. Reading purposes are probably best stated in the question form, which provides specific and clear direction for students.

3. If Mr. Hernandez takes into consideration his students' reading levels and interests, he is demonstrating a concern for students as individuals. If he is supportive of students' reading efforts (no matter how meager) and emphasizes their growth (no matter how small), he is demonstrating his concern for individuals. By doing these things and showing an enthusiasm for his subject area, he is building positive attitudes toward school, teachers, and subject area.

4. Knowledge of results can be provided immediately after students have completed their reading assignments by (a) providing self-correction answer keys, (b) placing students in pairs or small groups for comparing answers and discussing, or (c) holding teacher-pupil conferences. You may have thought of additional acceptable techniques that provide immediate feedback.

5. Success can be guaranteed through (a) writing a teacher-student work contract wherein the amount and quality of work is agreed upon in advance; (b) making a grade contract, which guarantees an agreed-upon grade for a specified quantity and/or quality of work; (c) pairing a reluctant reader with a good reader to work together in completing the assignment; (d) assigning material that is at or below the reading level of the reluctant reader and providing a single, short-range purpose for the assignment; (e) providing class time for reading the assignment.

If your answers agree with the sample answers in content or intention—congratulations! You have reached the end of this Study Guide and should now be ready for the Posttest.

One word of caution about motivation strategies before we close. Motivation strategies, like most other strategies, do not achieve their height of effectiveness until they have been applied consistently over a long period of time. The reason for this is simple: motivation factors are not discrete entities, but rather are interrelated factors. When manipulated by a teacher, each factor interacts with other factors. Ultimately the cumulative effect is that a need is created in even some of the most reluctant readers. This effect takes time to achieve, so do not become disappointed or give up using the strategy if your results are not immediate.

Final Comment

From this module you have acquired a strategy that should help you motivate more students in your subject area. The application of this strategy is left up to you as a teacher. No one may ever know if you apply or forget the strategy. But we hope that you will feel a professional and ethical responsibility to apply the motivational strategy presented in this module. If you do, we think you will accomplish more of your instructional objectives and many of your students will remember you as someone who cared.

Posttest

Directions: Read each of the following statements, and complete each Posttest item as directed.

1. Write a one-word synonym for *motivation*. List two sources of motivation.
2. List the eight major affective and cognitive factors influencing motivation.
3. List the core factors in the motivation strategy presented in this module. Write the motivation acronym presented in this module.
4. List and explain the application of this strategy, to enhance the appeal of the following subject area reading assignment.

Reading Assignment

> Mr. Davis is a physical education teacher interested in familiarizing his classes with football theory. He is about to assign to be read pages 22–31 from a basic textbook in sports. The current topic under study is The Fundamentals of Football, which consists of such subtopics as (a) time and periods of play, (b) kickoff, (c) scrimmage, (d) passing, (e) downs, and (f) scoring.

Posttest Answers

1. Some appropriate synonyms for *motivation* are *need* and *desire*. Two sources of motivation are intrinsic motivation (from within) and extrinsic motivation (from without).
2. The major affective and cognitive factors are:

Affective	*Cognitive*
Interest	Purpose
Attitude	Short-term goals
	Adjustments for reading levels
	Success
	Usefulness of knowledge
	Knowledge of results

3. The core factors in the motivational strategy introduced in this module are: *Purpose, Attitude, Results,* and *Success.* The key-word, mnemonic device to aid retention of the core factors is the acronym PARS.
4. The procedure for modifying the "Fundamentals of Football" reading assignment is:

   a. Establish the *purposes*: Prepare general and specific purposes for reading assignment. These purposes should be as questions.

   b. Adjust your *attitude*: Consider the needs and interests of individual students, be supportive of individual efforts, and be enthusiastic about your subject area. Be positive!

c. Provide *results*: Provide immediate knowledge of results through self-correction devices, small group discussions, or teacher-pupil conferences.

d. Ensure *success*: See to it that every individual student succeeds on some part of the reading assignment.

If any of your answers and the sample answers disagree in content or intention, recycle through the discussion of the specific components or the example reading assignment on U.S. involvement in World War II. If you are still having difficulty, see your instructor.

Selected Bibliography

Ausubel, D. P. "A Teaching Strategy for Culturally Deprived Pupils: Cognitive and Motivational Considerations." In *Teaching Reading in High School: Selected Articles*, edited by R. Karlin. Indianapolis: Bobbs-Merrill, 1969.

Bergman, J. R. "A New Tool Designed to Develop Positive Attitudes Toward Reading." *Reading Improvement* 14, no. 2 (Summer 1977): 70–73.

Betts, E. A. "Capture Reading Motivation." *Reading Improvement* 13, no. 1 (Spring 1976): 41–46.

Crisculo, N. P. "Convincing the Unconvinced to Read: 12 Strategies." *Journal of Reading* 21, no. 3 (1977): 219–21.

Darling, D. "Evaluating the Affective Dimension of Reading." *Perspectives in Reading*. Vol. 8. Edited by T. C. Barrett. Newark, Delaware: International Reading Association, 1967.

Dinkmeyer, D., and Dreikus, R. *Encouraging Children to Learn: The Encouragement Process*. Englewood Cliffs, New Jersey: Prentice-Hall, 1963.

Estes, T. H, "A Scale to Measure Attitudes Toward Reading." *Journal of Reading* 15, no. 2 (1971): 135–38.

Haimowitz, B. "Motivating Reluctant Readers in Inner-city Classes." *Journal of Reading* 21, no. 3 (1977): 227–30.

Heathington, B. S. "What to Do about Reading Motivation in the Middle School." *Journal of Reading* 22, no. 8 (1979): 709–13.

Hovious, M. "Motivating Junior High Readers." *Journal of Reading* 17, no. 5 (1974): 373–75.

Kohl, H. R. *Teaching the Unteachables*. New York: New York Review, 1967.

Krathwohl, D. R. et al. *Taxonomy of Educational Objectives: Handbook II, Affective Domain*. New York: David McKay, 1964.

Mason, G. E., and Mize, J. M. "Twenty-Two Sets of Methods and Materials for Stimulating Teen-Age Reading." *Journal of Reading* 21, no. 8 (1978): 735–41.

Mueller, D. L. "Teacher Attitudes Toward Reading." *Journal of Reading,* 17, no. 3 (1973): 202–5.

Seaton, H. W., and Aaron, R. L. "Modification of Pupil Attitude Toward Reading Through Positive Reinforcement Scheduling." *Reading Improvement* 15, no. 2 (Summer 1978): 96–100.

Smith, C. B.; Smith, S. L.; and Mikulecky, L. *Teaching Reading and Subject Matter in the Secondary School*. New York: Holt, Rinehart and Winston, 1978.

Welker, W. A. "Reading and the High School Student: An Attitudinal Approach to Reading." *Reading Improvement* 13, no. 2 (Summer 1976): 98–100.

MODULE **10**

Identifying and Helping
Problem Readers

Contents

Prospectus
  Rationale
  Objectives
  Resources and Time Required
Pretest
Branching Program Alternatives for Pretest Responses
Enabling Element 1: *Characteristics of Problem Readers*
Enabling Element 2: *Possible Causes of Reading Failure*
Enabling Element 3: *Using Nontesting Devices to Identify
      Possible Causes of Failure*
Enabling Element 4: *Referring and Helping Problem Readers*
Posttest
  Posttest Answers
Selected Bibliography

Prospectus

Rationale

One problem that constantly frustrates content area teachers is students who are reading far below grade level. These students often appear uninterested, rebellious, withdrawn, slow, or unmotivated. Usually, students who are poor readers do not complete assignments, attempt to copy from other students, and fail to take part in class discussions. You may wonder why these students even come to school.

This module is designed to (1) help you develop a better understanding of such students and (2) provide practical suggestions for identifying, helping, and referring students who are experiencing reading problems. The students with reading problems can survive—and learn—in content area classes. Their teachers must understand the symptoms and causes of reading problems, identify factors that may be interfering with the students' responsiveness to reading, be aware of sources of help, and have ideas for teaching students who cannot read the commonly used written materials. These competencies, along with the commitment to help students succeed, will enable students to perform better and learn more in your content area.

Objectives

Terminal Objective

You will identify problem readers and factors that may be interfering with their responsiveness to reading tasks, and adapt your instructional procedures to help problem readers succeed in your content areas.

Specific Objectives

1. You will describe the characteristics of problem readers and indicate your three major responsibilities for helping problem readers succeed in your content area classes.
2. You will list and explain by categories those factors that may cause reading failure.
3. You will use nontesting devices to identify factors that may cause reading failure.
4. You will indicate appropriate referral sources for students who manifest certain symptoms, and you will state guidelines and techniques for adapting instruction to help problem readers succeed in the content classes.

Resources and Time Required

All materials required for completion of this module are included. It would be most helpful if you talked with the school nurse, librarian, reading specialists, guidance counselor, school psychologist, and assistant principal in charge of curriculum to determine what specific support sources are available. Some discussions with the various resource personnel will enhance your accomplishment of the objectives in this module. The estimated time to complete the starred core Enabling Activities is two to four hours.

Pretest

Directions: For each question, determine the word that indicates your belief regarding your competency. If you are in doubt, choose NO.

1. Undoubtedly, you have problem readers in your classes. Can you define the term *problem reader* and describe your three major responsibilities in helping such readers?   YES   NO
2. Many factors determine how well students learn to read. Can you state and explain six major factors that influence reading achievement?   YES   NO
3. Content teachers share the responsibility for determining factors that may be interfering with students' responsiveness to reading. Do you have an observation checklist, personal inventory, and other nontesting devices useful for identifying possible causes of reading failure? Are you using them?   YES   NO
4. All teachers can help problem readers succeed if appropriate assistance is provided. Do you know the specialists to whom problem readers should be referred? Do you have guidelines and techniques to help problem readers succeed in your classes?   YES   NO

Branching Program Alternatives
for Pretest Responses

1. A problem reader is a student who is not able to read at grade level and therefore cannot read the content area materials commonly used in your classes. If you are not sure of the typical behaviors of problem readers or your role in identifying, referring, and helping problem readers, complete Enabling Element 1. If you are familiar with these behaviors and know your three major responsibilities for helping problem readers, you are ready for Enabling Element 2, which deals with factors contributing to reading failure.

2. The six major factors that influence reading achievement are similar to those that influence success in any academic area. If you are familiar with the six factors (physical condition, language development, environment, aptitude, social-emotional problems, and educational background), then go right on to Enabling Element 3. See Enabling Element 2 if you need to refresh your memory or learn a mnemonic device to help you remember the factors.

3. If you have your own checklist, personal inventory, and other nontesting devices that you are using to identify possible causes of reading failure, go to Enabling Element 4. If you need such nontesting instruments, you will find sample devices in Enabling Element 3.

4. Do you know to whom you should refer a student who exhibits certain educationally inhibiting behaviors, and are you aware of guidelines and techniques for helping problem readers in your classroom? Enabling Element 4 is designed to alleviate teacher and student frustration by providing alternative strategies to help such students. If you want to "make it through the day," as well as actually help students succeed, do Enabling Element 4.

Enabling Element 1
Characteristics of Problem Readers

Specific Objective 1

You will describe the characteristics of problem readers and indicate your three major responsibilities for helping problem readers succeed in your content area classes.

Enabling Activities

*1. Read Study Guide 1 to determine typical problem reader behaviors and also to learn a general definition of the term *problem reader*.

---

*Indicates core Enabling Activity.

2. At a departmental faculty meeting or with the entire faculty in your school, discuss who is responsible for teaching basic reading skills to those students who are reading below grade level. Will the English teachers assume this responsibility? Should special developmental reading classes be established in the school? Is there a need for some special remedial reading classes in the school? Is there a sufficient number of reading classes in your school to provide for the number of students who are not reading on grade level?

3. List the names of ten students you have or have had who can be classified as problem readers. After each name, write two or three adjectives that describe them as students. Analyze your list to determine what common characteristics the students have or had. Also, think about the differences among the students, and list possible reasons for the differences. Why is it that some students learn to cope better with their problems?

4. Look at the achievement scores in reading if they are available for your students. You would expect one-third of the students to be reading *below* grade level, one-third of the students *on* grade level, and one-third of the students *above* grade level. What percentage of your students are reading below grade level according to the results of a standardized achievement test in reading?

*5. Think about how problem readers feel in your class. What would it be like to be unable to complete the reading assignments and therefore be unable to participate in class discussions? What would it be like to be given a test that you could not read? What would it be like to be asked to read in front of your peers? Would you withdraw and say nothing, or would you try to save face by making fun of a situation or by creating some disturbance so as to avoid the unpleasant situation? Would you be inclined to cheat by looking at someone else's work? Can you begin to feel the frustrations of a problem reader? If so, are you committed to doing something about them?

Study Guide 1

By the time students enter middle or secondary schools, they should be able to use an appropriate strategy for attacking unfamiliar words. They should be able to comprehend different types of written materials and have an extensive reading vocabulary. Students at this level can use different study strategies and employ a flexible reading rate. These students should be developing many and varied tastes and interests in reading and critically evaluating what they read. Finally, it is hoped that students who enter middle and secondary schools will consider reading to be an important source of pleasure and knowledge.

Obviously, not all students exhibit these behaviors when they complete elementary school. Some students are behind even in the first grade. You will be able to readily identify problem readers if you first administer an informal suitability survey. You will find that some students will miss most of the comprehension questions on the informal suitability survey, which you administer as a group test. When you meet with these

*Indicates core Enabling Activity.

students to administer your informal suitability survey on an individual basis, you will find them embarrassed to read aloud to you. Some of the students may even refuse to do so because they are ashamed that they are unable to read materials corresponding to their present grade level. As a content area teacher, you have a right to be concerned about these students' chances of success in your class—especially if reading assignments are frequently used as a way of helping students obtain information and ideas.

Problem Reader Defined

A reading specialist would define *problem reader* as a student who is reading two years below *expected* reading level. For example, a student who is expected to read at the ninth-grade level according to his aptitude, and yet is reading at the seventh-grade level, would be classified as a problem reader. If this student is in the seventh grade, he is not much of a problem reader to the content area teacher. Conversely, if this student is in the ninth grade, he is a "problem" to the content area teacher—the student will have difficulty reading some of the commonly used reading materials. A student having this inability is truly a "problem" in your eyes.

For content area teachers, then, *problem reader* can be defined *as a student who is reading below grade level and therefore is unable to read the materials you commonly use in your content area classes* (even though you implement ideas from the previous modules). These students need remedial reading instruction in a special class within the school or at a private reading clinic. You may think it would be wise for these students to drop out of your class until they are able to meet the prerequisite reading level, but you realize this is impossible. The problem reader also feels discouraged realizing he or she is unable to complete all of the course requirements regardless of motivation. One of your major concerns then as a content area teacher should be identifying and helping these students in your classes.

Characteristics of Problem Readers

A summary of the characteristics of problem readers follows. An array of these behaviors will be evident, although one student will not exhibit all of the behaviors. In fact, you can lessen their rate of occurrence by assigning materials suitable for the students' reading levels. For example, if you were to use a textbook written at the eleventh-grade level to teach a group of eighth-grade students, many students would manifest characteristics of problem readers. To prevent this from occurring, determine the readability levels of the materials you commonly use. Remember that a problem reader is a student who is not reading on grade level and therefore is unable to read the content area materials you commonly use. You can create many problem readers in your class if you use textbooks or other reading materials written at a higher readability level than the grade of intended use. Generally, the problem reader

Has Inadequate Word-Pronunciation Skills. When you ask a problem reader to read orally during administration of an informal suitability survey, you will notice that the student fails to use context clues. Problem readers tend to skip hard words or guess at unfamiliar words, rather than analyze the word to see if there is a prefix, suffix, or stem. These students generally ask someone what the word is, rather than use the other steps in the word-pronunciation strategy (described in Module 8).

Has a Limited Vocabulary. The major reason problem readers have difficulty understanding materials is that their vocabularies are limited. Problem readers do know the meanings of some words in the content area, but most of their definitions could be classified at the specific level. They will understand some words at the functional level of understanding, but rarely do they have conceptual definitions for words used in your content area.

Has Low Level of Comprehension. Problem readers have difficulty answering the higher level questions you ask to check comprehension. Frequently, problem readers can answer recall or recognition questions, but fail to answer questions involving translation, application, analysis, synthesis, or evaluation. A large part of the difficulty is caused by the lack of vocabulary. However, when given the meanings of the words, problem readers still have difficulty arriving at correct answers.

Does Not Apply Study Skills or Strategies. When teachers make reading assignments, problem readers usually approach the assignment by attempting to read the first page. Problem readers do not survey the materials or develop questions to be used as purposes in reading. Problem readers rarely take time to recite, since they did not really have any particular questions in mind.

Observe, refer, and help problem readers.

Likewise, these students spend very little time reviewing material they have read. In addition to having poor study strategies, the problem reader has not developed the study skills which are necessary to read materials in your content area.

Appears Uninterested or Lazy. Problem readers are *not motivated* during class sessions and frequently make you wonder why they are even in school. No matter how effective you are in applying the PARS motivational strategy, the problem reader fails to read the assignment because it is too difficult. Some problem readers withdraw and try to "hide" from you when you are asking questions as a part of the class discussion; whereas others overact by making fun of the situation. Many problem readers have irregular attendance because they feel inadequate in classroom situations. This irregular attendance continues to hinder their academic progress.

Quite frankly, it is not going to take you long to recognize problem readers in your classes. You will identify them early if you use the Informal Suitability Survey and the reading skills tests, which were described in Modules 3 and 4 respectively. If you do not use these assessment devices, when you make reading assignments in your classes or administer quizzes, the above characteristics will be evident. What are you expected to do as a content area teacher?

The Content Area Teacher's Responsibilities

We do not want you to stop working on the objectives of your content area. It is your responsibility to help the students achieve the objectives of your particular area. It is not your responsibility to teach children how to read, but rather to teach them how to do math problems, develop concepts in social studies, achieve objectives in physical education, or whatever your particular content area is. There are three responsibilities, though, that you can accept to help the problem reader succeed in accomplishing the objectives in your class. If you believe in your students, and especially have an extra concern for the students who are problem readers, you can help them accomplish the objectives of your classes.

Identify. Your first task is to *identify* those factors that may be causing the reading failure. Your students, if given a choice, do not want to be problem readers. They would like to be able to read the materials with ease! Rather than just classifying or describing these students as lazy, uninterested, or "turned-off" to schooling, you must try to identify what factors are influencing their lack of reading achievement. Behavior is *caused*; therefore you must look for factors influencing a student's lack of response to reading instruction. (The next Study Guide deals with six factors that influence reading achievement and provides nontesting devices to help identify factors hindering a particular student's progress.) If you can identify factors causing a student's reading problem, you may be able to find help to overcome those factors hindering progress.

Refer. Your second responsibility is to *refer* students to colleagues in specialized areas. The school nurse, guidance counselor, media specialist, administrators, school psychologist, and reading teachers may be able to provide special assistance to help eliminate some of the factors causing the student's reading problems. You must be willing to work with your colleagues as a team member because humans are simply too complex for one person to know all the answers. Rather than giving oversimplified answers to the student or the parent as to why the student is having a reading problem or saying that the student will "grow out of it," you must seek the help of colleagues who may have some information or expertise that goes beyond yours. Your second responsibility then is to refer problem readers. (Some specific ideas to help you are suggested in Enabling Element 4 of this module.)

Help. Your responsibility is only beginning when you have referred problem readers. You cannot fold your arms and say, "I have done my part." The student is still coming to you in class to accomplish the objectives of your content area. Your third responsibility then is to *help* the problem reader achieve these objectives by adapting some of your instructional techniques to help problem readers succeed in your classes. You may adapt by using low-level reading materials, using more audio-visual aids to help problem readers get information and ideas, administering oral tests, having the students help each other, and/or making differentiated reading assignments (as suggested in Module 3). Although these adaptations do require some extra efforts on your part, you will be surprised at the repertoire of ideas and materials you will be able to develop if you are sincere about helping problem readers succeed. You will find that your students can achieve many of your objectives when they get the information and ideas via some technique other than reading. Problem readers are especially skillful in getting information by listening to tapes, looking at pictures, participating in class discussions, and by using such audio-visual aids as films, filmstrips, and overhead transparencies.

You may be thinking that it would be great if every student could read the materials in your content area with ease. This is an ideal, and we have not and probably never will reach this stage. Therefore, your responsibility is to (1) identify problem readers and the factors that may be hindering their progress in reading, (2) refer these students for specialized help, and (3) make adaptations in your instructional strategies to help them achieve your vital objectives. Now go to Enabling Element 2 to find out why some students are not able to read on grade level.

Enabling Element 2
Possible Causes of Reading Failure

Specific Objective 2

You will list and explain by categories those factors that may cause reading failure.

Enabling Activities

*1. Read Study Guide 2. Identify and be able to explain the six major factors that influence reading achievement.

2. In addition to discussing how emotional problems can cause reading failure, discuss how reading failure can influence emotional problems.

3. Elementary school teachers often receive the total blame for reading failure. Discuss why this is unjust.

*4. Usually a student's failure in reading is due to a number of interrelated factors. Describe some students who can be classified as problem readers, and indicate the various factors that may be working together to cause the reading problems.

5. Some reading specialists believe the environment is the most important factor influencing reading achievement. Do you agree with this statement? Can parents of middle-school and secondary-school students help their children in reading? In what ways? How can these suggestions be communicated to parents?

Study Guide 2

Content teachers can be of valuable assistance if they know some of the reasons students fail to read on grade level. This information can be used to help problem readers succeed, even though they are experiencing reading problems. As you read the descriptions of possible causes of reading failure, try to think of ways you can identify these factors in your students. Remember that problems are often caused by two or more interrelated factors rather than by one isolated factor.

Physical Condition

A number of physical factors correlate with failure in reading. Disabilities in vision and hearing can produce reading problems. For example, a student may have difficulty obtaining a clear image from materials printed on the chalkboard or in the textbook. Reduced visual acuity, fusion difficulty, and eye-muscle control problems are just a few of the visual disabilities that correlate with reading failure. Likewise, students with insufficient hearing or discrimination usually have problems in reading because they misunderstand the teacher's directions and explanations.

The general health of the student is also an important factor in learning to read. Students who have not had a proper diet or sufficient rest may experience difficulty in reading, which is a highly abstract task requiring a high degree of concentration. These students generally have poor attendance, and they may have experienced many childhood illnesses, which resulted in extended absences from school. In some cases, specific illnesses such as glandular disturbances or thyroid dysfunctions may hinder academic achievement. Other students may take inappropriate drugs or substances that influence their hearing, vision, and general health.

---

*Indicates core Enabling Activities.

Language Development

The relationship between language development and success in reading is obvious. Students who have a meager vocabulary, poorly developed sound–symbol relationships, and a weak grasp of the grammar base of the language have considerable difficulty with reading.

Not all students grow in height and weight at the same rate. Likewise, not all students develop language facility at the same rate or have excellent models of language. Students who mature slowly are likely to arrive at school too immature for the academic task of reading. Likewise, students who have not heard standard English will experience difficulty when they read unfamiliar language patterns and words. Thus, some students fall behind in reading—and remain behind—because of the maturational factors and substandard-language models.

Environment

Reading requires students to bring meaning to printed symbols. To find meaning is only possible, however, when students have had some experiences related to what they are reading. Students who have not had many real or vicarious experiences are at a disadvantage when reading. For an example, if a student is reading a selection concerning a country he has visited, he is likely to get more meaning from what he is reading than another student who has never been out of the city in which he was born.

Parents are also a part of the environment and set an example for their children. Those parents who read frequently and enjoy reading as a source of information and pleasure are most likely to convey these attitudes to their children. Conversely, students who come from homes where there are no reading materials may experience difficulty in learning to read because they have not learned to value this task.

Aptitude

There is a high positive correlation between reading achievement and intelligence among high-school students and adults because many of the factors measured by present-day intelligence tests are the same factors required for success in reading. For example, most intelligence tests measure visual memory, auditory memory, the ability to make judgments, and general information and vocabulary—all very important in learning to read. A student who does not seem to have the aptitude for learning to read as well as some other students usually falls behind in reading. However, students with less than average intelligence can still learn to read as long as opportunities are provided and the instructional methods are adapted to their aptitudes.

Social-Emotional Problems

Social-emotional factors also influence reading achievement. Some students fail in reading because they are overwhelmed with social and emotional problems resulting from poor relationships with friends and family. Reading difficulties sometimes result from personal problems brought about by inappropriate relationships with parents, siblings and peers. Symptoms associated with social and emotional problems (such as a short attention span, preoccupation, and lack of desire to stay with a task) are the same behaviors associated with academic failure.

Educational Background

Schools have also caused many reading problems among students. It is common to hear high-school teachers blame elementary-school teachers for poor reading instruction, and sometimes they are right. However, many factors influence poor reading achievement. Previous teachers may have used unsuitable materials, methods, or may have neglected some students who attended irregularly and seemed unmotivated by reading. With large numbers of students in the classroom, teachers find it impossible to provide for all the individual differences and cannot do as much as they would like to do, or need to do, to help each student. The result is that students' reading levels and needs for specific skills have not been properly determined and/or remediated.

PLEASE Remember the Factors

These six factors work together to either help or hinder progress in reading. It is essential that teachers consider all of them when determining why some students have failed to learn to read as well as expected.

A mnemonic device that may help you remember these factors is the acronym PLEASE. Each letter in this acronym represents one of the major factors influencing reading achievement:

P—physical condition—health, hearing, vision, nutrition
L—language development—vocabulary, grammar, sentence structure
E—environment—home, attitudes toward reading, motivation
A—aptitude—visual memory, auditory memory, judgment, general information
S—social-emotional problems—relationships with peers, family, and self
E—educational background—quality of teaching, appropriateness of materials, class
   size

Perhaps you will remember this acronym because it is the plea made by problem readers—Please! Your task is to *PLEASE identify*, *PLEASE refer*, and *PLEASE help* problem readers. The other study guides in this module will aid you as you perform these tasks.

Enabling Element 3
Using Nontesting Devices to Identify Possible Causes of Reading Failure

Specific Objective 3

You will use nontesting devices to identify factors that may cause reading failure.

Enabling Activities

*1. Read Study Guide 3. Compare the advantages and disadvantages of the different devices you can use to identify possible causes of reading failure.

*2. Try the Observational Checklist with some of the students in your class who are problem readers. Can you identify some explanations for the reading failures of these students? Remember, the more you use the checklist, the more automatic your observations will become. Periodically reread the checklist to refresh your memory.

3. Duplicate the Incomplete Sentences and Personal Inventory forms; have your students complete them. Think of ways to use this information for adapting instruction.

4. Talk with teachers in your building to determine who will use the different devices. It is suggested that all teachers use the Observational Checklist as a guide to observing and talking with students, and that others (such as homeroom teachers) who have the major responsibility for certain students use the Personal Inventory and Incomplete Sentences. Adapt these suggestions to your particular school.

5. Share some of the results of the personal inventories with the school librarian. Responses to items 7, 9, 13, and 20 may provide valuable information for selecting books, magazines, and other materials for the library or media center.

Study Guide 3

If the factors that seem to be interfering with students' responsiveness to reading can be identified, then students can be given appropriate help. Even though content area teachers are not expected to provide remedial reading instruction for problem readers, they can be of valuable assistance in determining the factors that are hindering progress. Four useful devices for identifying PLEASE factors are included in this module.

Teachers need to employ different techniques for gathering information about problems because students are different. Some students are eager to talk with teachers; talking and listening to these students is appropriate. Others will avoid talking about themselves. In these cases, the teacher must be able to observe or use paper and pencil

---

*Indicates core Enabling Activities.

inventories to gather information. Presented in this Study Guide are an Observational Checklist, guidelines for interviewing students, and two paper and pencil inventories.

Using an Observational Checklist

The checklist on the next page is designed to provide guidelines for observing students who are experiencing reading difficulties. If you read the checklist periodically, you will be sure to have these factors and specific behaviors paramount in your mind as you are observing students. Keep in mind the mnemonic device presented in Study Guide 2—PLEASE. Each one of the letters in this acronym refers to one of the major reasons for reading failure:

P-physical factors, L-language development, E-environmental factors, A-aptitude, S-social-emotional, E-educational factors. Some observable behaviors are listed for each one of these factors.

You are not expected to complete this checklist for each of your students. The purpose of the checklist is to guide your observations of students as you try to identify possible causes that may be hindering them. Often your observations are the keys for identifying the causes of reading problems. PLEASE keep these factors in mind so you can help identify possible reasons for students' lack of responsiveness to instruction.

**Observational Checklist for Identifying
Possible Causes of Reading Failure**

Directions: Which area(s) seem to be interfering with the students' responsiveness to reading? Underline specific behaviors you observe, and add comments as necessary.

_____ *P—Physical Factors*   *Comments:*
    When the student is reading, does she
        Lose her place?
        Rub her eyes?
        Blink excessively?
        Tilt her head so as to use only one eye?
        Complain of blurred print, headaches, or watering eyes?
    When you speak to the student, does she
        Tilt her head?
        Cup her ear?
        Appear inattentive?
        Ask you to repeat directions?
    Does she appear well rested and generally healthy?
    What is her attendance record?

_____ *L—Language Factors*   *Comments:*
    When she speaks, does she
      Have a meager vocabulary?
      Use poor sentence structure?
    Does the student make frequent spelling errors that indicate
      a lack of knowledge of sound–symbol relationships?
    Does she have a past history of poor performance in lan-
      guage-related courses?
    If you have had occasions to talk with the parents and
      siblings, did you notice anything helpful for interpreting
      the student's language background?

_____ *E—Environment Factors*   *Comments:*
    Does the student talk about places she has visited or events
      that she has experienced?
    Does the student have any books, magazines, or other
      reading materials of her own?
    Do her parents seem interested in her and accept her?
    Is education valued by the family?

_____ *A—Aptitude Factors*   *Comments:*
    Does the student ask questions?
    Does she have a fairly good background of information?
    Is she able to draw conclusions and make sound judgments
      based on given facts?
    Does she learn things rapidly and remember what she has
      learned?
    Is she able to see similarities and differences in concepts?

_____ *S—Social-Emotional Factors*   *Comments:*
    Is the student accepted by her family and peers?
    Is she able to get along with others?
    Does she have a positive self-concept?
    Is she able to control her emotions and concentrate long
      enough to complete a task?

_____ *E—Educational Factors*   *Comments:*
    Does the student have positive or negative attitudes toward
      the school?
    Does she have purposes for learning?
    Has the student experienced success or failure in most
      academic areas?
    Has the student been enrolled in any remedial reading
      programs?
    Are the materials available appropriate for the student?

Using a Personal Inventory

Consider using or adapting the following Personal Inventory if you would like to quickly gather more information about your students. You can administer a Personal Inventory to the students for whom you have the major responsibility. As you read the items, notice that they are designed to gather information concerning the six major factors influencing reading achievement and academic progress in general.

Notice that the directions indicate that a student can leave blank those items he or she does not wish to answer. You should make note of these items and then use observation as a device to gather more information concerning the items. As with all devices, remember that the responses indicate the feelings of the students on that particular day. The students' answers must be combined with other samples of behavior before any conclusions or judgments are made.

After administering the inventory, use the guidelines provided for interpreting the information. Keep in mind, however, that some responses may provide information concerning two or more factors.

Personal Inventory

Name _____ Date _____
Address _____ Age _____
Telephone _____

Directions: The following questions are designed to help me get to know you. Write your answers in the blanks provided. If you are not sure of some answer, or do not want to answer some question, simply leave it blank.

1. What other schools have you attended? _____
   _____

2. Are you supposed to wear glasses? _____ If yes, when did you first get them?
   _____

3. Do your eyes bother you when you read or write? _____ In what way? _____
   _____

4. Is your hearing (circle one) excellent, good, fair, or poor?

5. Is your health (circle one) excellent, good, fair, or poor?

6. How many hours do you sleep each night? _____
   _____

7. Do you read for pleasure? _____ If yes, name some of the recent books or magazines you have read. _____
   _____

8. Is your reading (circle one) excellent, good, fair, or poor?

9. What is the most interesting topic you like to study? _____
   _____

10. What is the least interesting topic you must study? _____
_____

11. How much time do you usually spend each day studying outside of school? __

12. List some of the places that you have visited outside of (city) _____
_____
_____

13. What interests do you have outside of school? _____
_____
_____

14. What school activities do you enjoy? _____
_____
_____

15. How do you get along with your parents? _____
_____
_____
_____

16. Circle the word that shows how most teachers think of you as a student: excellent, good, fair, or poor.

17. Is your vocabulary: excellent, good, fair or poor?

18. Is your spelling: excellent, good, fair, or poor?

19. Do you have a place to study at home? Please describe it.
_____
_____

20. What kinds of responsibilities would you like to have as an adult?
_____
_____
_____
_____

21. How do you get along with the other students in this class? Do you know these students well? Who are your favorite students?
_____
_____
_____
_____

22. Why do some people like you? _____
_____
_____

23. Are there some people who do not like you? _____
Why? _____
_____

24. What is your father's occupation? _____
What is your mother's occupation? _____

25. What language is usually spoken in your home? _____
_____

26. Do your parents talk with you about school? _____ If so, what kinds of things do they ask? _____
_____
_____

Guide to Interpreting Information
From the Personal Inventory

Major Factor	*Questions Designed to Provide Information*
Physical Condition	2, 3, 4, 5, 6
Language Development	8, 17, 18, 25
Environment	12, 19, 24, 26
Aptitude	9, 10, 13, 20
Social-Emotional Problems	15, 21, 22, 23
Educational Background	1, 7, 11, 14, 16

Incomplete Sentences

Some teachers like to use incomplete sentences such as the following to gather information about students. The teacher who has the major responsibility for certain students may be the one who will administer the incomplete sentences. When interpreting responses to incomplete sentences, it should be remembered that the student's responses only represent feelings on a particular day. Before making any rash judgments, more information should be gathered by consulting the guidance counselor, cumulative records, personal inventory, other teachers, and information from the talks you might have with the student.

Incomplete Sentences

Name _____ Date _____

Directions: Quickly complete the following sentences. Write down the first thing that enters your mind. There are no right or wrong answers.

1. Reading is _____
2. I like to _____
3. My friends _____
4. I feel _____
5. The best magazine _____
6. Elementary school was _____
7. My eyes _____

8. My ears _____

9. My parents _____

10. Education is _____

11. I have been to _____

12. I wish I could _____

13. When I read to others _____

14. I am liked by _____

15. School is _____

16. My teachers _____

17. Books are _____

18. I sleep _____

19. When I finish school _____

20. My home _____

21. I need help in _____

22. My best subject is _____

23. Spelling is _____

24. Teachers usually _____

Although responses vary, in general you will find the following guides useful as you analyze the responses to the incomplete sentences. Certain responses will necessarily fit more than one classification; however, we have tried to make them as discrete as possible. For example, one student may complete item 4 with "I feel tired." Another student may say, "I feel lonely." In the first case the item refers to a physical factor, and the second response concerns the social-emotional factors. It will be necessary to adapt the following guidelines to the students' responses.

Guidelines for Analyzing the
Incomplete Sentence Responses

Factor	*Number of Sentence That May Provide Information*
Physical	4, 7, 8, 18
Language	1, 13, 17, 23
Environment	5, 10, 11, 13, 20
Aptitude	12, 19, 21, 22
Social-Emotional	2, 3, 9, 14
Education	6, 15, 16, 24

Talking and Listening to Students

Some students are eager to share information with their teachers if the teachers seem interested in them. Talking to and listening to students can be a useful technique to gather information concerning the six factors influencing reading achievement. All teachers have some responsibility to listen to students because different students relate better to different teachers. If all the teachers on the staff are aware of the importance of listening to students and are perceptive as they listen and talk to students, the staff will be better able to help the students. For example, some students will relate to the physical education teacher on the field, but not relate at all to the English teacher in the classroom; whereas, another student will relate better to the English teacher and avoid face-to-face encounters with the physical education teacher.

Many of the questions in the Personal Inventory form can be used in talking with students. Of course, the questions will be phrased differently and asked in a natural sequence as the conversation develops. A teacher who is aware of the six major categories, however, can organize the responses of the students into meaningful categories for interpretation.

When talking to students, you must be sincere and present an attitude of concern. Ask questions in such a way that students realize you are not "meddling," but rather trying to help them. You will want to aid the students in accepting themselves as they are, and yet provide hope for improvement. Help the students realize that reading and success in academic areas are important, but that there are other important things in life, too. Listed below are sample questions you can use to gather information during a *natural* conversation with the student.

Sample Questions That Can Be
Used When Talking With Students

Physical Condition. Have you ever had any trouble with seeing or hearing? What illnesses have you had? How many hours do you sleep in a day?

Language. What language do your parents speak? Did they graduate from high school? College? Do you have any problems in learning to spell, read, or write?

Environment. What places have you visited while on vacation? How do your parents feel about your school activities? Can you study at home?

Aptitude. What things do you do best? Do you want to do better in school? Why? Do you think you can learn to read better?

Social-Emotional. Who are your best friends? How well do you get along with your family? What kinds of things make you happy? Frustrated? Sad?

Education. What kind of student were you in elementary school? Have you ever been in a special reading class? Do your teachers generally like you?

Final Comment

In addition to using these nontesting devices to determine possible causes of reading failure, you can also use some of the reading skills tests presented in Module 4, Diagnosing Reading Skill Needs. These skill tests will help you further identify special reading difficulties that may be remediated. Likewise, if you use an Informal Suitability Survey, you will be doing your part to help find appropriate materials for problem readers. One testing or nontesting device is simply insufficient. You need a battery of devices to enable you to gather information that will in turn enable you to help students. For practical ideas on what to do with information that you have gathered, go on to Enabling Element 4.

Enabling Element 4
Referring and Helping Problem Readers

Specific Objective 4

You will indicate appropriate referral sources for students who manifest certain symptoms, and you will state guidelines and techniques for adapting instruction to help problem readers succeed in the content classes.

Enabling Activities

*1. Read Study Guide 4. Identify possible resource persons to whom problem readers can be referred. Also make note of ways you can help such students in your classes.

*2. Talk with the school nurse, psychologist, and guidance counselors to determine the specific services they offer and the procedures for initiating referral. Ask about professional services that are free to low-income families.

*3. Talk with the reading specialist and developmental reading teachers to determine what reading services are offered in the school. What other types of reading instruction should be offered?

 4. Discuss guidelines for referring students for special help. What are the school and county guidelines for referring problem readers? You should not refer students to specialists outside the school without the advice and consent of the appropriate person. Often the guidance counselor, assistant principal, school psychologist, or some other resource person is able to use more elaborate screening devices to determine if referrals are in fact necessary.

 5. Talk with your colleagues about ways of involving parents in home–school tutoring programs for problem readers.

 6. Read the Teacher Daily Dozen Checklist. Note one item which you would like to improve. Brainstorm with your colleagues and review previous modules to determine specific ways in which you can implement the behavior.

Study Guide 4

If you have identified problem readers and perhaps determined some of the factors that may be interfering with their responsiveness to reading, what is the next step? Should you discontinue teaching your content area and begin teaching reading? Obviously, this is neither possible nor desirable.

There are two additional ways content teachers can help problem readers. First, you need to refer students to the proper sources of help. You are not expected to teach

---

*Indicates core Enabling Activities.

beginning reading skills, diagnose or prescribe glasses or hearing aids, or act as a full-time guidance counselor. You need and must have help of specialists! Second, even though you are not expected to teach primary-grade reading skills, there are some adaptations you can make in your instructional strategies to help problem readers. You do have some responsibility to help students who are reading two years or more below their grade level to succeed in your content area while they are trying to overcome their reading deficiencies. Problem readers can succeed in content areas if you make these minor adaptations. Suggestions for referral and ideas for adapting instructional strategies are presented for each one of the major factors that influences reading achievement. PLEASE use referrals and the following guidelines and techniques—they help!

Helping Students with Physical Problems

1. Refer the student to the school nurse for further screening. Perhaps a visual, hearing, or health problem has been missed or has developed recently. If drug or substance abuse is evident, refer the student to the school counselor.

2. Encourage the student to wear glasses or a hearing aid if prescribed. Help the student accept herself as she is by being honest with her concerning any physical limitations.

3. Suggest short periods of work when doing close work, such as reading and writing. Direct the student to set a time limit for studying.

4. Have the student sit near the chalkboard, screen, or generally where the action is. Do not pay too much attention to her so as to make her feel awkward and unusual.

5. If necessary, contact the librarian to see if books with larger print are available. You might also see if cassettes are available or could be made for those students who have a difficult time reading, but yet are able to listen and comprehend.

6. Remember not to turn your back on students when speaking or to put your hands in front of your face. Often teachers are not conscious of habits that may interfere with their teaching effectiveness. Evaluate yourself continuously to see if you are articulating and maintaining good eye contact.

7. It might be helpful to write key vocabulary words on the chalkboard and discuss the meaning and pronunciations of the words using the suggestions in Modules 5 and 8.

8. If the student is experiencing health problems that are hindering her attendance, you might ask the visiting teacher to contact the parents. It may be necessary to adjust the assignments and number of credits according to the capabilities of the student.

Helping Students with Language Problems

1. Refer the student to a remedial reading specialist or remedial English classes. When doing so, share the information you have gathered about the student's reading skills and habits.

2. Give oral tests if possible. Often you can administer tests orally while the other

students are taking the written exams. If this is not possible, see if a parent volunteer can help you.

3. Provide information on cassettes or have others read to students for whom suitable materials are not available. Often students can listen and understand what they may not be able to read.

4. Repeat the student's responses using correct grammar and good sentence structure. Realize that you alone are not going to change the student's use of language overnight; however, if all teachers make conscientious efforts, and if the student desires to improve, it is possible to change language patterns.

5. Use many visual materials to expand concepts. The old saying "a picture is worth a thousand words" may be trite, but it is very true.

6. Correct spelling errors by going over the frequently missed words. Point out the sounds that may be confusing to the students.

7. To help students increase their vocabularies at higher levels, use the ideas in Module 5. Many problem readers only have specific understandings of words.

8. Suggest some self-study books designed to improve spelling, reading, or writing. Many times these books include practical exercises and essential information valuable for improving spelling, writing, and reading.

Helping Students with Environmental Problems

1. Use many visual and auditory aids to help the students develop concepts. Students can develop many concepts through vicarious experiences when direct experiences are not possible.

2. Refer the student to the guidance counselor if physical abuse is evident. Child abuse agencies rely on teachers for referrals; however, you should talk with the appropriate authority before making referrals to outside agencies.

3. Praise the student sincerely for ideas, good suggestions, and so forth. Do not overdo the praise so as to make the student feel that you really do not have confidence in her.

4. Be available to parents if they express concern. Many times parents are interested in their children and want them to do better.

5. Have confidence in the student. Expect her to do her best and show disappointment when you do not get her best efforts.

6. Make the students aware of the various resources that are available to them at school and public libraries. If you use many reading materials in your classes, arrange visits to the libraries to inform students of what materials are available and how to locate them. Provide opportunities for the students to browse and use some of the materials that are interesting to them.

7. Help students realize the value of having a place for study and good study habits. Provide specific suggestions on how they can study in your content area. Suggest places in the school or community where they can study and at the same time enjoy the company of other people if desired.

8. Read or tell stories about famous people who have been successful even though they came from a detrimental environment. Magazines and newspaper articles often include such examples. Remember, you are not going to change attitudes in one day; however, if you take advantage of teaching opportunities on a daily basis, the change will occur.

Helping Students with Social-Emotional Problems

1. Refer the student to the guidance counselor or school psychologist. Some students have problems requiring special analysis and guidance. After the student has met with the guidance counselor and/or the school psychologist, talk with them to determine what recommendations they have for helping the student in the classroom.

2. Avoid antagonizing the student. Avoid that which tends to ''set off'' the student.

3. Determine the student's strengths and praise her sincerely. At the same time, help the problem reader face her weaknesses and set goals for improving herself.

4. Be ready to listen to the student. Not all students are ready to talk; but when they do, they are generally trying to get advice from you.

5. Give responsibilities that are of interest to the student. Differentiate your assignments according to interests and abilities.

6. Accept the student as she is. You may not like what she does, but you can still like her as a person.

7. Use discussion groups and group dynamic techniques to help students develop skill in working with and accepting others. Often students form stereotypes and develop cliques that hinder social activities. It is important for teachers to help students appreciate the differences in their classmates.

8. Help students plan schedules that allow time for social involvement as well as studying. Help the students accept the fact that most students enjoy socializing and yet must spend some of the time studying if they are going to succeed academically. Plan flexible schedules with the students.

Helping Students with Less Aptitude for Reading

1. Refer the student to the school psychologist for an individual intelligence test to determine special aptitudes. An I.Q. score is not as meaningful as the scores for factors of intelligence that the test measures. Determine special areas in which the student might have a better aptitude, such as in visual or auditory memory, and then capitalize on these strengths as you teach the student or give suggestions for studying.

2. Use many visual materials, first-hand experiences, and concrete objects when teaching. Keep in mind that reading is a highly abstract task; it requires the person to form mental images from the printed symbols. Many times students who demonstrate low aptitude have not had as many experiences as others.

3. Adjust materials to capabilities according to results of the Informal Suitability Survey.

4. Grade on an individual rate of progress if at all possible.

5. Encourage the students by creating pride in achievement. Help students realize the value of a job well done.

6. Help the students develop confidence in what they can do and be, rather than emphasizing what they cannot do or become. Remember, there are aptitudes for many different types of skills.

7. Remember the importance of repetition and practice. Most students, and especially those with low aptitude toward reading, need many practice and reinforcement activities to learn new concepts or skills.

8. Identify the most important concepts, attitudes, and skills you believe students need to have in your content area. Concentrate on these objectives so that the students will learn the things most helpful in life.

9. Divide the students in your class into teams to complete some assignments. Make sure there are students from different achievement and aptitude levels on each team. You can have the teams, rather than individuals, compete with one another to complete certain assignments.

Helping Students from Educationally Poor Backgrounds

1. Make sure you are providing materials the students are capable of reading. Apply some of your newly developed skills in administering and interpreting Informal Suitability Surveys.

2. Use the different teaching strategies that were suggested for word meaning and word pronunciation skills. Since vocabulary is an important factor for comprehension, identify the most important specialized words in your content area and emphasize these. Have the students keep a record of new words they are learning.

3. If you need to use many materials that require reading, have an excellent reader put the most important sections of the commonly required reading materials on cassettes. These might be kept in the library or classroom for use by poor readers. Use audio-visual aids that will help the students develop concepts without reading.

4. Summarize the most important material on a handout written at a low reading level. Review Module 2 for specific suggestions on how to write materials at specified reading levels.

5. Ask the librarian or department chairman for books or other supplemental materials that are written at lower reading levels and also contain the concepts and skills you are trying to teach. You may want to establish centers that focus on interesting topics or skills.

6. Introduce assignments with a purpose so the students will have specific information to find. Discuss with them how the assignments will help and demonstrate to them strategies for studying.

7. Have more involvement activities during class sessions. Students can learn from each other while they do group research and have discussions. Simulation type activities in which students actually apply newly acquired skills or concepts are very appropriate for problem readers. Role playing and dramatization can also be helpful in making your class sessions come alive.

8. Use the textbook illustrations, pictures, and charts to explain the content of your subject area. Often graphic aids along with your comments or questions can provide the essential information found in the text. Supplement this material by inviting resource people to your classroom.

9. Outline or teach the students to outline some of the most important information in the course. Many times comprehension is aided if the thoughts are well organized as is required when outlining. A skill group might help to teach this skill or other important skills that problem readers have not developed.

You are certainly not expected to change problem readers into mature readers in the short period of time that you have with them. However, you should have a positive attitude toward problem readers and believe that they can succeed in your classes if you make the minor adaptations that were suggested above. Your attitude and effective teaching techniques will enable problem readers to develop better concepts via success; and this, too, will help them grow in reading achievement.

Putting It All Together

Keep in mind that usually more than one factor influences reading achievement. A student may be plagued by social-emotional problems that are triggered by physical problems. These two problems may in turn result in educational problems for the student. The following checklist is designed to help you "put it all together to get the job done" as you try to help problem readers. The checklist is a daily dozen checklist, rather than a series of steps that you can follow in helping problem readers. The emphasis is on *continual* effective teaching as the prescription for helping problem readers in your classroom. Use the checklist to continually evaluate yourself to make sure you are not contributing to the delinquency of problem readers. This is what teaching content area related reading skills is all about!

Teacher Daily Dozen Checklist

_____ 1. Am I using materials the students are capable of handling? Do I use my department chairman and librarian as resources for getting such materials?

_____ 2. Have I identified the most important concepts for my students? Am I teaching the concepts, skills, and attitudes that will make their lives better?

_____ 3. Am I using a variety of activities in the classroom rather than just reading? Do I use activities such as simulation, role playing, resource people, discussions, and audio-visual aids?

_____ 4. Do I differentiate my assignments according to the needs of the students? After having used Informal Suitability Surveys, am I using the information to provide appropriate materials? Do I give suggestions for students on how to read the materials?

_____ 5. Do I accept my students as they are? Do I avoid labeling them? Have I determined their most important strengths, and are my instructional techniques designed to maximize them?

_____ 6. Do I refer students who need specialized help? Am I aware of the support services available in the school and community?

_____ 7. Do I identify and demonstrate enthusiasm for my content area? Am I stimulating the students' interests and curiosity?

_____ 8. Am I continually observing students to determine factors which may be helping or hindering their academic achievement? Have I used this information to actually help the students?

_____ 9. Do I take time for myself? Am I able to enjoy many experiences outside of school that will make me a better teacher in the classroom?

_____10. Am I actually helping my students increase their vocabularies and develop appropriate strategies for word pronunciation, comprehension, and study?

_____11. Am I aware of the reading skills required for reading materials in my content area? Do I help students learn to read these specialized types of materials, or am I just assuming that anyone can read them? Do I use skill groups and skill centers to provide for individual differences?

_____12. Am I implementing the PARS (Module 9) strategy for motivating reluctant readers? Is my attitude one that will be influencing the students to succeed in my classes? Do I have faith in students?

Posttest

Directions: The following questions are designed to measure your accomplishment of the objectives in this module. Read each item and respond as directed.

1. Describe the characteristics of problem readers and list your three major responsibilities for helping problem readers succeed in content area classes.
2. List the six major factors that influence reading achievement. After each factor, provide a specific example of how it can help or hinder reading achievement.
3. Read the following description of a fifteen-year-old problem reader, and identify two factors that may be causing the reading failure.

When Tom comes to your class he seems to want to "goof off." He does not pay attention when you are talking and never completes the assignments you make. When provide time for him to begin his textbook reading assignment in class, he doesn't even open his book. You found the major textbook was too difficult for him when you surveyed the suitability of the textbook for students. Yet when you read the textbook he is able to understand with 100 percent accuracy.

According to Tom's cumulative record, he received a prescription for glasses when he was in the fourth grade; yet you have never seen him wear them. As you think back, you have noticed that he squints when looking at the chalkboard.

Even though Tom fools around in class once in awhile, he does ask good questions. He is friendly and outgoing in his manner; however, you noticed he does not have many close friends in this class. He is always courteous when you talk with him individually.

When Tom's homeroom teacher administered the incomplete sentences (Study Guide 3) to the class, Tom was one of the first students to complete the sentences. Read his responses, which follow.

Tom's Responses to the Incomplete Sentences
 1. Reading is a rip off.
 2. I like to watch television.
 3. My friends are OK.
 4. I don't like these questions.
 5. The best magazine is *Popular Mechanics*.
 6. Elementary school was fun.
 7. My eyes are OK.
 8. My ears are on my head.
 9. My parents work.
10. Education is a drag.
11. I have been to New York.
12. I wish I could find a job.
13. When I read to others I get nervous.
14. I am liked by my dog.
15. School is a drag.
16. My teachers are smart.
17. Books are hard.
18. I sleep in on Saturdays.
19. When I finish school I will make more money.
20. My home is near the expressway.
21. I need help in math.
22. My best subject is shop.
23. Spelling is OK.
24. Teachers usually like me.

4. Indicate two possible referral sources and two ways you could help Tom in your class.

Posttest Answers

1. A problem reader can be defined as a student who is reading below grade level and therefore is unable to read commonly used content area materials. Although the

characteristics of problem readers vary, the following behaviors are frequently typical of problem readers:

a. Lacks systematic method for pronouncing unknown words.

b. Has a limited vocabulary in speaking, writing, listening and reading.

c. Experiences difficulty in comprehending materials.

d. Has not developed a study strategy or specialized study skills necessary for success in content areas.

e. Displays a negative attitude towards reading assignments.

2. The six factors that influence reading achievement are:

a. Physical Condition

b. Language Development

c. Environment

d. Aptitude

e. Social-Emotional Problems

f. Educational Background

Physical factors can help or hinder reading achievement in many ways. Excellent visual and auditory skills are prerequisites for the reading task. Likewise, good physical health enables a person to learn. If a student has visual, health and/or auditory problems, the chances for success in reading are limited.

Language development can influence reading achievement, too. Students who were generally slow in the development of language skills, or do not have adequate models to learn standard English, fall behind during the early years of school. Concentrated efforts to improve language can help the student become a better reader.

The environment is one of the most important factors in reading achievement. The student who does not have books or other reading material along with a place to study at home is hindered. Progress in reading is made more difficult by parents who do not support the schools or the student. Conversely, parents who overprotect their child or put their child under too much pressure can hinder achievement, too.

Reading is highly correlated with intelligence as measured by present-day academic aptitude tests. The student who is below average in those factors that influence reading (visual memory, auditory memory, and vocabulary) experiences difficulty in learning to read because reading requires these aptitudes.

Social-emotional factors can help or hinder reading achievement. Reading requires a great deal of concentration and thinking. The student who is plagued with social-emotional concerns may not be able to put forth the required concentration. Also, a student who feels incapable of learning will have a more difficult time learning to read.

Students who are fortunate enough to have enthusiastic, dedicated teachers who diagnose to determine appropriate objectives and activities will have a better chance of succeeding in reading. Teachers who neglect the problem reader contribute further to the cause.

3. A visual defect may be influencing Tom's responsiveness to instruction. Glasses were prescribed when he was in the fourth grade, but he does not wear them. He seems to avoid accepting this limitation according to his response to item 7. Accord-

ing to the description, Tom does not have friends in your class. Likewise, his responses to items 4 and 14 may indicate possible social-emotional problems. It could be he is "goofing off" to gain acceptance from peers. Also, he may not be wearing his glasses because he does not want to appear different from his peers. The interaction effects of poor vision and lack of appropriate peer relationships could be contributing to his lack of responsiveness to instruction.

4. At this time Tom should be referred to the school reading specialist to determine the extent of his reading disability and to suggest instructional materials that would be most beneficial for him. You might also refer Tom to his counselor, who might provide some insights to his "acting-out" behavior and negative self-concept. The school nurse could screen his vision again and talk with him about the visual defect. Try to give attention to Tom and motivate him by using the questions he asks in class. Involve him in activities that do not require reading. Perhaps you might have Tom listen to some tapes that include sections of the textbook you would like him to understand. If possible, relate some of your content area objectives to Tom's interest in cars, math, and industrial arts.

Final Comment

This module was written to provide you with some explanations of why certain students are problem readers. The techniques for adapting instruction for such students are outlined in this module and were extended in previous modules. These techniques will enable you to help the problem reader develop the skills and knowledge of your content area. It is hoped that you will apply the ideas in this module to help problem readers become more successful in your classes. Simply because a student is a problem reader it does not follow that he or she cannot succeed in school. Of course, the student's success depends upon the most important factor in the educational process—you!

If you have correctly completed all Posttest items, you are finished with the module. If not, see your instructor for help, or return through the Enabling Elements as needed.

Selected Bibliography

Aukerman, R. C. *Reading in the Secondary School Classroom*. New York: McGraw-Hill, 1972.

Behrens, H. D., and Maynard, G. *The Changing Child: Readings in Child Development*. Glenview, Illinois: Scott Foresman, 1972.

Brooks, B. D., and Merino, S. "Strategies for Teaching Within a Bicultural Setting." *Reading Improvement* 13, no. 2 (Summer 1976): 86–91.

Cushenbery, D. C. *Remedial Reading in the Secondary School*. West Nyack, New York: Parker, 1972.

Forgan, H. *Help Your Child Learn to Read*. Toronto: Pagurian Press Ltd., 1975.

Hafner, L. E. *Improving Reading in Middle and Secondary Schools*. 2nd ed. New York: Macmillan, 1974.

Karlin, R. *Teaching Reading in High School*. 2nd ed. Indianapolis: Bobbs-Merrill, 1972.

Mangieri, J. N. "A Secondary Reading Program That Worked." *Reading Improvement* 15, no. 1 (Spring 1978): 10–12.

Mercer, C. D. *Children and Adolescents with Learning Disabilities*. Columbus, Ohio: Charles E. Merrill Publishing Co., 1979.

Otto, W., and Smith, R. J. *Corrective and Remedial Teaching*. Boston: Houghton-Mifflin and Co., 1980.

Ramsey, W. Z., ed. "Organization for Individual Differences." *Perspectives in Reading*. Vol. 9. Newark, Delaware: International Reading Association, 1967.

Rossman, J. F. "Remedial Readers: Did Parents Read to Them at Home?" *Journal of Reading* 17 (1974): 622–25.

Strang, R. *Reading Diagnosis and Remediation*. Newark, Delaware: International Reading Association, 1968.

———; McCullough, C. M.; and Traxler, A. C. *The Improvement of Reading*. New York: McGraw-Hill, 1967.

Wilson, R. M. *Diagnostic and Remedial Reading for Classroom and Clinic*. 4th ed. Columbus, Ohio: Charles E. Merrill Publishing Co., 1981.

Index

Affective factors in motivation, 261
Alteration of readability, 12, 38, 41–42, 47–52
Application and analysis questions, 155–56, 158
  sample skills test, 112
  strategy for answering, 170–71
Aptitude factors in reading failure, 289, 293
  adaptations to, 302–3
Articles, readability of
  altering, 38, 41–42
  determining, 26–27
Art students, reading skills for, 98
  sample test, 112–13
Attitude, as motivational factor, 261, 267, 269, 273
Audio-visual aids in vocabulary instruction, 141

Branching Program, definition of, 3
Business education, reading skills for, 99
  sample test, 111–12

Classification Scheme for Reading Questions, 151–64
  categories of questions in, 107–8, 154–59
  question-answering strategies, 170–72
  writing of questions with, 160–64
Cognitive factors in motivation, 261–63
Comprehension, 97, 150–85
  checking (see Informal Suitability Survey)
  Classification Scheme for Reading Questions, 151–64
  in problem readers, 285
  question-answering strategies, 164–82
  sample tests, 112–13
  sources of test items, 107–8
  in specific content areas, 98–105
  and SQ3R Study Strategy, 199

Connotative word meanings, 141
Context clues to pronunciation, instruction in, 246

Dale-Chall Readability Formula, 12, 13
Differentiated reading assignments, planning, 82–87, 262
Drama students, reading skills for, 105

Educational factors in reading failure, 290, 293
  adaptations to, 303–4
Emotional factors in reading failure, 289–90, 293
  adaptations to, 302
Enabling Elements, definition of, 3
English students, reading skills for, 99–100
Environmental factors in reading failure, 289, 293
  adaptations to, 301–2
Evaluation questions, 157, 158
  strategy for answering, 171–72
Extrinsic motivation, 257, 258

Fay, Leo, 206, 211
Foreign languages, reading skills for, 100
Fry's Graph for Estimating Readability, 8, 12, 13–21
  with articles, 26–27
  as check on writing, 53, 54
  with fewer than 100 words, 27–29
  informal application of concept, 29–30
  Raygor's graph compared to, 42–43, 46
  with textbooks, 24–26

Grade levels, as readability measurement, 11
  altering, 48–52, 54–55
  estimating, 12, 13, 43 (see also Fry's Graph)
Graphs for estimating readability (see also Fry's Graph)
  Raygor's, 42–46

Health students, reading skills for, 100
Homemaking students, reading skills for, 101
Humanities, SQ3R Study Strategy for, 198–204

Index use, sample plan for teaching, 195–98
Individualized (differentiated) reading assign-
    ments, 82–87, 262
Industrial arts, reading skills for, 101
Informal Suitability Survey, 60–92, 283–84
    administration of, 75–76
    application of concept, 71–72
    chart of results, 81–82
    construction, 67–72
    group, 76, 78
    implementation of results, 82–89
    individual, 76–77, 78–79
    number needed, 65–66, 71
    purpose, 60, 64, 72
    samples, 64–65, 68–69, 70–71
    scoring, 77–80
Interest, as motivational factor, 261
Intrinsic motivation, 257, 258

Klare, G.R., 10, 11–12

Language factors in reading failure, 289, 293
    adaptations to, 300–301
Letters to parents, 42

Mathematics, reading skills for, 102
    SQRQCQ Study Strategy, 210–17
    test, sample, 110
Meaning (see Comprehension; Vocabulary)
Modular format, 2–4
Motivation, 254–78
    definition, 257
    factors influencing, 260–63
        core factors, 266–70, 271–74
    problem readers' lack of, 286
    questionnaires for students, 258–59, 264–65
    sources, intrinsic versus extrinsic, 257–58
    statements of, 69
    strategy for, 266–70
        incorporation into assignments, 270–75
Music students, reading skills for, 102–3
    sample test, 112

Objectives
    definition, 2–3
    terminal, checklist of, 4–5

Parents, letters to, 42
PARS motivational strategy, 267
    activities for implementing, 268–70
    incorporation into assignments, 271–75
Physical education, reading skills for, 103–4
Physical factors in reading failure, 288, 292
    adaptations to, 300
Posttest, definition of, 3
PQRST Study Strategy, 205–10
Prefixes, in pronunci....on, 225, 226, 228, 240–41
    tests, 114, 231, 232, 236
Problem readers, 89, 280–309
    characteristics, 284–86
    definition of, 284
    factors influencing, 288–90
        adaptations to, 300–304
        identifying, 286, 291–98
    helping, 88, 287, 300–305
    identifying, 283–84, 286
    referral of, 287, 299–300, 301, 302
    teacher's responsibilities toward, 286–87
Pronunciation skills, 98, 222–51
    problem readers' lack of, 284–85
    in specific content areas, 98–105
    strategy, 224–29, 237–49
    test of, 231, 233–34
    tests, 231–36
        samples, 114–15
        sources of items, 109
Prospectus, definition of, 3
Purpose, as motivational factor, 262, 267,
    268–69, 271–72

Question-answering strategies, 164–75
    teaching, 175–82
Quick Test of Word Pronunciation, 231, 232,
    235–36
    record form for, 231, 233, 234, 239

Raygor's graph, 42–46
Readability, 11
    alteration, 12, 38, 41–42, 47–52
        in writing process, 53–55

Readability (*continued*)
  of articles, 26–27, 38, 41–42
  estimating, 10, 12, 13, 42–46 (*see also* Fry's
    Graph; Informal Suitability Survey)
  factors influencing, 11–12 (*see also* Sentence
    length; Word difficulty)
  formulas, 10, 12, 13 (*see also* Fry's Graph)
    limitations, 13
    Raygor's graph, 42–46
    uses, 12
  as motivational factor, 262
  textbooks, 24–26, 42
  in writing of materials, 12, 38, 41, 52–55
    letters to parents, 42
Reading aloud, word recognition errors in, 77,
    78–80
Reading assignments, differentiated, 82–87, 262
Reading problems, solving (*see* Motivation; Prob-
    lem readers)
Reading questions (*see also* Classification Scheme
    for Reading Questions)
  strategies for answering, 164–82
Reading skills, 94–122 (*see also* Comprehension;
    Pronunciation skills; Study skills and
    strategies; Vocabulary)
  categories of, 97–98
  for specific content areas, 98–105
  teaching of, 120
  tests (*see* Tests, reading skills)
Reading styles, 202
Recognition and recall questions, 154, 158
  sample skills test, 112–13
  strategy for answering, 170
Reference-book use
  for pronunciation, 247
  skills test for, 113
Reluctant readers, motivating (*see* Motivation)
Results, knowledge of, as motivational factor,
    262–63, 267, 269, 273
Robinson, Francis, 199

Santos Classification Scheme for Reading Ques-
    tions (*see* Classification Scheme for Reading
    Questions)
Science, reading skills for, 104
  PQRST Study Strategy, 205–10
  sample test, 111

Sentence length, as readability factor, 12
  alteration, 48, 49–50, 51
  formulas using, 12, 13, 15, 18
Set, multiple meanings of, 135
Short-term goals, as motivational factor, 262
Simulation activities, 140
Skill groups and skill centers, 120
Skills, reading (*see* Reading skills)
Social-emotional factors in reading failure,
    289–90, 293
  adaptations to, 302
Social sciences, SQ3R Study Strategy for,
    198–204
Social studies, reading skills for, 104–5
Spache, George, 206
Spache Readability Formula, 12, 13
Speech students, reading skills for, 105
SQ3R Study Strategy, 198–204
SQRQCQ Study Strategy, 210–17
Stems of words, 240–41, 242
  isolation of, 226–27, 243
  syllabication, 227, 243–46
Strategies (*see also* Study skills and strategies)
  motivational, 266–70
    incorporation into assignments, 270–75
  question-answering, 164–82
  vocabulary-building, 136
  word-pronunciation, 224–29, 237–49
    test of, 231, 233–34
Study skills and strategies, 97, 188–220
  general skills list, 192
  PQRST Strategy, 205–10
  problem readers' lack of, 285–86
  sample tests, 113–14
  sources of test items, 108–9
  in specific content areas, 98–105
  SQ3R Strategy, 198–204
  SQRQCQ Strategy, 210–17
  teaching of skills, 193–98
Success, as motivational factor, 263, 267, 270,
    273–74
Suffixes, in pronunciation, 225, 226, 228, 241–42
  tests, 114, 231, 232, 236
Suitability survey for materials (*see* Informal
    Suitability Survey)
Syllabication, 227, 243–46
Syllables, number of, as readability factor, 15

Syllables (*continued*)
  counting, 17, 20
  reduction, 49
Symbols, mathematical, test of, 110
Synthesis questions, 156, 158
  strategy for answering, 171

Test questions, readability of, 41
  determining, 28, 54
Tests, reading skills, 106–18
  administering and scoring, 118
  mastery level, 115
  parts, 109–11
  pronunciation, 114–15, 231–36
  recording of results, 118–19
  samples, 110, 111–15
  sources of items, 107–9
Textbooks
  aids to use of, 87–88
  readability of (*see also* Informal Suitability
    Survey)
    altering, 42
    determining, 24–26
  study aids in, using, 193–98
    sample test, 113–14
Translation questions, 154–55, 158
  strategy for answering, 170

Usefulness of knowledge, as motivational factor,
  263

Vocabulary, 124–47
  activities for teaching, 136–45
  generic, 97
  guidelines for teaching, 132–36
  levels of meaning in, 127–31, 137, 142
    activities for developing, 138–41
  of problem readers, 285
  questions about, in Informal Suitability
    Survey, 70
  sample tests, 111–12
  size of, and age, 127
  sources of test items, 107
  for specific content areas, 98–105
  types of, 126–27

Word difficulty, as readability factor, 12, 13
  alteration, 48–50, 51
  long words, counting of, 43
  syllables, number of, 15, 17, 20
Word meaning (*see* Vocabulary)
Word recognition (*see also* Pronunciation)
  errors, 77, 78–80
Writing of materials, 12, 38, 41, 42, 52–55

Harry W. Forgan is currently a Professor of Education at the University of Miami, Coral Gables, Florida. He earned his Bachelor of Education, Master of Education, and Doctor of Philosophy at Kent State University. He has written five books concerning reading methods and has coauthored four books. The companion text for this book, *Developing Competencies in Teaching Reading,* was coauthored with Charles Mangrum. He has written a book for parents, *Help Your Child Learn to Read,* and several practical handbooks published by Goodyear Publishing Company: *The Reading Corner, Phorgan's Phonics, Read All About It!, Getting Ready to Read,* and *The Reading Circle.* Dr. Forgan has been a classroom teacher and serves as a consultant to many school systems, teacher centers, and professional reading associations. He continues to work with students in elementary, junior high, and high schools in Dade County, Florida.

Charles T. Mangrum II is Professor of Education and Chairperson of the Graduate Reading Area at the University of Miami, Coral Gables, Florida. Dr. Mangrum did his advanced graduate work at Indiana University. He has taught in both elementary and secondary schools and served as a Reading Consultant for an elementary and junior high school district. He served as Editor of the *Reading Aids Series* published by the International Reading Association and Editor of the *Florida Reading Quarterly* published by the Florida State Reading Council. He is a past President of the Florida State Reading Council. He is coauthor of *Developing Competencies for Teaching Reading in the Elementary School and Middle School* published by Charles E. Merrill. He is coauthor of a multimedia program for primary grades that teaches, through language, our alphabet and the sounds that each letter represents. This program is published by Bowmar-Noble and is called LETTER SOUNDS ALL AROUND. He is a contributor to journals, presentor at conferences, and a consultant to schools.

Other Reading Books of Interest

Principles and Practices of Teaching Reading, 5th edition
Heilman, Blair and Rupley

Diagnosis and Remediation for Classroom and Clinic, 4th edition
Wilson

Teaching Content Area Reading Skills, 2nd edition
Forgan and Mangrum

Programmed Reading for Teachers
Wilson, Hall, Gambrell, Coley, Campbell, Johnson

Phonics in Proper Perspective, 4th edition
Heilman

Locating and Correcting Reading Difficulties, 3rd edition
Ekwall

Analytical Reading Inventory, 2nd edition
Woods and Moe

Phonics for Teachers of Reading, 3rd edition
Hull

Teaching Reading as a Language Experience, 3rd edition
Hall

The Development of Language and Reading in Young Children,
2nd edition
Pflaum

Programmed Word Attack for Teachers, 3rd edition
Wilson and Hall